Textbook 1

课本（上册）

Zoom In: Intermediate Chinese in 118 Hours

118 小时突破中级中文

主　编：LIQUN SU（苏立群）
副主编：WEI-SAN SU（胡未三）
编写者：LIQUN SU（苏立群）
WEI-SAN SU（胡未三）
LU CAI（蔡璐）

MP3
www.sinolingua.com.cn

SinolinguA
华语教学出版社

First Edition 2021

ISBN 978-7-5138-2067-7

Published by Sinolingua Co., Ltd
24 Baiwanzhuang Street, Beijing 100037, China
Tel: (86) 10-68320585 68997826
Fax: (86) 10-68997826 68326333
http://www.sinolingua.com.cn
E-mail: hyjx@sinolingua.com.cn
Facebook: www.facebook.com/sinolingua
Printed by Beijing Hucais Culture Communication Co., Ltd

Printed in the People's Republic of China

前言 Preface

During my twenty years of teaching at SOAS (School of Oriental and African Studies, University of London), I began to develop an interest in different ways of teaching Chinese as a written language. My book *Mastering Chinese Characters: A Modern Approach* was published in 2014 by the Commercial Press. I've now compiled a new series of textbooks which is an update called the *Zoom In* series (including *Elementary Chinese in 60 Hours* 1 & 2, *Intermediate Chinese in 118 Hours* 1 & 2, *Advanced Chinese in 337 Hours* 1 & 2 with accompanying workbooks).

The traditional way to teach written Chinese has been to take each character apart and trace the roots of its radicals to their sources. Though being well-accepted by Chinese students who are already familiar with their own history and culture, this approach has not been particularly effective for foreign students learning the language from scratch. In hindsight, this strategy was perhaps both too academic and too localised. It tended to assume the student possessed a basic knowledge of China such as its national and folkloric heritage, its geography, social values and codes of behaviour.

In an attempt to avoid similar pitfalls, it became something of an obsession of mine to figure out an alternative way to inspire and support foreign students in a way which does not require prior knowledge of Chinese. The resulting series of textbooks is an attempt at this more intuitive approach, that employs fresh visual tools. Since both pictures and sound are regular components of Chinese characters, we have included a cartoon to match each character, supported by a short piece of text in English which students are encouraged to read aloud. Whatever proved most helpful to the class or individual ended up on these pages, as I believe the priority should always be given to practical use over established convention.

In accordance with the Chinese saying, "Give a man a fish and you feed him for a day; teach a man to fish and you feed him for a lifetime. Knowledge is the best charity," the book encourages students to follow the method and pursue their own learning goals as far as their interest dictates.

The first 22 lessons are dedicated to character learning while the later lessons (Lessons 23-44) include two parts. “Part 1 Combining Characters” is about making words or phrases. All 270 characters learned in the first 22 lessons are used to form words and phrases. “Part II Compose Sentences” is about using words and phrases to form five sentences. The first three sentences are simple and the last two are longer and more difficult. After finishing the whole book, students should be able to know 1,500 words or phrases and read 810 simple sentences, while those with strong language ability could master as many as 1,350 sentences.

A workbook is also designed to help students memorize Chinese characters and word combinations as well as helping to construct sentences with those words. The book also provides a story of some 6,500 words for students to read.

This series has been used in the classroom for more than two years. If students spend 2 hours per week in a total of 22 weeks (totally 44 hours) either taking a course or by self-study, they could pass easily the test for mid-low level of Chinese language.

In the West there exists tremendous interest in learning Chinese. In order to follow this trend, I would suggest a couple of things: Firstly, to remind Chinese language teachers that a spoken language and its written form are intimately connected. In other words, to teach the spoken language, it is paramount to teach reading and writing at the same time. Secondly, our attention should be given more to children and teenagers, for whom Chinese has become one of the most popular subjects at school. It is with this age group in mind that we hope to take on a serious subject in a relaxed and playful manner.

As this volume is soon to be put into publication, I would like to thank Simona Bryant for her very helpful contribution to proofreading the English part. Special thanks go to Mr. Kevin Munns for his recording of the English in the book. His high standard of English has greatly helped improve this book!

David Su Liqun

前言

Preface

任教英国伦敦大学亚非学院（School of Oriental and African Studies，University of London）的 20 年期间，我一直都在寻找一种向欧美学生介绍汉字的方法。“突破中文”系列教材是在《汉字图解学习手册》（Mastering Chinese Characters: A Modern Approach，商务印书馆 2014）的基础上运用更新思路编写的。该系列教材共分六个级别：《60 小时突破初级中文（上、下册）》、《118 小时突破中级中文（上、下册）》和《337 小时突破高级中文（上、下册）》，每个级别含课本和练习册各一册。

《118 小时突破中级中文（上册）》课本的第一部分（字篇，第一课到第二十二课）学习汉字。

在对外汉语教学的数十年中，曾不断有人尝试过以“图片解析汉字”的方法来编写教材，不过总体来说收效不明显，原因是这些书对汉字的解释过于“学术化”与“地域化”。“学术化”是指“以文解文，以字解字”，忽略了学习者是外国人，他们对中国是“零知识”；“地域化”是指著书者大多对欧美受众群体的社会及价值观缺乏切身的了解，因而，在文化的沟通和语言的表达两个方面都受到了局限。这套“突破中文”系列教材尽量避免这些短处，而采用的方法是：第一，把学生领回到甲骨文、金文和籀文时代——对这个久远的时光隧道本书不是用“引证”和“六书”去充填，而是通过卡通画的形象并结合汉字后面的故事把这些字“激活”来启发、引导学生；第二，采用了以“声”加深学生对“形”记忆的特殊模式，即每一个汉字都设计了“把汉字说出来”的一条，就是用一句地道的英文把这个汉字的形、声、义都归纳、融合进去，达到“只要记得住这句话，就知道这个字的意思、写法和发音”的目的。此外，课本还提供了书写的笔顺，鼓励学习者“唱字”，“横竖撇捺，点勾折提”边写边唱。

课本的第二部分（词句篇，第二十三课到第四十四课）是学习汉字的组构功能，即以字组词、以词组句、以句组段、以段组章的规律。

解释这个规律之前，需要先把这套书何以取名“Zoom In（趋真向实法则）”或称“Natural Flow（自然顺序法，简称‘序法’）”做一个说明。

什么是这个“趋真向实法则”（或“自然顺序法”）呢？众所周知，大自然里有两个相互独立又相互制约的元素，一个是时间，一个是空间。宇宙中的万物在穿过时间隧道时都在改变其空间的位置；所以这个“自然顺序法”是时间先于空间，而时间自身的顺序是由无限的长到有限的短，空间自身的顺序是由无限的大到有限的小。人类的生活也不例外，这两个元素的规则影响着我们的万千世界。耐人寻味的是这个“自然顺序法”从数千年以前就反射到中华民族的语言（汉语）中，汉语的“序法”规则就是建立在这个基础之上的。

具体来说，两个或两个以上的汉字首尾相接的法则，在表达时间时是“由长到短”，表达空间时是由“大到小”。更具体来说，这个“序法（自然顺序法）”反映到汉语的字词与句子的组构方面，都是从广义到狭义，从整体到局部，从一般到具体，从前到后，从上到下，等等。

中国古代的智者说：“给人一条鱼，你只喂他一天；教给一个人会钓鱼，你就养活了他一辈子；授人以技能是最好的助人方式。”基于汉语这种简单易懂的“序法”，课本的第二部分（第二十三课到第四十四课）就是把这个“序法”用在“以字组词，以词组句”上——教授学习者钓鱼的技能！

于此，后二十二课的内容都是使用第一部分学习的 270 个汉字加上初级课本上、下册学的 348 个汉字去组构词、短语的，而且，每个汉字都给出五个使用该汉字的句子，其中前三句比较简单，后两句相对长些、复杂些。在本书的最后一课结束的时候，学生能够认读 1500 个单词或短语，可以掌握 810 个简单句子；对于那些语言能力强的人，可以达到 1350 个句子。此外，每本还配有练习册，提供记忆汉字和字词扩充及中英句子互翻的练习。为了增加学生的成就感，本书还附有一篇长达 6500 个汉字的小说供学生阅读欣赏。

《118 小时突破中级中文（上册）》（含课本及练习册）从完成初稿到最终提交用了两年多的时间，其间，它已被作为课堂教材试用过多次。粗粗统计的结果是，如果学生每周上课或自学 2 小时，经过 22 周 44 个小时的学习，通过中等低阶水平的考试是绰绰有余的。

苏立群

目录

Contents

字篇

目录 Contents

词句篇

目录 Contents

附录

字篇

阿 **Prefix** ā;ē Radical/Component 阝 ear	349

Prefix ā;ē 阿

Ancient form

(cliff) + (curved river) = prefix

Catchphrase

This meandering river flowing at the foot of the cliff is the Ah River. The **Prefix** is 阿 ā/ē. (The prefix is used before names.)

Stroke order

啊 **WOW** ā;á;ǎ;à Radical/Component 口 mouth	350

WOW ā;á;ǎ;à 啊

Ancient form

(mouth) + (cliff) + (curved river) = wow

Catchphrase

WOW, the curved river is really beautiful. **WOW** is 啊 à. (It is an interjection for expressing surprise or praise.)

Stroke order

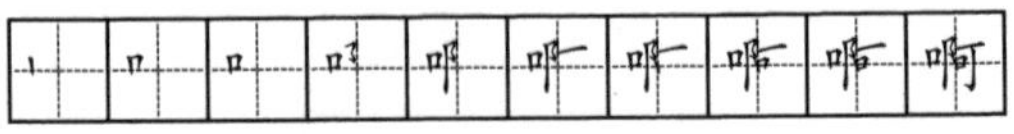

矮 **SHORT** ǎi Radical/Component 矢 arrow	351

SHORT ǎi 矮

Ancient form

(arrow) + (crop) + (girl) = short

Catchphrase

This little girl picking grain in the wheat field is even **SHORT**er than an arrow. **SHORT** is 矮 ǎi.

Stroke order

安 **PEACE/SAFETY** ān Radical/Component 宀 roof/house	352

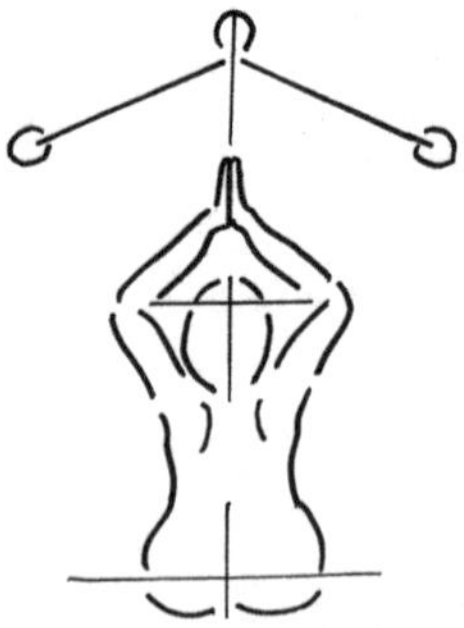

PEACE/SAFETY ān 安

Ancient form

(roof/house) + (woman) = peace/safety

Catchphrase

When there is a woman in the house, the home will be **PEACE**ful. **PEACE/SAFETY** is 安 ān.

Stroke order

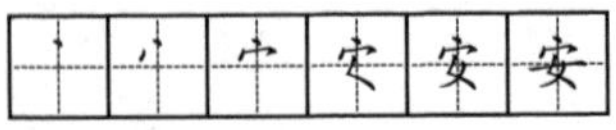

把 **HOLD** bǎ 353
Radical/Component 扌 hand

HOLD bǎ 把

Ancient form

(hand/arm) + (snake/reptile) = HOLD

Catchphrase

When you grab a snake with your bare hand, you have to **HOLD** it close to its head; otherwise, it is dangerous. **HOLD** is 把 bǎ.

Stroke order

一	扌	扌	扌	扣	扣	把

般 **TYPE/LIKE** bān 354
Radical/Component 舟 boat

TYPE/LIKE bān 般

Ancient form

(boat) + (hand with tool) = type/like

Catchphrase

In the water towns of south China, people use the waterways **LIKE** the public roads. **TYPE/LIKE** is 般 bān.

Stroke order

′	丿	舟	舟	舟	舟	舟	舡	般	般

搬 **MOVE** bān 355
Radical/Component 扌 hand

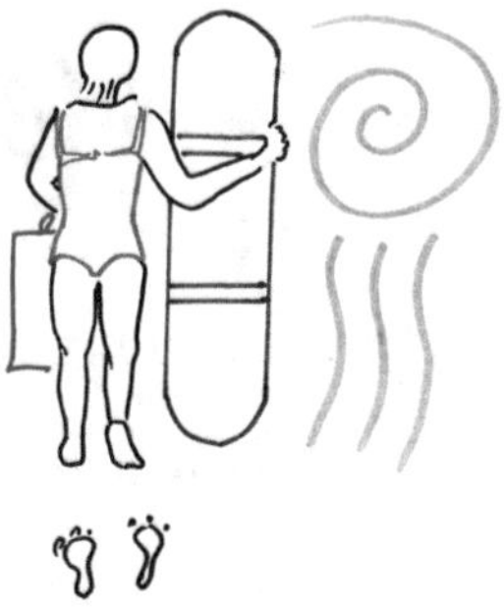

MOVE bān 搬

(hand) + (boat/board) + (hand with tool) = move

Catchphrase

This surfer is **MOV**ing to a beach with big waves. **MOVE** is 搬 bān.

Stroke order

一	扌	扌	扌	扌	扌	扌	扌	捎	搬	搬	搬	搬

板 **BOARD** bǎn 356
Radical/Component 木 wood/tree

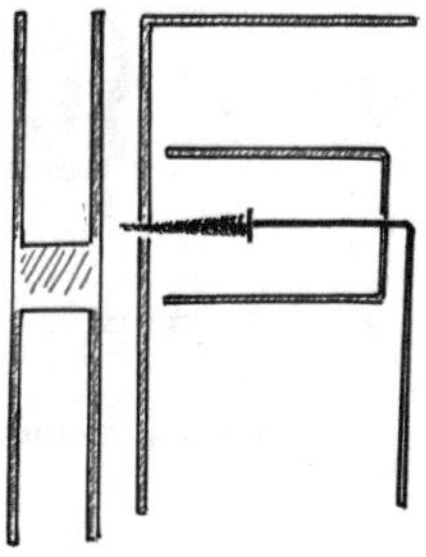

BOARD bǎn 板

(wood) + (tool and hand) = board

Catchphrase

Someone is holding a tool to fix several wooden **BOARD**s to the wall. **BOARD** is 板 bǎn.

Stroke order

一	十	木	木	朩	朳	杤	板

办（辦）DEAL/DO/MANAGE bàn — 357

Radical/Component 力 strength/power

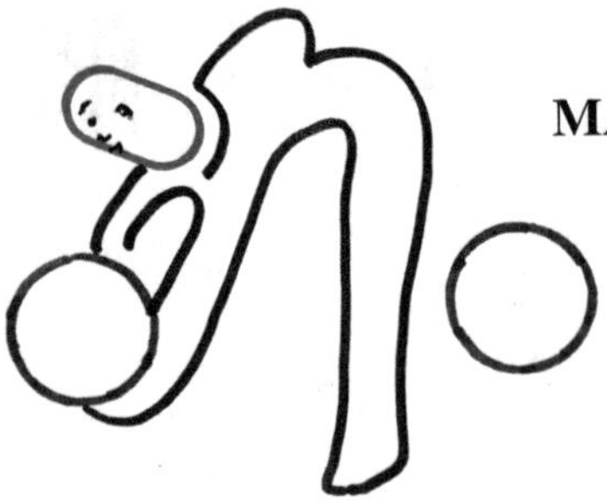

DEAL/DO/MANAGE bàn 办

Ancient form

Traditional form 辦

Catchphrase

It takes a lot of effort to **DEAL** with things. Sometimes **DO**ing something is like moving a big round stone from one side to the other. **DEAL/DO/MANAGE** is 办 bàn.

Stroke order

𠃌	力	力	办

半 HALF bàn — 358

Radical/Component 十 ten/cross shape

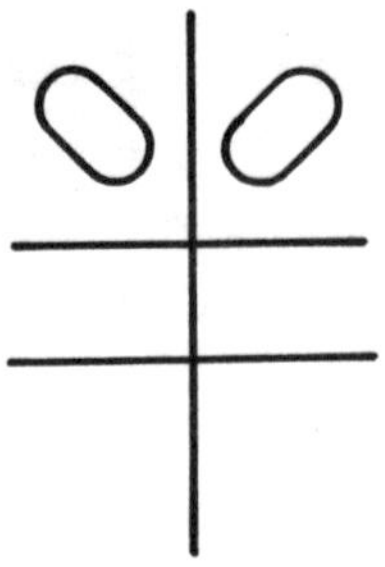

HALF bàn 半

Ancient form

Catchphrase

This character is split in **HALF**. Each side is the mirror image of the other. **HALF** is 半 bàn.

Stroke order

丶	丷	㐅	兰	半

包 WRAP bāo — 359

Radical/Component 勹 wrap

WRAP bāo 包

Ancient form

(wrap) + (energy) = wrap

Catchphrase

Energy **WRAP**ped by something on the outside is temporarily trapped inside. **WRAP** is 包 bāo.

Stroke order

丿	勹	勺	匀	包

饱（飽）FULL bǎo — 360

Radical/Component 饣 food/eat

FULL bǎo 饱

Ancient form Traditional form 飽

(food/eat) + (energy) = full

Catchphrase

This man has eaten all the food in the basket and now he is really **FULL**. **FULL** is 饱 bǎo.

Stroke order

丿	𠂊	饣	饣	饣	饣	饣	饱

361 被 QUILT bèi

Radical/Component 衤 cloth

QUILT bèi 被

Ancient form

(cloth) + (skin) = quilt

Catchphrase

Throughout civilization, the skins of animals have been cut into pieces to make **QUILT**s for people. **QUILT** is 被 bèi.

Stroke order

丶	㇇	礻	礻	礻	衤	衤	衤	衤	被

362 鼻 NOSE bí

Radical/Component 鼻 nose

NOSE bí 鼻

Ancient form

(nose) + (air) = nose

Catchphrase

The **NOSE** is very sensitive, and sometimes wearing a mask is useless against air pollution. **NOSE** is 鼻 bí.

Stroke order

丿	𠂆	白	白	自	自	自	鼻	鼻	鼻	鼻	鼻	鼻	鼻

363 必 MUST bì

Radical/Component 心 heart

MUST bì 必

Ancient form

(heart) + (a sharp object) = must

Catchphrase

A surgery **MUST** be done that a needle **MUST** be inserted in your heart. **MUST** is 必 bì.

Stroke order

丶	心	心	必	必

364 变(變) CHANGE biàn

Radical/Component 又 again

CHANGE biàn 变

Ancient form Traditional form 變

(equal/also) + (again) = change

Catchphrase

The Book of **CHANGE**s, or *I-Ching*, reflects the philosophy of **CHANGE**s of ancient Chinese. **CHANGE** is 变 biàn.

Stroke order

丶	亠	亠	亣	亦	亦	变	变

冰 ICE bīng 365

Radical/Component 冫 ice/cold

ICE bīng 冰

Ancient form 

(ice) + (river) = ice

Catchphrase

Ah, there are two blocks of **ICE** in the water. The weather is so cold! **ICE** is 冰 bīng.

Stroke order

才 JUST cái 366

Radical/Component 扌 hand

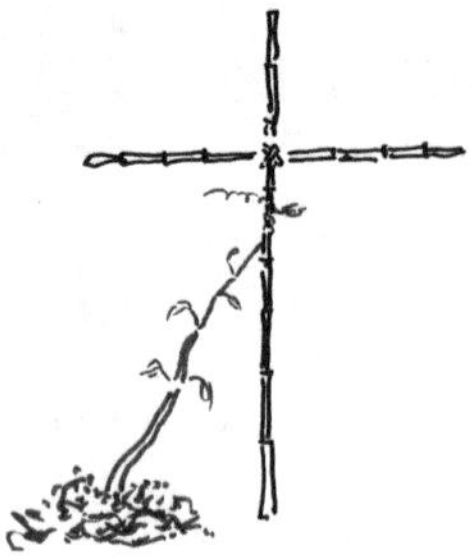

JUST cái 才

Ancient form 

Catchphrase

JUST as soon as the seeds sprout, it will naturally climb up the cross-shaped frame. **JUST** is 才 cái.

Stroke order

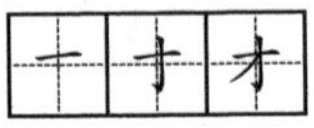

参(參) PARTICIPATE cān 367

Radical/Component 厶 private/personal

PARTICIPATE cān 参

Ancient form 

Traditional form 參

(opened mouth) + (sound waves) = participate

Catchphrase

I have prepared a music playlist. Would you let me **PARTICIPATE** in your party, so we can dance to it? **PARTICIPATE** is 参 cān.

Stroke order

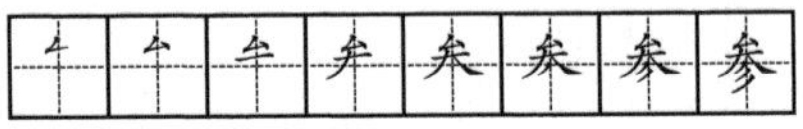

草 GRASS cǎo 368

Radical/Component 艹 grass

GRASS cǎo 草

Ancient form 

(grass) + (morning sun) = grass

Catchphrase

The morning sun illuminates the **GRASS**. **GRASS** is 草 cǎo.

Stroke order

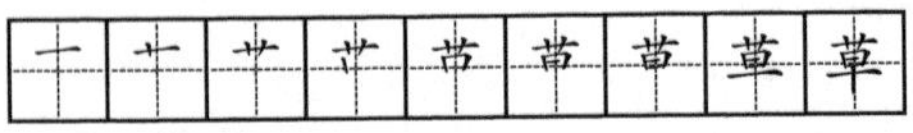

层(層)STOREY/LAYER céng — 369
Radical/Component 尸 corpse

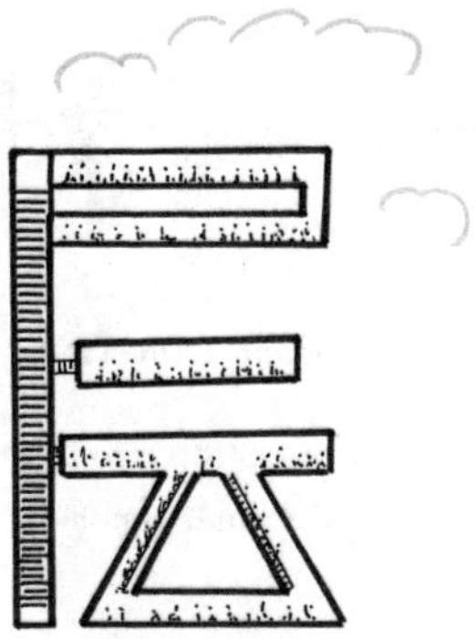

STOREY/LAYER céng 层

Ancient form　Traditional form 層

(the shape) + (cloud) = storey/layer

Catchphrase

Wow, there are so many people walking up and down in this five-**STOREY** building! **STOREY/LAYER** is 层 céng.

Stroke order

查 CHECK chá — 370
Radical/Component 木 wood/tree

CHECK chá 查

Ancient form

(tree) + (morning) = check

Catchphrase

In order to protect this tree, somebody needs to climb up every morning to **CHECK** if there are any pests. **CHECK** is 查 chá.

Stroke order

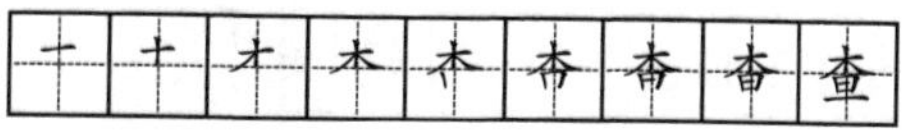

差 BAD chà; DIFFERENCE chā — 371
Radical/Component 工 work

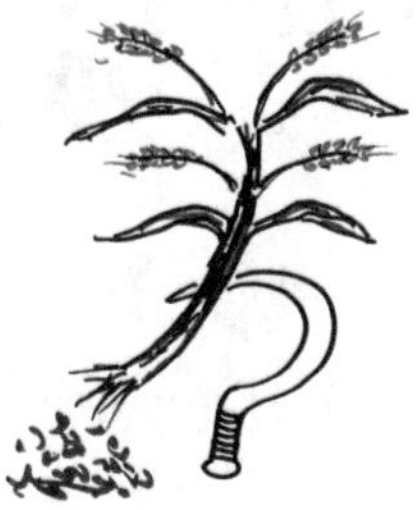

BAD chà;
DIFFERENCE chā 差

Ancient form

(crop) + (work) = bad

Catchphrase

A person uses a tool to cut some of the **BAD** crops in the field to feed the sheep. **BAD** is 差 chà; **DIFFERENCE** is chā.

Stroke order

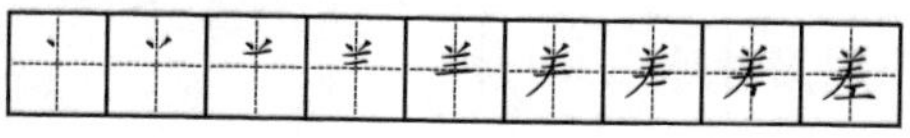

尝(嘗)TASTE cháng — 372
Radical/Component 小 small/tiny

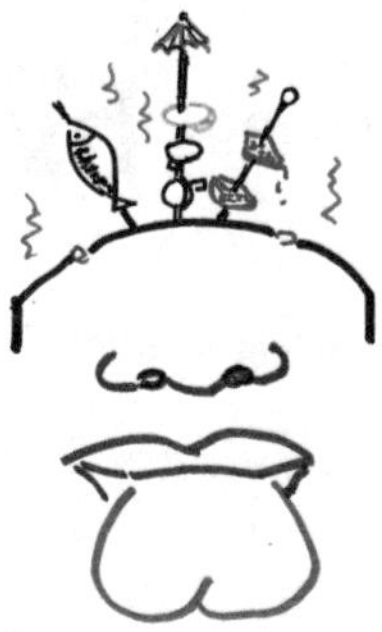

TASTE cháng 尝

Ancient form　Traditional form 嘗

(favourite/fashion) + (taste) = taste

Catchphrase

There are only three meat skewers on the barbecue, but so many customers all want a **TASTE**. How can we have enough? **TASTE** is 尝 cháng.

Stroke order

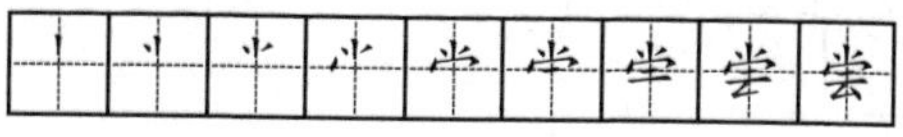

超 SURPASS chāo 373

Radical/Component 走 walk

SURPASS chāo 超

Ancient form

(walk) + (call out) = surpass

Catchphrase

This athlete is a super charismatic role model. His strict training ensures he always **SURPASS**es others and wins the gold medal. **SURPASS** is 超 chāo.

Stroke order

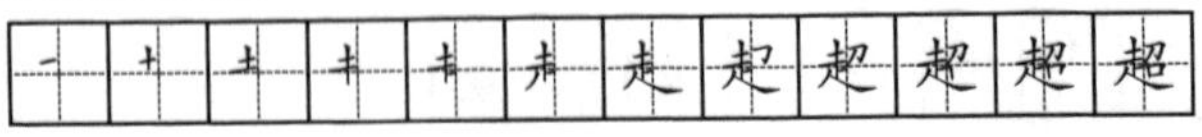

衬 INNER LINING chèn 374

Radical/Component 衤 cloth

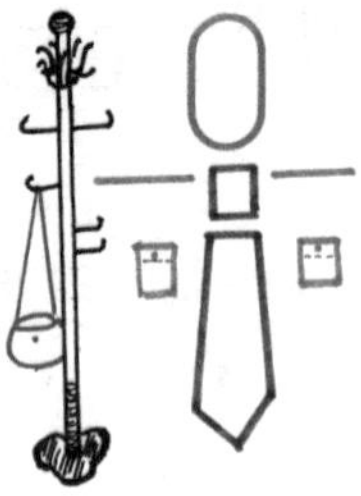

INNER LINING chèn 衬

Ancient form

(cloth) + (inch/the right size) = inner lining

Catchphrase

In ancient times, there was an **INNER LINING** inside the coat, and later it developed into a shirt. **INNER LINING** is 衬 chèn.

Stroke order

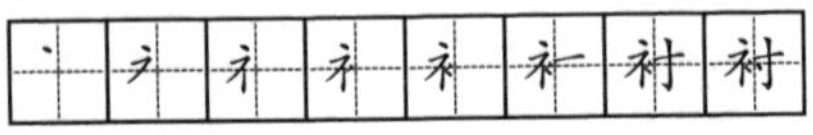

成 BECOME chéng 375

Radical/Component 戈 weapon

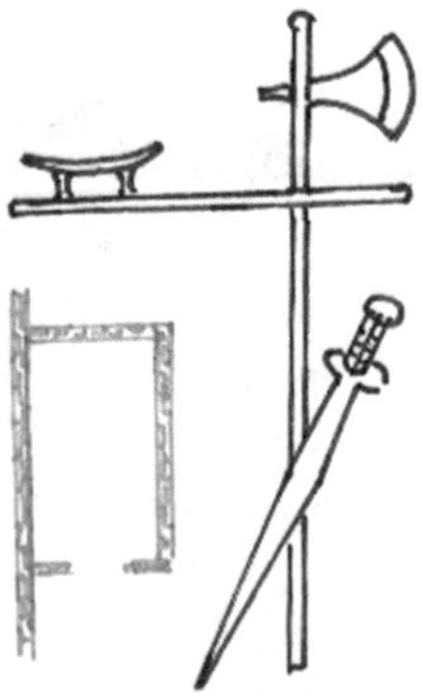

BECOME chéng 成

Ancient form

(knife) + (dagger axe) = become

Catchphrase

In ancient times, knives, daggers and axes **BECAME** the main weapons in warfare. **BECOME** is 成 chéng.

Stroke order

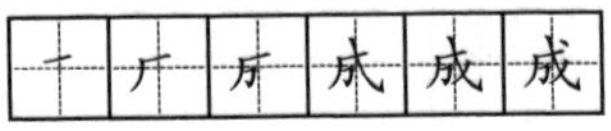

城 CITY/WALL chéng 376

Radical/Component 土 soil/land

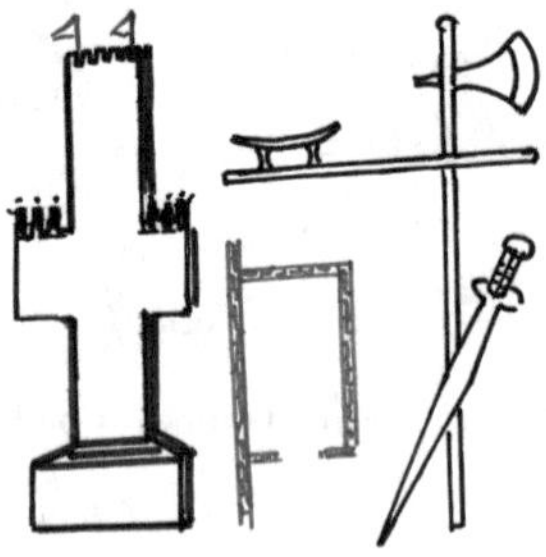

CITY/WALL chéng 城

Ancient form

/(watchtower) + (weapon) = wall/city

Catchphrase

Ancient armies needed weapons and watchtowers to defend their **CITY**. **CITY/WALL** is 城 chéng.

Stroke order

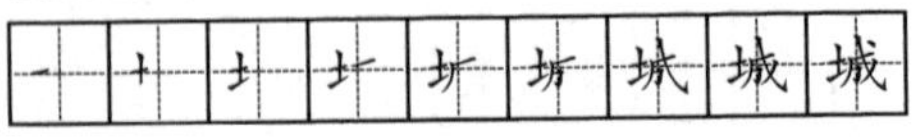

迟(遲) LATE chí 377
Radical/Component 辶 walk

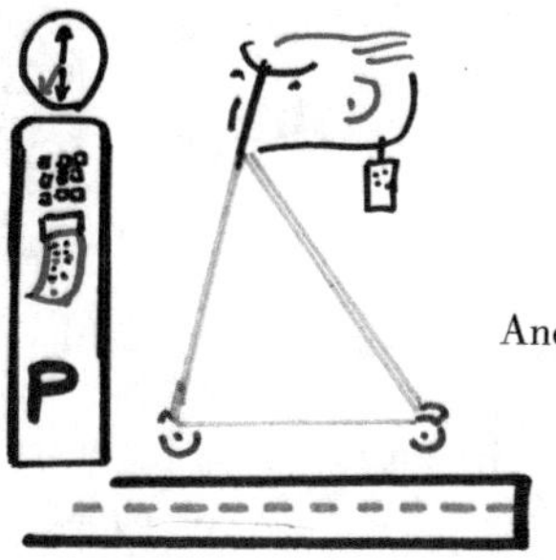

LATE chí 迟

Ancient form Traditional form 遲

辵(walk) + 尺(measure)
= late

Catchphrase

I don't understand why this parking meter says that I am **LATE**. I am just a small trolley that walked here. **LATE** is 迟 chí.

Stroke order

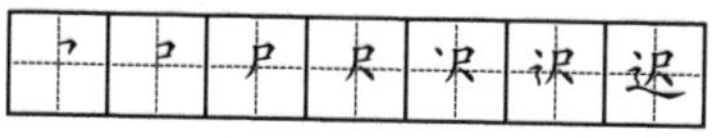

除 EXCEPT chú 378
Radical/Component 阝 cliff

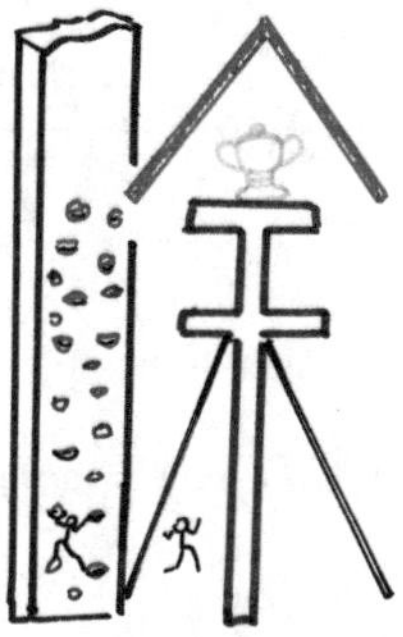

EXCEPT chú 除

Ancient form

阜(cliff) + 余(I/the rest)
= except/divide

Catchphrase

No one **EXCEPT** me can climb up this high wall to get the trophy. **EXCEPT** is 除 chú.

Stroke order

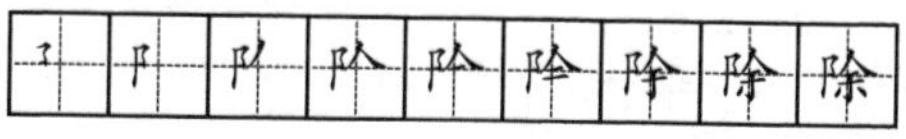

楚 CLEAR chǔ 379
Radical/Component 木 wood/tree

CLEAR chǔ 楚

Ancient form

林(trees) + 疋(footprint) = clear

Catchphrase

I am walking the right way, so I can **CLEARly** see the two big trees in front of me. **CLEAR** is 楚 chǔ.

Stroke order

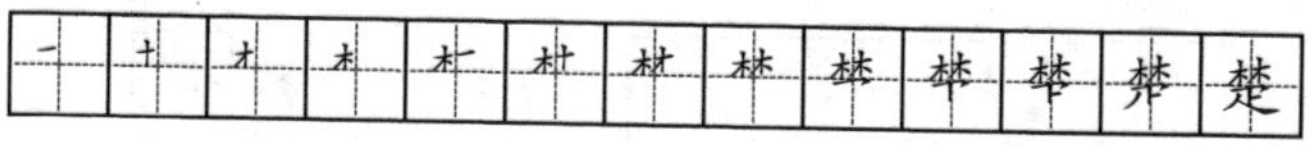

船 BOAT chuán 380
Radical/Component 舟 boat

BOAT chuán 船

Ancient form

舟(boat) + 㕣(water & shout)
= boat

Catchphrase

That man fell into the water and was calling for help. A **BOAT** passed through the rapids to save him. **BOAT** is 船 chuán.

Stroke order

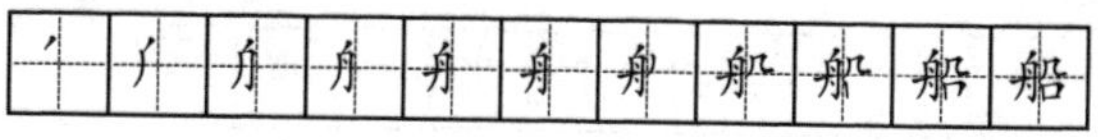

春 SPRING chūn 381
Radical/Component 日 sun

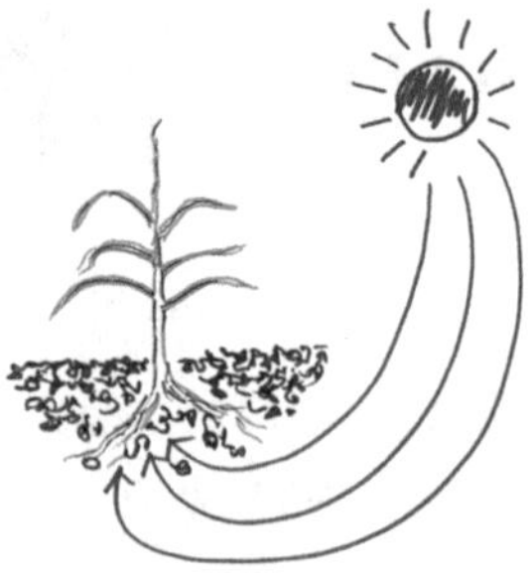

SPRING chūn 春

Ancient form

(plant) + (sun) = spring

Catchphrase

The sun nourishes the land and life begins to stir. It is **SPRING**. **SPRING** is 春 chūn.

Stroke order

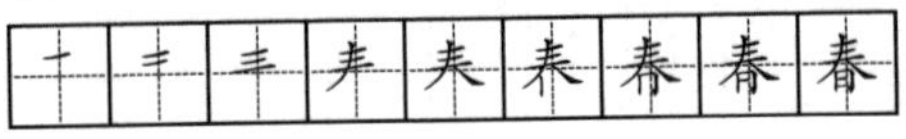

词(詞) WORD cí 382
Radical/Component 讠 language

WORD cí 词

Ancient form　Traditional form 詞

(language) + (manage) = word/phrase

Catchphrase

To manage and express the meanings of language, you use **WORD**s. **WORD/PHRASE** is 词 cí.

Stroke order

聪(聰) CLEVER cōng 383
Radical/Component 耳 ear

CLEVER cōng 聪

Ancient form　Traditional form 聰

(ear) + (brain & heart) = clever/smart

Catchphrase

People who listen with their ears and use their brains must be **CLEVER**. **CLEVER/SMART** is 聪 cōng.

Stroke order

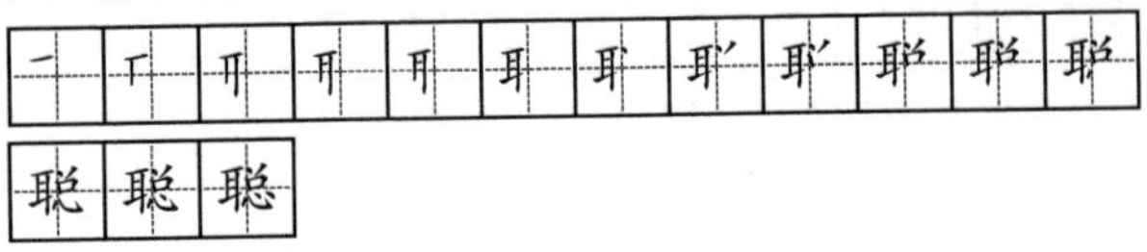

答 AGREE dā; ANSWER dá 384
Radical/Component ⺮ bamboo

AGREE dā; **ANSWER** dá 答

(bamboo) + (join) = answer

Catchphrase

How can I cross the river? The **ANSWER** is to join bamboo poles together to make a raft. **ANSWER** is 答 dá; **AGREE** is dā.

Stroke order

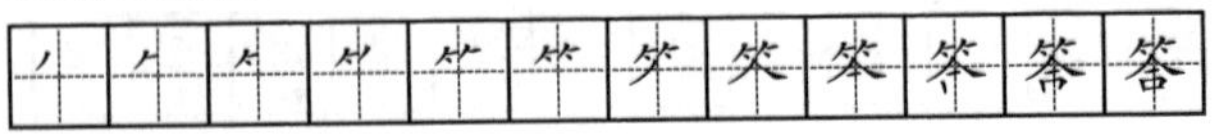

带(帶)**BELT** dài Radical/Component 巾 scarf/towel	385

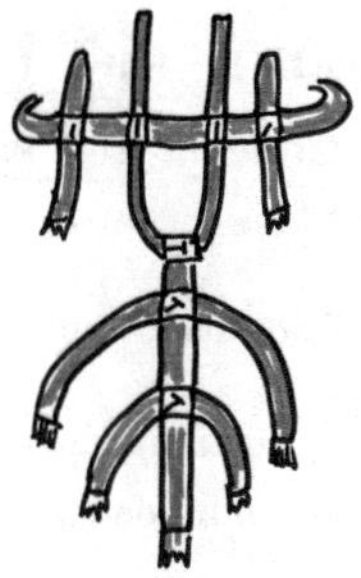

BELT dài 带

Ancient form  Traditional form 帶

(belts) + (bridle)
= belt

Catchphrase

In ancient times, a leather **BELT** was used to make a bridle for a horse. **BELT** is 带 dài.

Stroke order

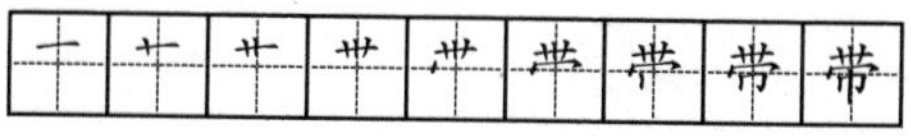

单(單) SINGLE dān 386
Radical/Component 十 ten/cross

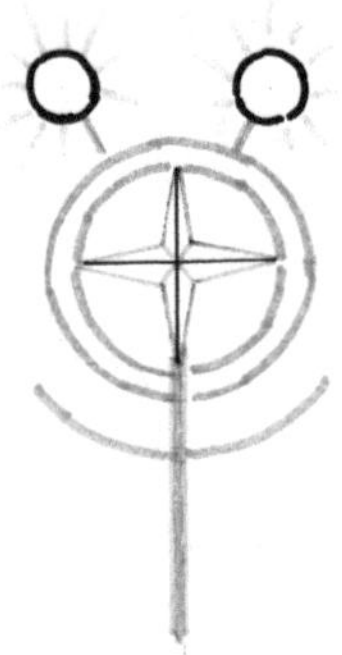

SINGLE dān 单

Ancient form Traditional form 單

(two handles) + 車(car) = single

Catchphrase

This is a **SINGLE**-speed brand-name bicycle with two mirrors. **SINGLE** is 单 dān.

Stroke order

丶 丷 丷 屰 当 肖 单 单

担(擔) WORRY dān; BURDEN dàn 387
Radical/Component 扌 hand

WORRY dān; **BURDEN** dàn 担

Ancient form Traditional form 擔

(hand) + 旦(morning sun) = worry/burden

Catchphrase

The heavy **BURDEN** of manual work begins as the sun rises each day, which makes me **WORR**ied. **WORRY** is 担 dān; **BURDEN** is dàn.

Stroke order

一 十 扌 扌 扣 扣 担 担

当(當) WHEN/BE dāng; PROPER dàng 388
Radical/Component 彐 dustpan

WHEN/BE dāng; **PROPER** dàng 当

Ancient form Traditional form 當

(small/tiny) + (opened container) = when/being

Catchphrase

WHEN you put two chocolate biscuits and a sugar stick on top of this three-layer cake, of course it will be delicious! **WHEN/BE** is 当 dāng; **PROPER** is dàng.

Stroke order

丨 丨 丬 当 当 当

灯(燈) LAMP/LIGHT dēng 389
Radical/Component 火 fire

LAMP/LIGHT dēng 灯

Traditional form 燈

火(fire) + 丁(T-shaped column) = light

Catchphrase

This oil **LAMP** hanging on a T-shaped pole is very strange and beautiful. **LAMP/LIGHT** is 灯 dēng.

Stroke order

丶 丷 火 火 灯 灯

地 LAND/SOIL dì; Grammatical Code de — 390
Radical/Component 土 soil/land/earth

LAND/SOIL dì; **Grammatical Code** de 地

Ancient form

(soil) + (snake) = land/soil/earth

Catchphrase

LAND is not only the home for humans, but for all the creatures of the world. **LAND/SOIL** is 地 dì.

Stroke order

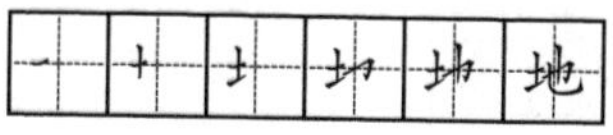

典 CLASSIC diǎn — 391
Radical/Component 八 eight-shape

CLASSIC diǎn 典

Ancient form

(music/books) + (repeating) = classic

Catchphrase

Reading all these **CLASSIC** books can help people learn. **CLASSIC** is 典 diǎn.

Stroke order

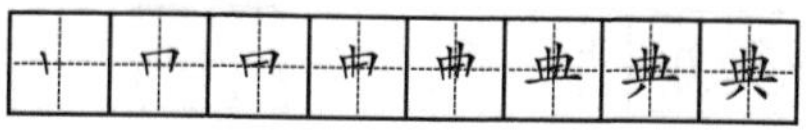

定 STABILITY dìng — 392
Radical/Component 宀 roof/house

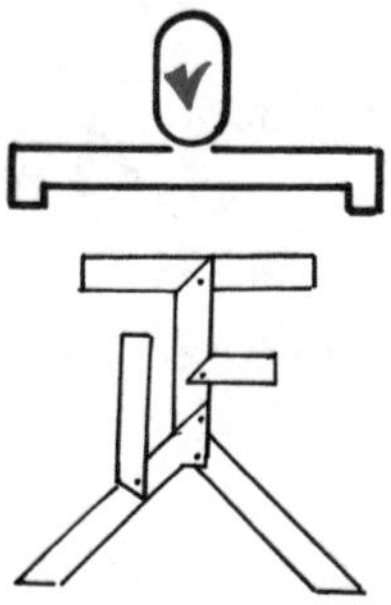

STABILITY dìng 定

Ancient form

(roof) + (correct) = stability

Catchphrase

The **STABILITY** of a house depends on a correct structure and solid foundation. **STABILITY** is 定 dìng.

Stroke order

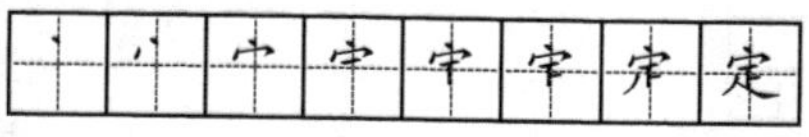

冬 WINTER dōng — 393
Radical/Component 夂 hand/tool

WINTER dōng 冬

Ancient form

(the circle ends) + (ice) = winter

Catchphrase

During **WINTER**, children will dress a snowman in a hat and scarf. **WINTER** is 冬 dōng.

Stroke order

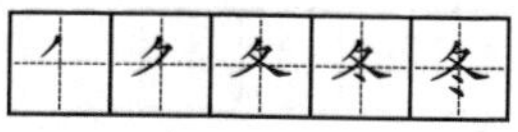

短 SHORT duǎn 394

Radical/Component 矢 arrow

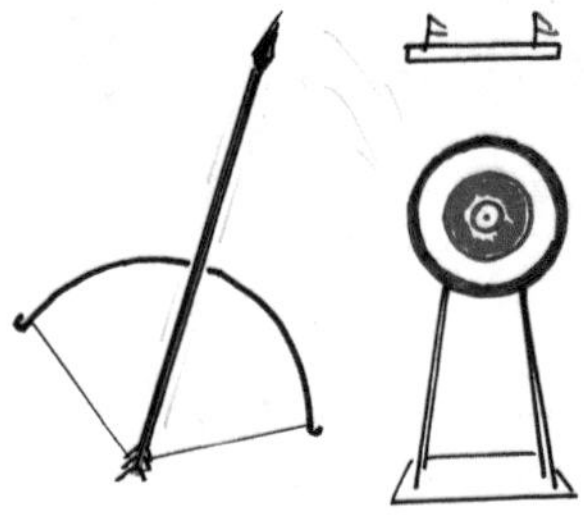

SHORT duǎn 短

Ancient form

(arrow) + (target/a small size like a bean) = short

Catchphrase

If you want the arrow to hit the centre of the target, it is best done from a **SHORT** distance. **SHORT** (distance) is 短 duǎn.

Stroke order

丿	𠂉	𠂉	午	矢	矢	矢	矩	矩	矩	矩	短

段 SECTION duàn 395

Radical/Component 殳 holding a tool to hit

SECTION duàn 段

Ancient form

(cutting work) + (hand with a tool to hit) = section

Catchphrase

It takes a while to cut an object into several **SECTIONs**. **SECTION** is 段 duàn.

Stroke order

丿	𠂆	𠂆	𠂆	阝	阝	阝	段	段

锻（鍛）FORGE duàn 396

Radical/Component 钅 metal/gold

FORGE duàn 锻

Ancient form   Traditional form 鍛

(metal/gold) + (dividing into sections) = exercise

Catchphrase

To **FORGE** a piece of metal and divide it into several sections is hard work. **FORGE** is 锻 duàn.

Stroke order

丿	𠂉	𠂉	乍	钅	钅	钅	钅	钅	钅	钅	钅	锻	锻

朵 Measure Word duǒ 397

Radical/Component 木 wood/tree

MW duǒ 朵

(bud) + (tree/twig) = MW

Catchphrase

A flower bud composed of many petals grows on the twig of a tree. **Measure Word** is 朵 duǒ.

Stroke order

丿	几	几	朵	朵	朵

饿(餓)HUNGRY è 398
Radical/Component 饣 eat/food

HUNGRY è 饿

Ancient form

Traditional form 餓

(eat/food) + (I/me) = hungry

Catchphrase

I am **HUNGRY**! There is food in front of me but I can't reach it. **HUNGRY** is 饿 è.

Stroke order

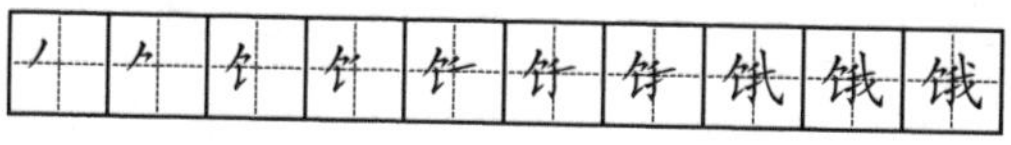

而 BUT ér 399
Radical/Component 而 but/beard

BUT ér 而

Ancient form

(mouth) + (beard) = but

Catchphrase

In Peking Opera, this kind of beard indicates not only that this person is elderly, **BUT** also that he is experienced. **BUT** is 而 ér.

Stroke order

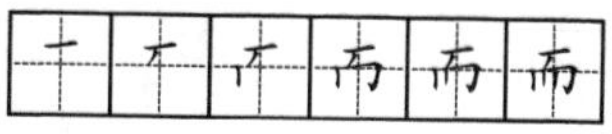

耳 EAR ěr 400
Radical/Component 耳 ear

EAR ěr 耳

Ancient form

Catchphrase

This character depicts a person's right **EAR**. **EAR** is 耳 ěr.

Stroke order

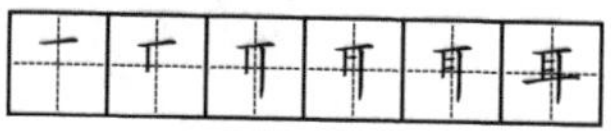

发(發/髮)LAUNCH fā;HAIR fà 401
Radical/Component 又 hand/again/once more

LAUNCH fā;
HAIR fà 发

Ancient form

Traditional form 發/髮

(foot) + (javelin)
= launch/set up

Catchphrase

With a spear, the man can set up and **LAUNCH** himself forward. **LAUNCH** is 发 fā. This man has no **HAIR**. **HAIR** is 发 fà.

Stroke order

法 METHOD/LAW fǎ; METHOD fá 402
Radical/Component 氵 water/river

METHOD/LAW fǎ;
METHOD fá 法

Ancient form 㳒

氵(water) + 去(go) = method/law

Catchphrase

An ancient **METHOD** for creating farmland was to check the field arrangement, wind direction, and drainage systems so as to ensure a good harvest of the crops. **METHOD/LAW** is 法 fǎ; **METHOD** is fá.

Stroke order

丶	丶	氵	汁	汢	汢	法	法

方 SQUARE fāng 403
Radical/Component 方 square shape/direction

SQUARE fāng 方

Ancient form 方

Catchphrase

In ancient northern China, some clans regarded the shape of a **SQUARE** as a spiritual symbol indicating integrity and majesty. **SQUARE** is 方 fāng.

Stroke order

丶	亠	亍	方

放 PUT fàng 404
Radical/Component 方 square/direction

PUT fàng 放

Ancient form 放

方(direction) + 攵(to be forced move) = put

Catchphrase

Under ancient law, criminals were **PUT** by force in the most desolate places to serve their sentences. **PUT** is 放 fàng.

Stroke order

丶	亠	亍	方	方	方	於	放

风(風) WIND fēng 405
Radical/Component 风 wind

WIND fēng 风

Ancient form 風 Traditional form 風

冂(kite) + 彡(air) = wind

Catchphrase

It is fun to make a kite with thin paper and let it float in the sky with the **WIND**. **WIND** is 风 fēng.

Stroke order

丿	几	风	风

附 AFFILIATE/ATTACH fù 406
Radical/Component 阝 wall

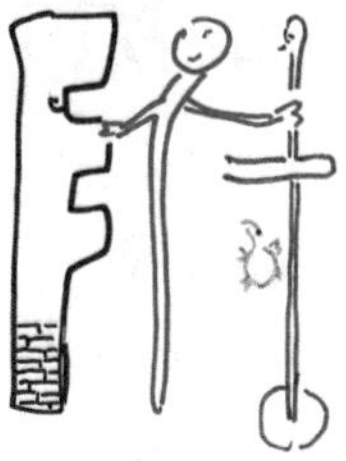

AFFILIATE/ATTACH fù 附

Ancient form

(wall) + (person) + (measure)
= affiliate/attach

Catchphrase

The homeowner said to the three: don't argue over every inch of space because we are all **AFFILIATEd** to each other, like a family. **AFFILIATE/ATTACH** is 附 fù.

Stroke order

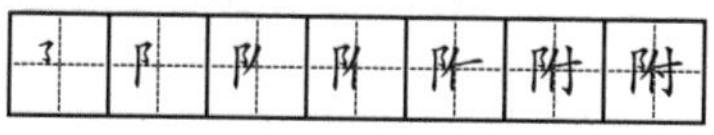

复(復/複) REPEAT fù 407
Radical/Component 夂 foot

REPEAT fù 复

Ancient form

Traditional form 復/複

(run away) + (repeated movement)
= repeat

Catchphrase

The long-distance runners must **REPEAT** the same lap around the track dozens of times to reach the red flag. **REPEAT** is 复 fù.

Stroke order

该(該) OUGHT TO/SHOULD gāi 408
Radical/Component 讠 language

OUGHT TO/ SHOULD gāi 该

Ancient form

Traditional form 該

(language) + (9 pm to 11 pm)
= ought to/should

Catchphrase

The tiny alarm clock tells you both that it is a quarter to eleven. You **OUGHT TO** go to sleep. **OUGHT TO/SHOULD** is 该 gāi.

Stroke order

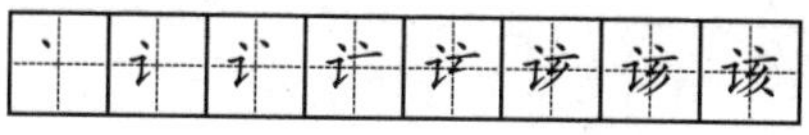

干(幹/乾) DRY gān; DO gàn 409
Radical/Component 干 dry/do

DRY gān; **DO** gàn 干

Ancient form

Traditional form 幹/乾

(rack) + ___ (arm) = dry/do

Catchphrase

This is a **DRY**ing rack with two arms, and this is the matter you need to **DO**. **DRY** is 干 gān; **DO** is gàn.

Stroke order

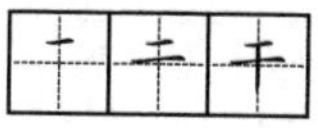

感 **FEELING** gǎn Radical/Component 心 heart	410

FEELING gǎn 感

Ancient form

(all/do the same) + (heart) = feeling

Catchphrase

The common people speak with one voice: they all **FEEL** grateful for the soldiers who are protecting their safety. **FEELING** is 感 gǎn.

Stroke order

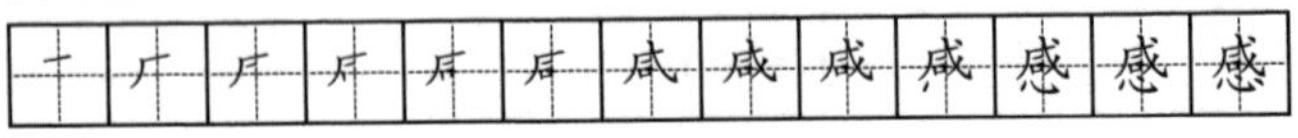

刚(剛) **JUST** gāng Radical/Component 刂 knife/sharp object	411

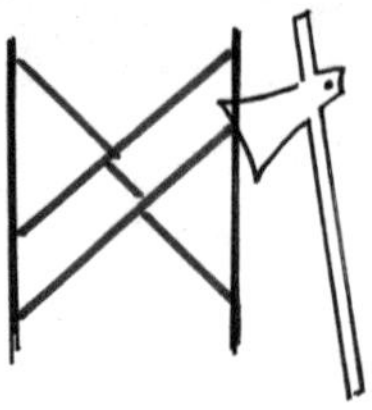

JUST gāng 刚

Ancient form

Traditional form 剛

(net) + (axe) = just

Catchphrase

This tempered glass is very strong. Although it has **JUST** been hit with an axe, it is still intact. **JUST** is 刚 gāng.

Stroke order

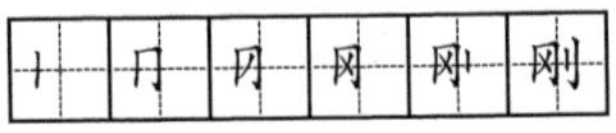

糕 **CAKE** gāo Radical/Component 米 rice	412

CAKE gāo 糕

(rice) + (lamb/tasty) + (fire) = cake

Catchphrase

This slowly-baked **CAKE**, made with rice flour and a little lamb fat, is my gift for my mother's birthday. **CAKE** is 糕 gāo.

Stroke order

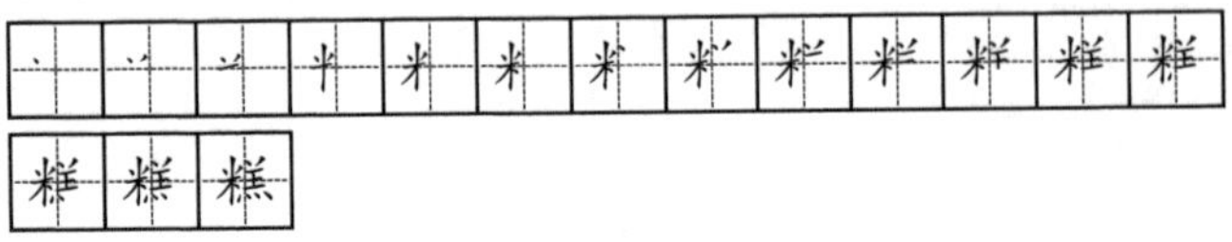

根 **ROOT** gēn Radical/Component 木 wood/tree	413

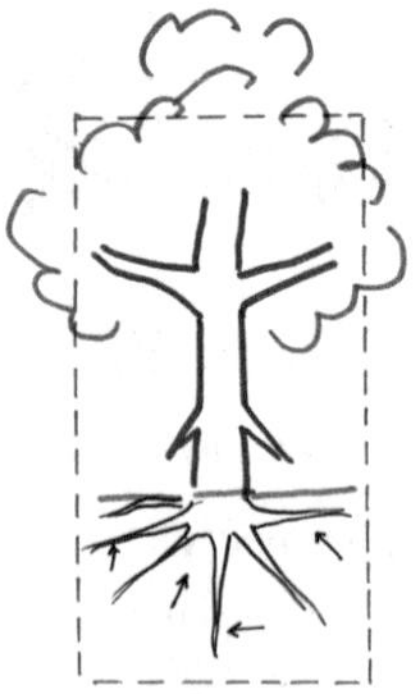

ROOT gēn 根

Ancient form

(tree) + (relevant/corresponding part to the radical) = root

Catchphrase

Above the trunk is the canopy, and below is the **ROOT**. **ROOT** is 根 gēn. (The left side of the character is a tree, and the character 艮 on the right side means "relevant or corresponding part", so this character refers to a part of a tree: its root.)

Stroke order

跟 HEEL/WITH/FOLLOW gēn — 414

Radical/Component 足 foot

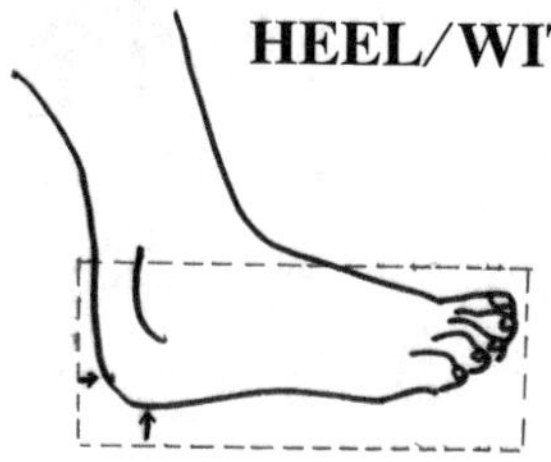

HEEL/WITH/FOLLOW gēn 跟

Ancient form

(foot) + (relevant/corresponding part to the radical) = heel

Catchphrase

The left side of the character is a foot, and the character 艮 on the right side means "relevant or corresponding part", so this character refers to a part of a foot: its **HEEL**. **HEEL/WITH/FOLLOW** is 跟 gēn.

Stroke order

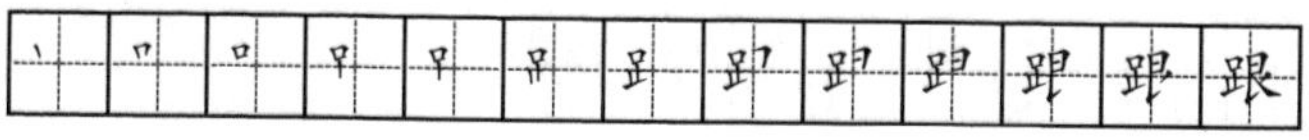

更 CHANGE gēng; MORE gèng — 415

Radical/Component 曰 talk

MORE gèng; **CHANGE** gēng 更

Ancient form

(suit) + (hand with thing) = change/more

Catchphrase

Before you go out, it's best to **CHANGE** in front of the mirror to make you look **MORE** smart. **CHANGE** is 更 gēng; **MORE** is gèng.

Stroke order

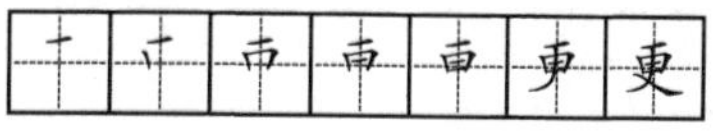

故 OLD gù — 416

Radical/Component 攵 rap by hand

OLD gù 故

Ancient form

(ancient) + (hand with tool) = old

Catchphrase

Ancient ruins always contain **OLD** classic stories that teach modern people what is right and wrong. **OLD** is 故 gù.

Stroke order

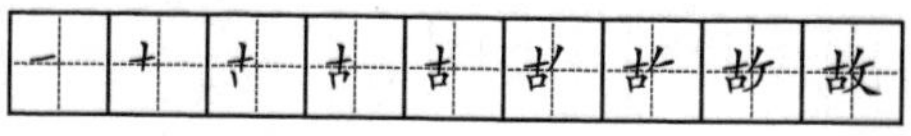

顾(顧) LOOK gù — 417

Radical/Component 页 face/head/page

LOOK gù 顾

Ancient form

Traditional form 顧

(bird) + (head to) = look

Catchphrase

Trains can rush out of a tunnel at any time. Birds know this and always **LOOK** carefully to avoid accidents. **LOOK** is 顾 gù.

Stroke order

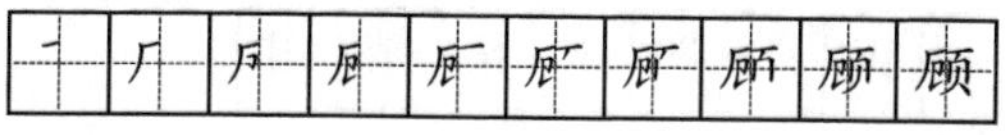

刮 BLOW guā 418
Radical/Component 刂 knife

BLOW guā 刮

Ancient form

(thousand mouths) + (knife)
= blow

Catchphrase

If a thousand mouths speak at the same time, it will **BLOW** into a great hurricane. **BLOW** is 刮 guā.

Stroke order

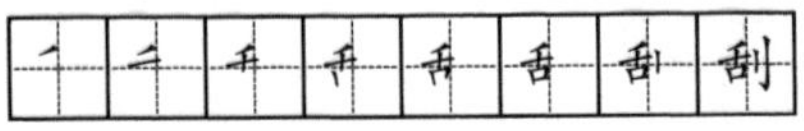

怪 STRANGE guài 419
Radical/Component 忄 psychology/heart

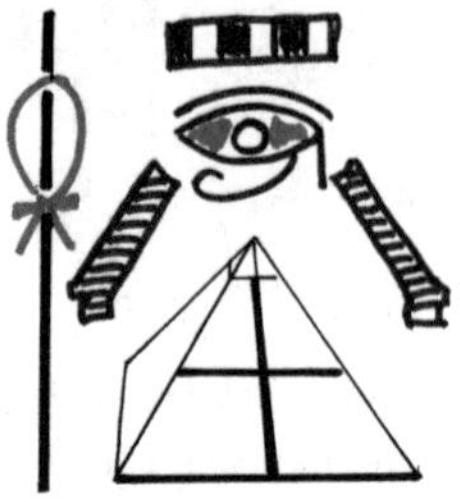

STRANGE guài 怪

Ancient form

(heart) + (powerful/unusual)
= strange

Catchphrase

There is a single eye on top of the pyramid, giving you a **STRANGE** and sacred feeling. **STRANGE** is 怪 guài.

Stroke order

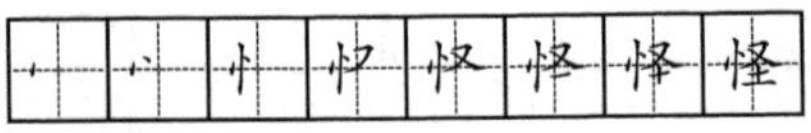

惯（慣）HABIT guàn 420
Radical/Component 忄 psychology

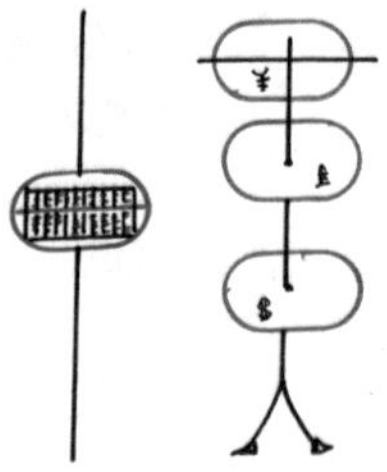

HABIT guàn 惯

Traditional form 慣

(heart) + / (money) = habit

Catchphrase

Regardless of how much money one has, it is a good **HABIT** to use it with good sense. **HABIT** is 惯 guàn.

Stroke order

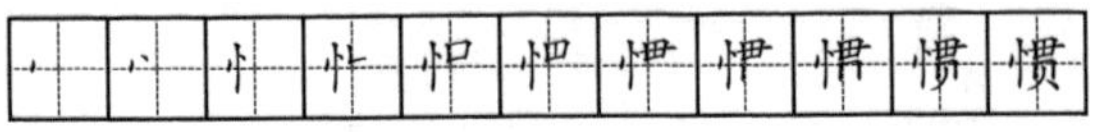

害 HARM hài 421
Radical/Component 宀 roof/house

HARM hài 害

Ancient form

(bows) + (mouth with arrow)
= harm

Catchphrase

HARMing others with harsh words is like shooting arrows from three bows at the same time. **HARM** is 害 hài.

Stroke order

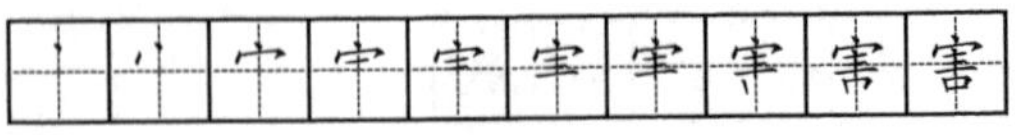

行 BUSINESS háng; WALK xíng — 422
Radical/Component 行 street/walk

BUSINESS háng;
WALK xíng 行

Ancient form 

Catchphrase

Banks occupy big **BUSINESS** buildings along commercial streets where potential customers walk by. **BUSINESS** is 行 háng; **WALK** is xíng.

Stroke order

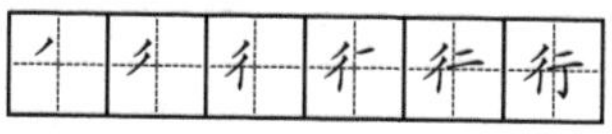

河 RIVER hé — 423
Radical/Component 氵 water/river

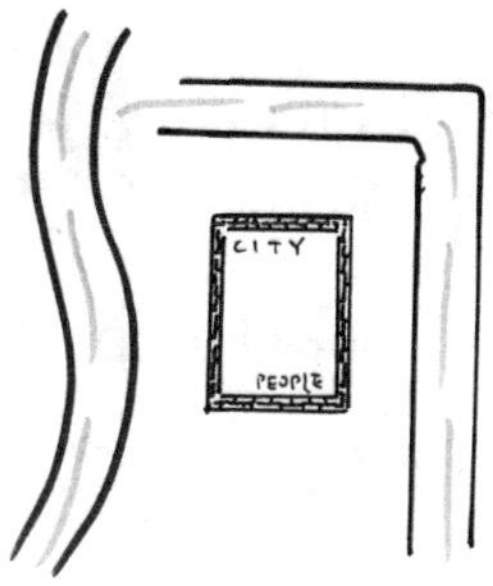

RIVER hé 河

Ancient form 

(water) + (curved river plus population) = river

Catchphrase

Ancient Chinese would build their towns near the gentle bend of a **RIVER**. **RIVER** is 河 hé.

Stroke order

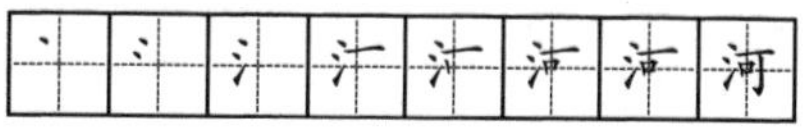

乎 Particle hū — 424
Radical/Component 丿 the first stroke

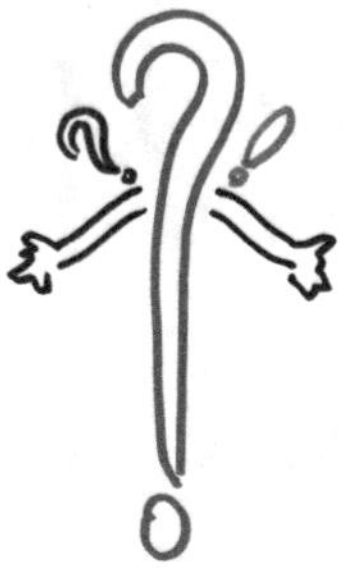

Particle hū 乎

Ancient form 

(air) + (instrument) = particle

Catchphrase

The **Particle** for interrogative or exclamatory sentences is 乎 hū.

Stroke order

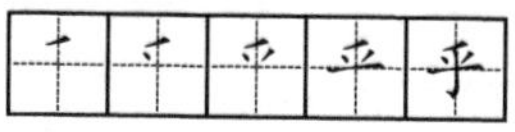

护(護) PROTECT hù — 425
Radical/Component 扌 hand

PROTECT hù 护

Ancient form 

Traditional form 護

(hand) + (window) = protect

Catchphrase

Cleaning your window keeps them looking nice and **PROTECT**s them from dirt. **PROTECT** is 护 hù.

Stroke order

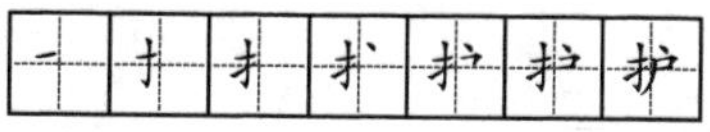

花 FLOWER huā 426
Radical/Component 艹 flower

FLOWER huā **花**

Ancient form

(soil and pedicel) + (pollen) = flower

Catchphrase

The right balance of chemical compositions in the soil makes the **FLOWER**s more beautiful. **FLOWER** is 花 huā.

Stroke order

一	十	艹	艹	芢	花	花

化 CHANGE huà 427
Radical/Component 亻 mankind

CHANGE huà **化**

Ancient form

(life) + (death) = change

Catchphrase

Zhuangzi, an ancient Chinese philosopher said that, the **CHANG**ing of life and death is repeated endlessly. **CHANGE** is 化 huà.

Stroke order

丿	亻	亻	化

画(畫) PAINTING/DRAWING huà 428
Radical/Component 田 field

PAINTING/ DRAWING huà **画**

Ancient form

Traditional form 畫

(hand with brush) + (landscape) = painting

Catchphrase

I often bring an easel to **PAINT** landscapes in the fields. **PAINTING/DRAWING** is 画 huà.

Stroke order

一	丆	币	币	亩	亩	画	画

坏 BAD huài 429
Radical/Component 土 soil/land

BAD huài **坏**

Ancient form

(soil) + (no) = bad

Catchphrase

If soil is **BAD**, then the land cannot be cultivated. **BAD** is 坏 huài.

Stroke order

一	十	土	圵	圷	坏	坏

环(環) CIRCLE huán — 430

Radical/Component 王 jade

CIRCLE huán 环

Ancient form 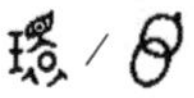

Traditional form 環

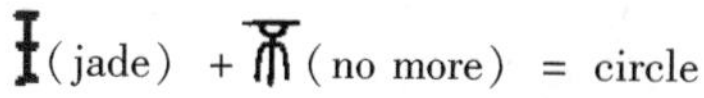

Catchphrase

No! This shape is wrong, I want to build a **CIRCUL**ar runway, not a runway at the airport! **CIRCLE** is 环 huán.

Stroke order

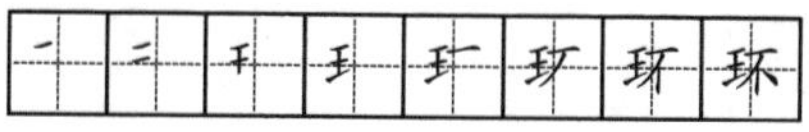

换 REPLACE huàn — 431

Radical/Component 扌 hand

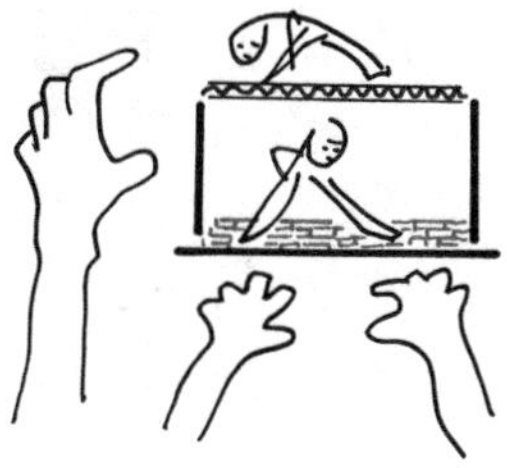

REPLACE huàn 换

Ancient form 

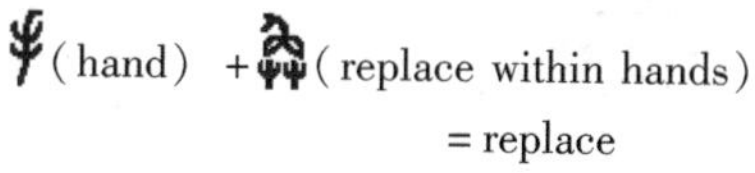

Catchphrase

After moving in, I **REPLACE**d the floor and tiles with my bare hands. **REPLACE** is 换 huàn.

Stroke order

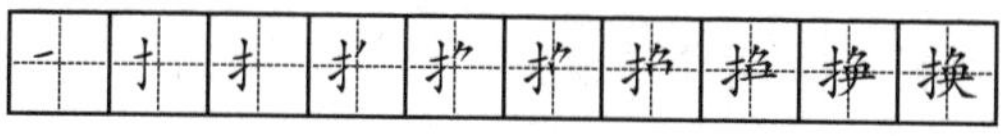

黄 YELLOW huáng — 432

Radical/Component 黄 yellow

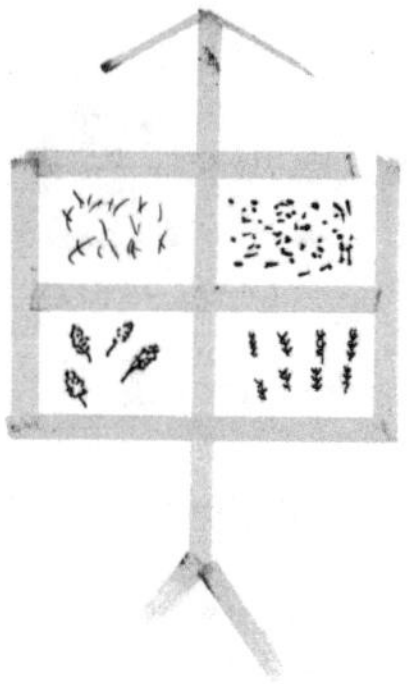

YELLOW huáng 黄

Ancient form 

Catchphrase

The fields of the Yellow River Basin are all **YELLOW**. **YELLOW** is 黄 huáng.

Stroke order

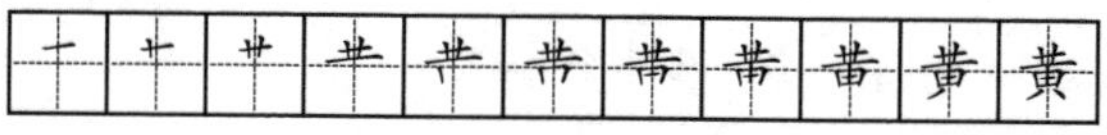

婚 MARRIAGE hūn — 433

Radical/Component 女 woman

MARRIAGE hūn 婚

Ancient form 

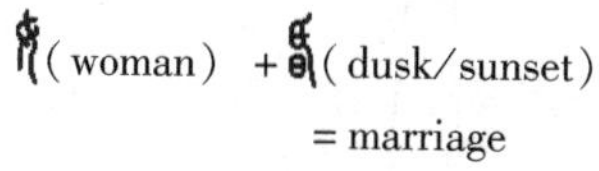

Catchphrase

In some parts of North China, women get **MARRIED** at sunset. **MARRIAGE** is 婚 hūn.

Stroke order

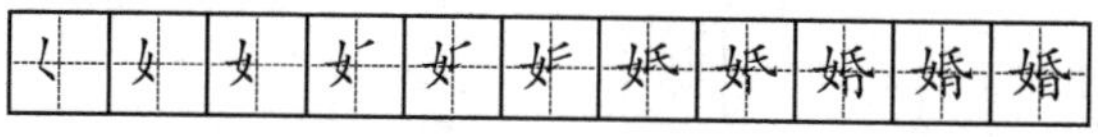

或 OR huò 434
Radical/Component 戈 axe

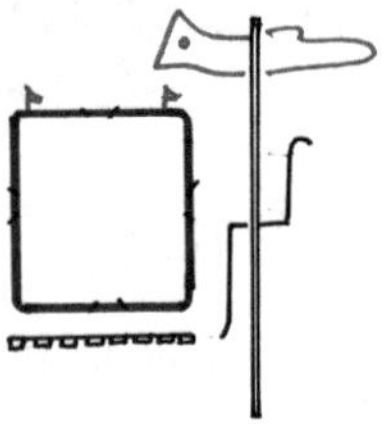

OR huò 或

Ancient form

(axe) + (one voice) = or

Catchphrase

Armed with only my axe and my voice, I shall fight and win **OR** I shall die. **OR** is 或 huò.

Stroke order

一 𠫓 𠫓 𠮛 𠮛 式 或 或

级(級) GRADE/LEVEL jí 435
Radical/Component 纟 silk

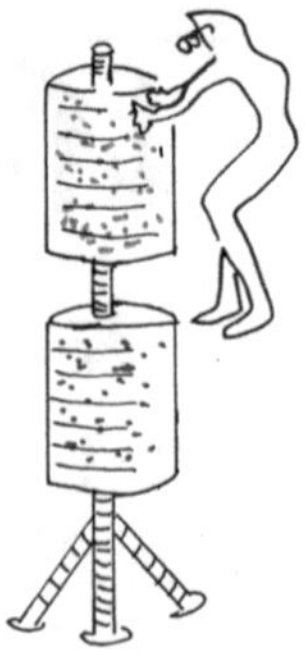

GRADE/LEVEL jí 级

Ancient form

Traditional form 級

(silk) + (grab/touch) = grade

Catchphrase

All silk products need to be checked by hand to be given the **GRADE** (there are **LEVEL**s A, B and C) before they go to market. **GRADE/LEVEL** is 级 jí.

Stroke order

𠃋 乡 纟 纠 级 级

极(極) EXTREME jí 436
Radical/Component 木 wood/tree

EXTREME jí 极

Ancient form

Traditional form 極

(tree) + (grab/hold) = extreme

Catchphrase

The snake on the bamboo tree is **EXTREME**ly hungry, and must eat the fruit to avoid death. **EXTREME** is 极 jí.

Stroke order

一 十 才 木 朸 极 极

急 HURRY/ANXIOUS jí 437
Radical/Component 心 heart

HURRY/ANXIOUS jí 急

Ancient form

(grab) + (heart) = hurry/anxious

Catchphrase

When people are in a **HURRY**, their hearts will beat faster than normal. **HURRY/ANXIOUS** is 急 jí.

Stroke order

𠂊 𠂊 刍 刍 刍 刍 急 急 急

438 己 SELF jǐ

Radical/Component 乙 self

SELF jǐ 己

Ancient form

Catchphrase

The crawling baby smiled at her **SELF** in the mirror. **SELF** is 己 jǐ.

Stroke order

439 记(記) TAKE NOTE jì

Radical/Component 讠 language

TAKE NOTE jì 记

Ancient form

Traditional form 記

(language) + (oneself) = take note

Catchphrase

One can build good language skills by **TAK**ing **NOTE** of what one says at all times. **TAKE NOTE** is 记 jì.

Stroke order

440 季 SEASON jì

Radical/Component 子 child

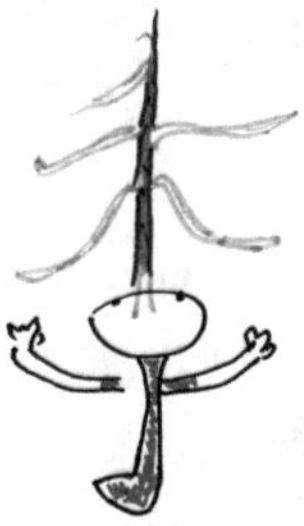

SEASON jì 季

Ancient form

(crop) + (child) = season

Catchphrase

Childhood is a time for growing, just like the growing **SEASON** of crops. **SEASON** is 季 jì.

Stroke order

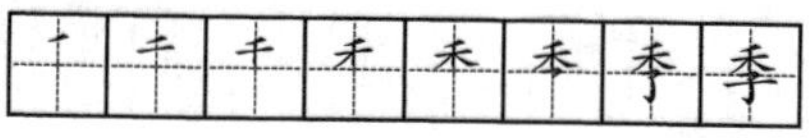

441 绩(績) ACHIEVEMENT jì

Radical/Component 纟 silk

ACHIEVEMENT jì 绩

Ancient form

Traditional form 績

(silk) + (in charge of finance) = achievement

Catchphrase

The owner of the silk factory has **ACHIEVE**d great wealth. **ACHIEVEMENT** is 绩 jì.

Stroke order

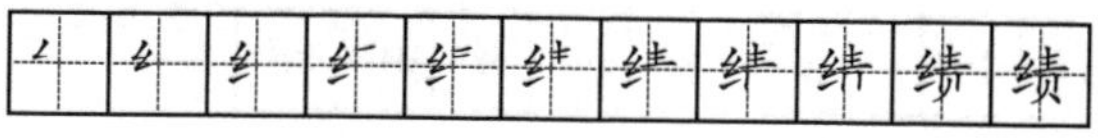

加 ADD jiā 442
Radical/Component 力 strength

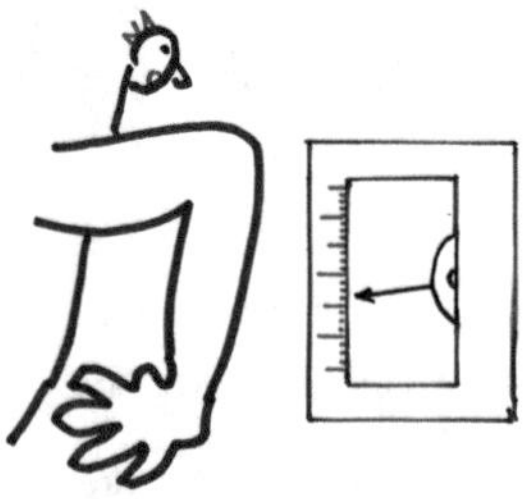

ADD jiā 加

Ancient form

(strength) + (mouth) = add

Catchphrase

In the gym, to increase your strength you must **ADD** more weight to the machine. **ADD** is 加 jiā.

Stroke order

㇇	力	力	加	加

假 FALSE jiǎ; HOLIDAY jià 443
Radical/Component 亻 man

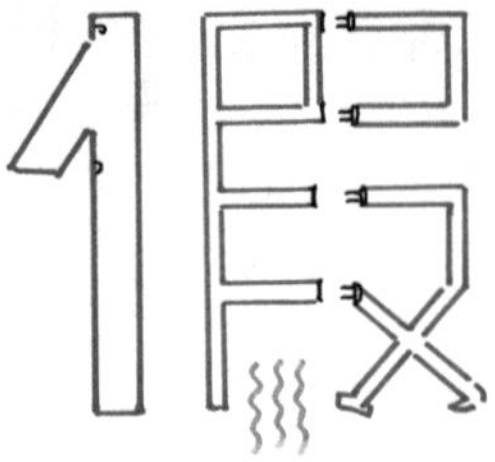

FALSE jiǎ; **HOLIDAY** jià 假

Ancient form

(man) + (recharging) = holiday

Catchphrase

The man needs a **HOLIDAY** to rest and recharge. **HOLIDAY** is 假 jià; **FALSE** is jiǎ.

Stroke order

ノ	亻	亻	仃	仴	佀	佀	佀	佀	假	假

检（檢）CHECK jiǎn 444
Radical/Component 木 wood/tree

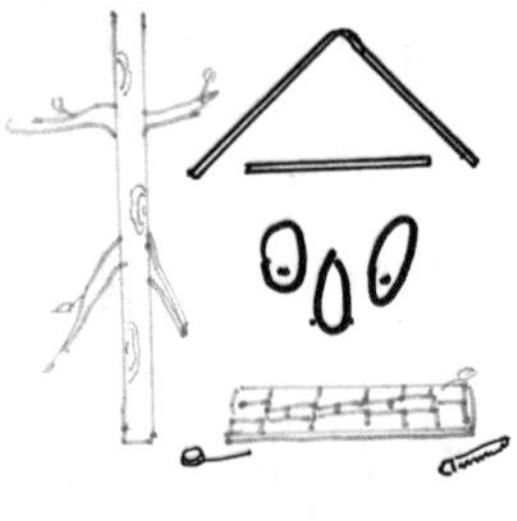

CHECK jiǎn 检

Ancient form

Traditional form 檢

(wood) + (look carefully) = check

Catchphrase

The wooden floor I made for my house should be **CHECK**ed carefully. **CHECK** is 检 jiǎn.

Stroke order

一	十	才	木	杈	松	松	松	检	检	检

简（簡）SIMPLE jiǎn 445
Radical/Component 竹 bamboo

SIMPLE jiǎn 简

Ancient form

Traditional form 簡

(bamboo) + (gap/space) = simple

Catchphrase

There is a gap between the two bamboo trees on my **SIMPLE** house. **SIMPLE** is 简 jiǎn.

Stroke order

ノ	𠂉	𠂉	𥫗	𥫗	𥫗	𥫗	筲	筲	筲	筲	简	简

健 SOUND/HEALTHY jiàn — 446

Radical/Component 亻 man

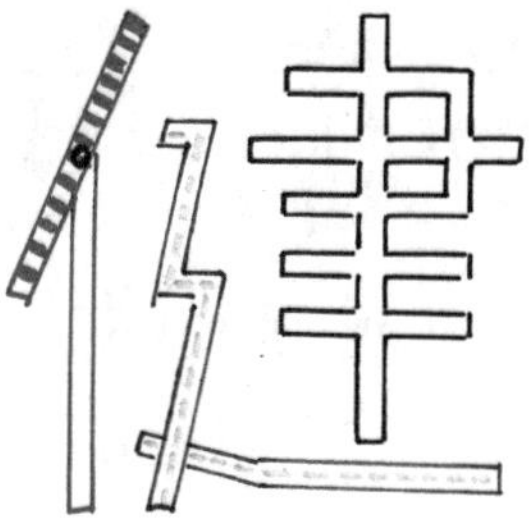

SOUND/ HEALTHY jiàn 健

Ancient form 

(man) + (road) (structure)
= sound/healthy

Catchphrase

The man chose a good spot next to the road to build the structure, so the foundation is very **SOUND**. **SOUND/ HEALTHY** is 健 jiàn.

Stroke order

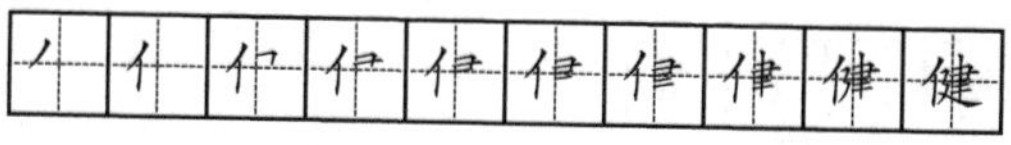

讲(講) SPEECH jiǎng — 447

Radical/Component 讠 language

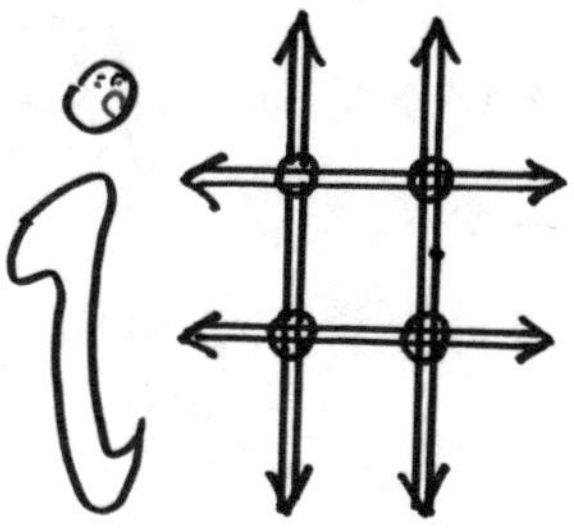

SPEECH jiǎng 讲

Ancient form 

Traditional form 講

(language) + (communicate)
= speech

Catchphrase

One method of communicating is through **SPEECH**. **SPEECH** is 讲 jiǎng.

Stroke order

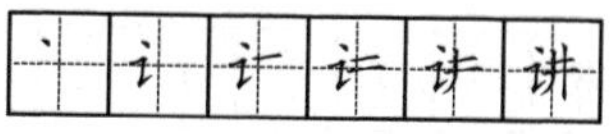

蕉 **BANANA** jiāo | 448
Radical/Component 艹 plant/grass/flower

BANANA jiāo 蕉

艹(plant) + 焦(bird and burn) = banana

Catchphrase

BANANA trees are dark brown like they'd been burned, and have birds sitting up in the leaves. **BANANA** is 蕉 jiāo.

Stroke order

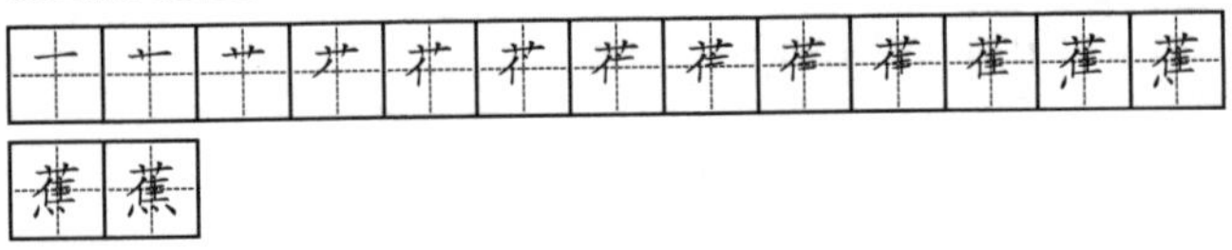

角 **HORN/CORNER** jiǎo; **ROLE** jué | 449
Radical/Component 角 horn/corner

HORN/CORNER jiǎo; **ROLE** jué 角

Ancient form 角

Catchphrase

This **HORN** was cut from the head of a bull. **HORN/CORNER** is 角 jiǎo; **ROLE** is jué.

Stroke order

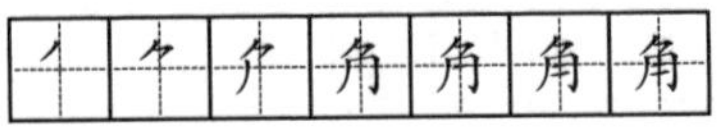

脚 **FOOT** jiǎo | 450
Radical/Component 月 organ/moon

FOOT jiǎo 脚

Ancient form 腳

(the shape of foot) + (the direction to leave) + (footstep) = foot

Catchphrase

Is it wise to wear beautiful shoes that are too small and hurt your **FOOT**? **FOOT** is 脚 jiǎo.

Stroke order

较(較) **COMPARISON** jiào | 451
Radical/Component 车 car

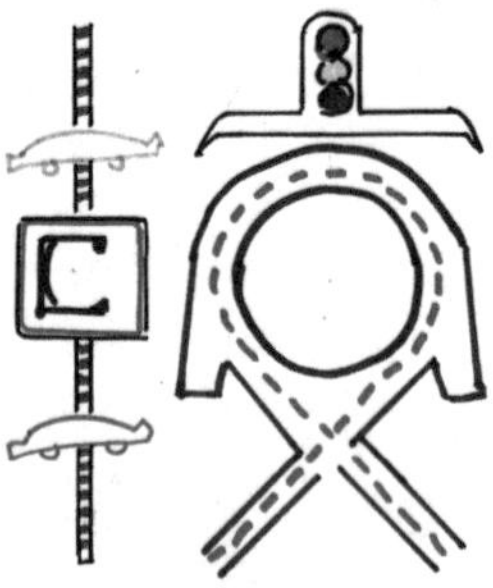

COMPARISON jiào 较

Ancient form 較 / 較 / 較

Traditional form 較

車(car) + 爻(competition) = comparison

Catchphrase

COMPAREd with normal streets, professional tracks are much better for car race competitions. **COMPARISON** is 较 jiào.

Stroke order

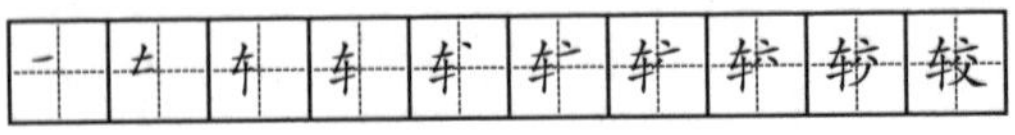

接 BRING IN/RECEIVE jiē — 452
Radical/Component 扌 hand

BRING IN/RECEIVE jiē 接

Ancient form

(hand) + (standing) + (woman)
= bring in/receive

Catchphrase

Traditional marriage customs require that the groom stand at the entrance of the bridal chamber and offer his hand to **BRING IN** the bride. **BRING IN/RECEIVE** is 接 jiē.

Stroke order

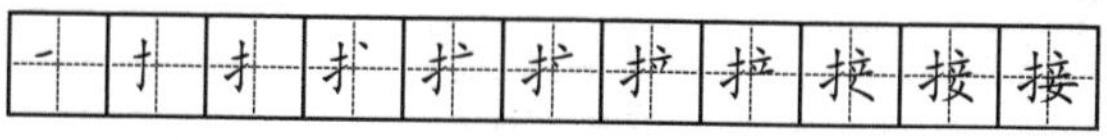

街 STREET jiē — 453
Radical/Component 行 walk

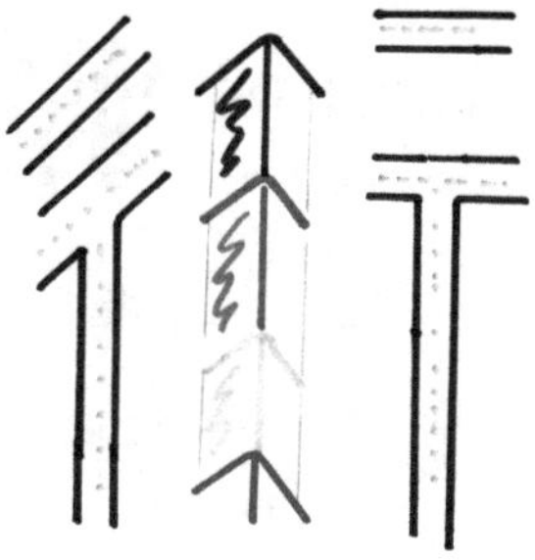

STREET jiē 街

Ancient form /

(roads/streets) + (stores)
= street

Catchphrase

Roads and **STREET**s formed around the stores. **STREET** is 街 jiē.

Stroke order

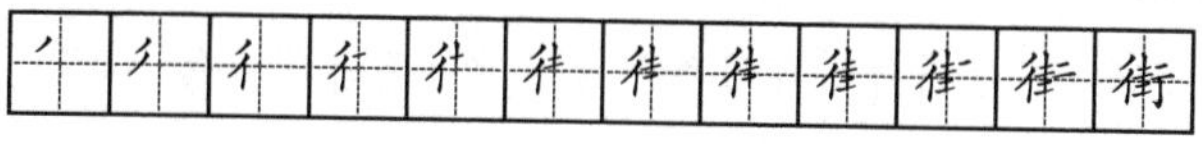

节(節) FESTIVAL jié — 454
Radical/Component 艹 plant/grass/flower

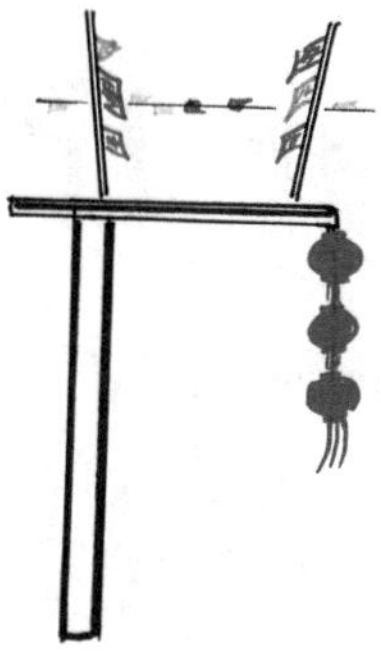

FESTIVAL jié 节

Ancient form

Traditional from 節

(plant/flower) + (pillar)
= festival

Catchphrase

Let's put up some flowers and hang three red lanterns on the side of the house to celebrate the Spring **FESTIVAL**. **FESTIVAL** is 节 jié.

Stroke order

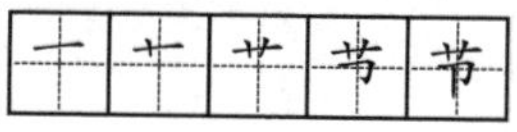

结(結) JOIN jié; PRODUCE jiē — 455
Radical/Component 纟 silk

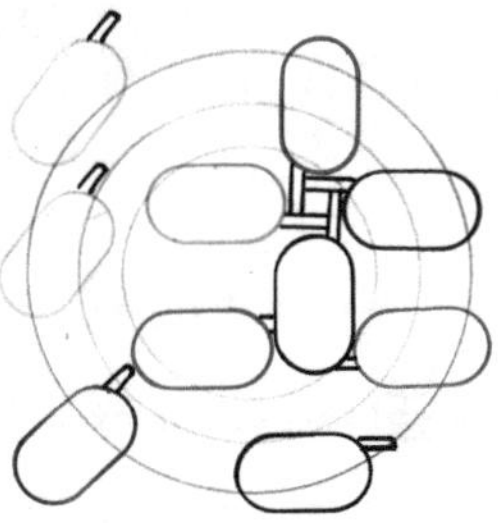

JOIN jié;
PRODUCE jiē 结

Ancient form

Traditional form 結

(silk) + (joyful, lucky)
= join

Catchphrase

Ten mobile phone users have **JOIN**ed together to form this chat group. **JOIN** is 结 jié; **PRODUCE** is jiē.

Stroke order

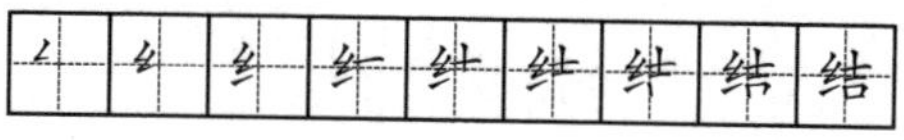

解 DISSECT jiě — 456

Radical/Component 角 horn

DISSECT jiě 解

Ancient form 解

角(horn) + 刀(knife) 牛(cow) = dissect

Catchphrase

When this cow was **DISSECT**ed, the horn was cut off first with a knife. **DISSECT** is 解 jiě.

Stroke order

丿	⺈	𠂊	角	角	角	角	角	角	角	解	解	解

界 BOUNDARY jiè — 457

Radical/Component 田 field/farmland

BOUNDARY jiè 界

Ancient form 界

田(farmland) + 介(in between) = boundary

Catchphrase

The arrow below indicates the **BOUNDARY** in between the different plots of farmland. **BOUNDARY** is 界 jiè.

Stroke order

丨	冂	日	田	田	畀	界	界	界

借 BORROW jiè — 458

Radical/Component 亻 man

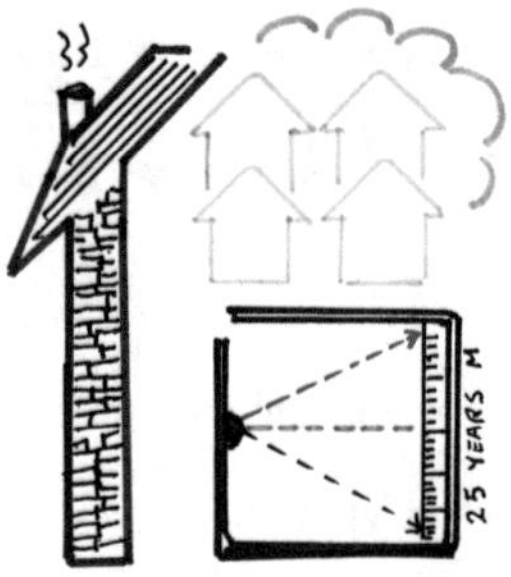

BORROW jiè 借

Ancient form 借

亻(man) + 昔(past days) = borrow

Catchphrase

Many people **BORROW** money from the bank to buy their house, but houses today are worth more now than in past days. **BORROW** is 借 jiè.

Stroke order

丿	亻	仁	什	件	件	供	借	借	借

斤 500 GRAMS jīn — 459

Radical/Component 斤 ax

500 **GRAMS** jīn 斤

Ancient form 斤/斤

厂(meat) + 斤(ax) = 500 grams (Chinese unit of weight)

Catchphrase

The butcher made three cuts of meat at 500 grams each! **500 GRAMS** is 斤 jīn.

Stroke order

丿	厂	斤	斤

净 CLEAN jìng | 460
Radical/Component 冫 ice

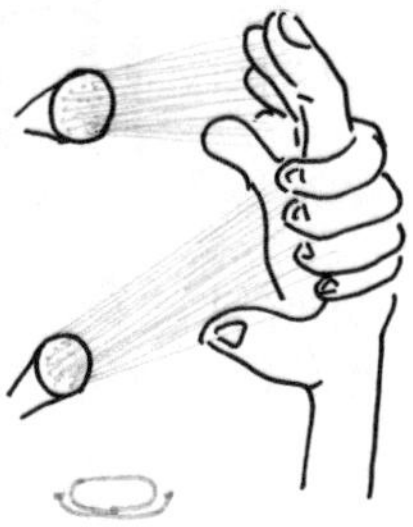

CLEAN jìng 净

Ancient form

氵(water) + 争(two hands compete) = clean

Catchphrase

The two hands compete for water to get **CLEAN**. **CLEAN** is 净 jìng.

Stroke order

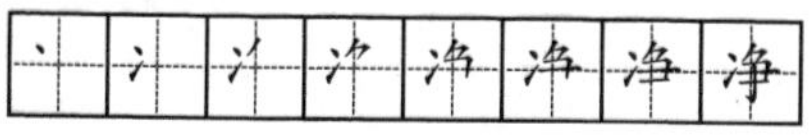

静 QUIET jìng | 461
Radical/Component 青 green

QUIET jìng 静

青(green/plants) + 争(two hands compete) = quiet

Catchphrase

The competition between plants is **QUIET** and peaceful. **QUIET** is 静 jìng.

Stroke order

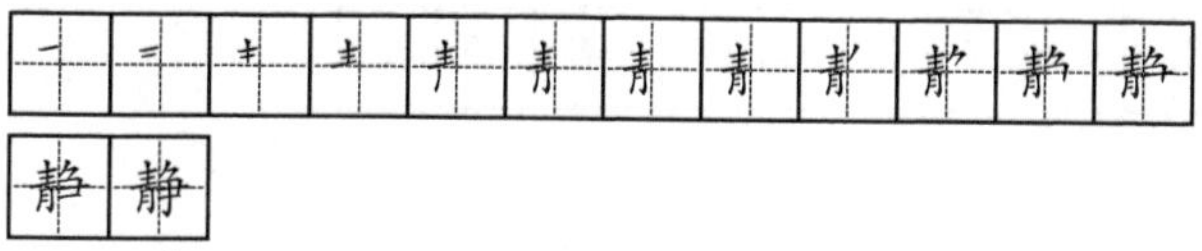

境 BORDER jìng | 462
Radical/Component 土 soil/earth

BORDER jìng 境

Ancient form

土(land) + 立(standing) + 竟(finish) = border

Catchphrase

A bird stands on a sign that establishes the **BORDER** between our land. **BORDER** is 境 jìng.

Stroke order

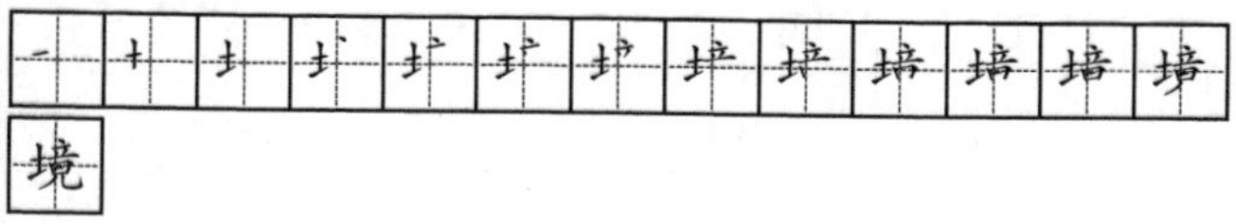

久 LONG jiǔ | 463
Radical/Component ノ the first stroke

LONG jiǔ 久

Ancient form

Catchphrase

The old man knows that acupuncture takes a **LONG** time to produce a curative effect. **LONG** is 久 jiǔ.

Stroke order

酒 ALCOHOL jiǔ 464
Radical/Component 酉 alcohol

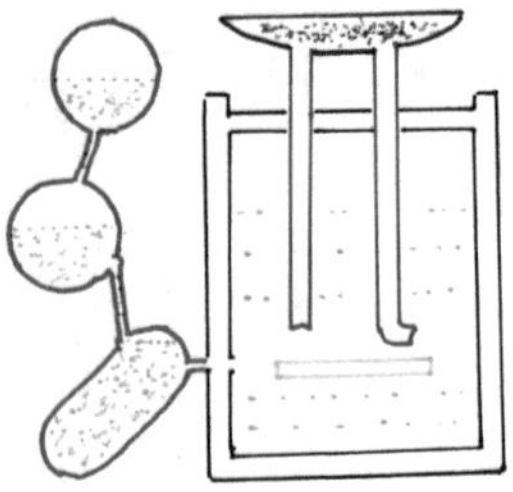

ALCOHOL jiǔ 酒

Ancient form

(liquid) + (container) = alcohol

Catchphrase

The water and **ALCOHOL** mixture must boil in a special container to be distilled. **ALCOHOL** is 酒 jiǔ.

Stroke order

丶	氵	氵	汀	沂	洏	洏	洒	酒	酒

旧(舊) OLD jiù 465
Radical/Component 日 day/sun

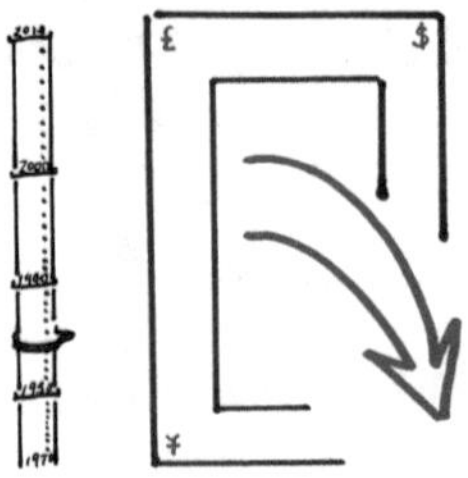

OLD jiù 旧

Ancient form

Traditional form 舊

Catchphrase

In the digital era, yesterday's technology is **OLD** today. **OLD** is 旧 jiù.

Stroke order

丨	丨丨	川	旧	旧

居 LIVE jū 466
Radical/Component 尸 emptied place

LIVE jū 居

Ancient form

(empty) + 古(unborn baby) = live

Catchphrase

The unborn baby **LIVE**s inside her mother's body where it used to be empty. **LIVE** is 居 jū.

Stroke order

尸	尸	尸	尸	尸	居	居	居

句 SENTENCE jù 467
Radical/Component 口 mouth

SENTENCE jù 句

Ancient form

(connecting) + (oral) = sentence

Catchphrase

One must connect words together orally to speak a **SENTENCE**. **SENTENCE** is 句 jù.

Stroke order

丿	勹	句	句	句

据 ACCORDING TO jù 468
Radical/Component 扌 hand

ACCORDING TO jù 据

(hand) + (live) = according to

Catchphrase

ACCORDING TO the feeling in her hand, the mother can judge if the baby in her womb is healthy. **ACCORDING TO** is 据 jù.

Stroke order

一	扌	扌	扩	护	护	护	护	护	据	据

决 DECIDE jué 469
Radical/Component 冫 ice/cold water

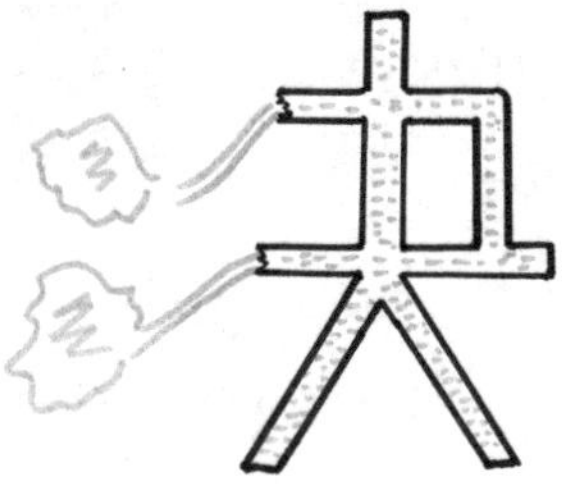

DECIDE jué 决

Ancient form

(water) + (container has broken) = decide

Catchphrase

The company has **DECIDE**d to dredge the water into the two lakes nearby. **DECIDE** is 决 jué.

Stroke order

丶	冫	冫	冫	决	决

卡 CARD kǎ; CLIP qiǎ 470
Radical/Component 丨 the first stroke

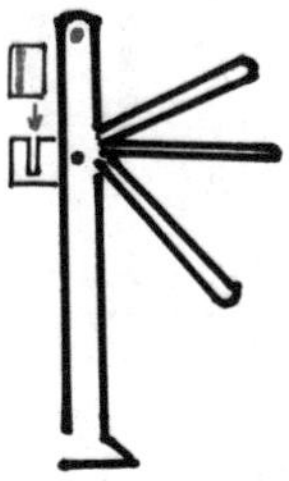

CARD kǎ; CLIP qiǎ 卡

上(up) + 下(down) = card

Catchphrase

You need to swipe your **CARD** to enter the building. **CARD** is 卡 kǎ; **CLIP** is qiǎ.

Stroke order

丨	卜	上	十	卡

康 HEALTH kāng 471
Radical/Component 广 broad

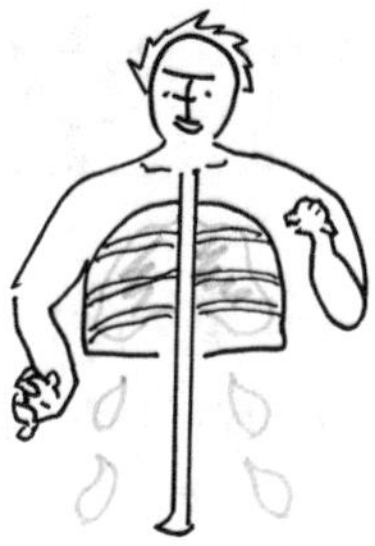

HEALTH kāng 康

Ancient form

(lung) + (air) + (two arms) = health

Catchphrase

For good **HEALTH**, you should exercise your arms which will inflate your lungs with air. **HEALTH** is 康 kāng.

Stroke order

丶	亠	广	户	庐	庐	庚	庚	康	康	康

渴 THIRSTY kě 472
Radical/Component 氵 water

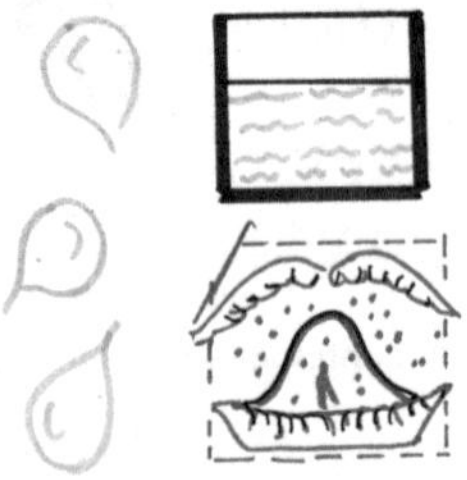

THIRSTY kě 渴

Ancient form

(water) + (so keen to) = thirsty

Catchphrase

I'm so **THIRSTY** that I could drink all the water in the pool upstairs! **THIRSTY** is 渴 kě.

Stroke order

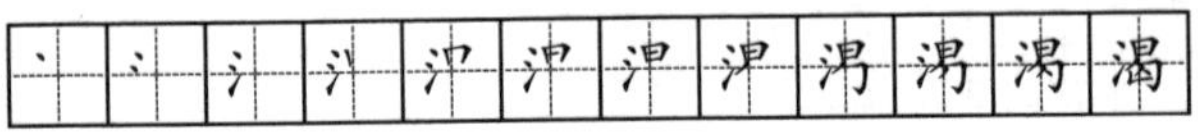

刻 ENGRAVE kè 473
Radical/Component 刂 knife

ENGRAVE kè 刻

Ancient form

(a name of traditional clock time) + (knife) = engraved

Catchphrase

This character which means a quarter of an hour exists in many Chinese idioms, so you should **ENGRAVE** this character into your mind. **ENGRAVE** is 刻 kè.

Stroke order

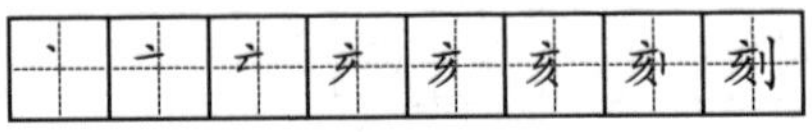

空 EMPTY kōng; BLANK kòng 474
Radical/Component 穴 cave

EMPTY kōng; **BLANK** kòng 空

Ancient form /

(cave) + (structure of building) = empty

Catchphrase

To design an ideal workplace, it is important to leave enough **EMPTY** space in the building for air to flow. **EMPTY** is 空 kōng; **BLANK** is kòng.

Stroke order

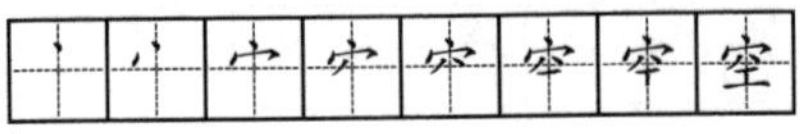

口 MOUTH kǒu 475
Radical/Component 口 mouth

MOUTH kǒu 口

Ancient form

Catchphrase

The character for **MOUTH** is shaped like a mouth. **MOUTH** is 口 kǒu.

Stroke order

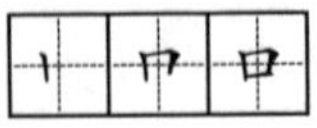

哭 CRY kū | 476
Radical/Component 口 mouth

CRY kū 哭

Ancient form

(eyes) + (facial expression) = cry

Catchphrase

The character for **CRY** looks like someone crying. **CRY** is 哭 kū.

Stroke order

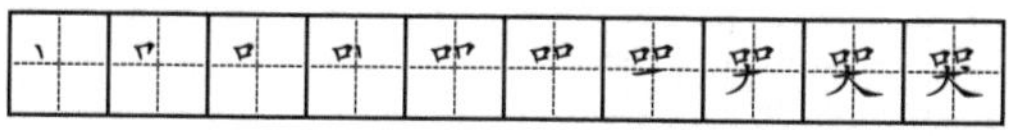

裤(褲) TROUSERS kù | 477
Radical/Component 衤 cloth

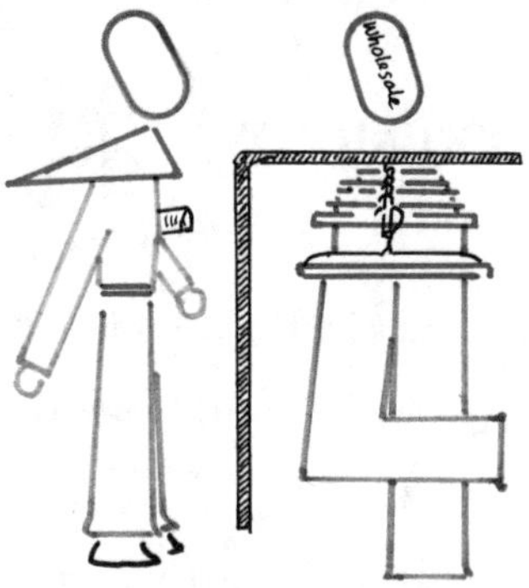

TROUSERS kù 裤

Traditional form 褲

(garment) + (warehouse) = trousers

Catchphrase

This man came to the warehouse to buy some new **TROUSERS**. **TROUSERS** are 裤 kù.

Stroke order

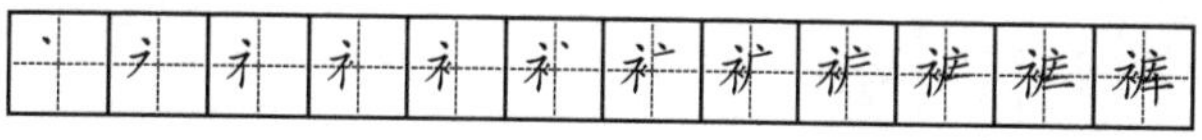

筷 CHOPSTICKS kuài | 478
Radical/Component ⺮ bamboo

CHOPSTICKS kuài 筷

(bamboo) + (fast) = chopsticks

Catchphrase

You can eat faster using bamboo **CHOPSTICKS**. **CHOPSTICKS** are 筷 kuài.

Stroke order

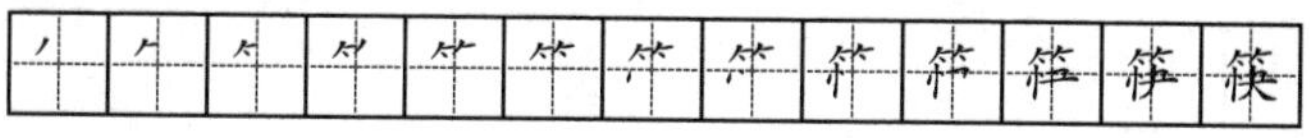

蓝(藍) BLUE lán | 479
Radical/Component 艹 leaf/flower/grass

BLUE lán 蓝

Ancient form Traditional form 藍

(certain leaves) + (monitor person) + (container) = blue

Catchphrase

The process of using certain leaves to make **BLUE** liquids is carefully monitored by a specialist. **BLUE** is 蓝 lán.

Stroke order

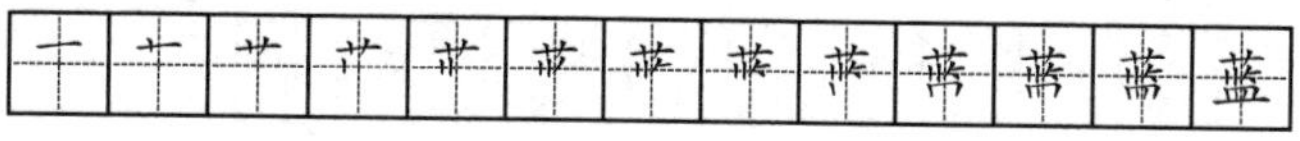

礼(禮) CEREMONY lǐ 480
Radical/Component 礻 spirit

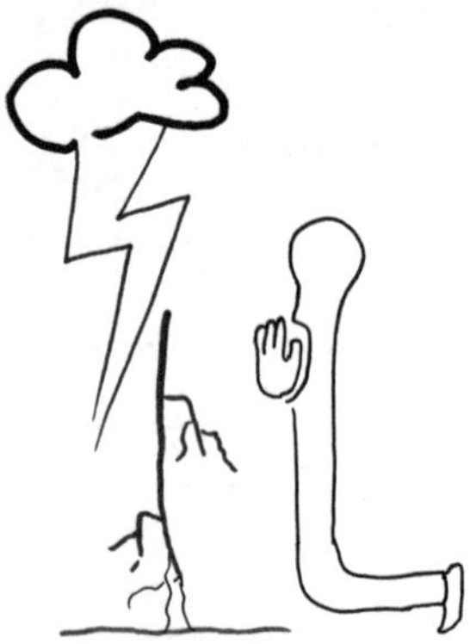

CEREMONY lǐ 礼

Ancient form　Traditional form 禮

(spirit) + (kneeling down) = ceremony

Catchphrase

People would kneel before thunder and lightning in an ancient **CEREMONY**. **CEREMONY** is 礼 lǐ.

Stroke order

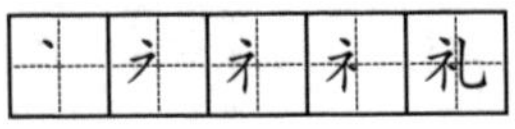

李 PLUM lǐ 481
Radical/Component 木 wood/tree

PLUM lǐ 李

Ancient form

(tree) + (boy) = plum

Catchphrase

The boy uses a pole to knock down **PLUMs** from the tree. **PLUM** is 李 lǐ.

Stroke order

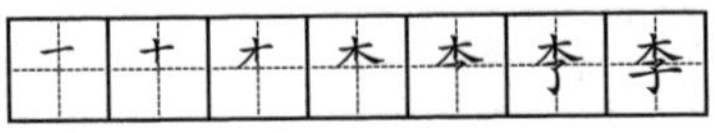

理 REASON lǐ 482
Radical/Component 王 jade

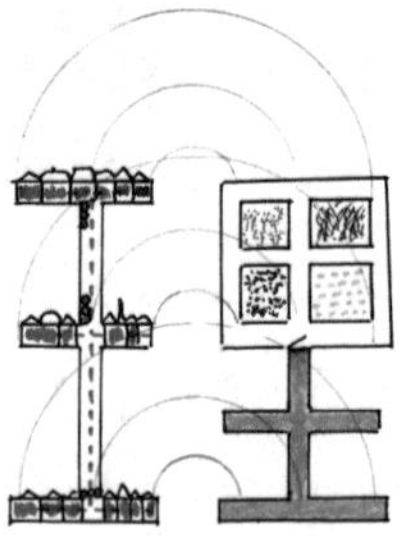

REASON lǐ 理

Ancient form

(shape of the character king) + (farmland) = reason

Catchphrase

There is a good reason why the three streets of neighbourhoods are next to the farmland and water channels. **REASON** is 理 lǐ.

Stroke order

力 FORCE/POWER lì 483
Radical/Component 力 power/strength

FORCE/POWER lì 力

Ancient form

Catchphrase

The elephant is a symbol of **FORCE**. **FORCE/POWER** is 力 lì.

Stroke order

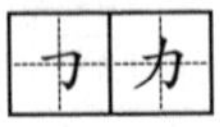

历 **EXPERIENCE** lì | 484

Radical/Component 厂 cliff/opened roof

EXPERIENCE lì 历

Ancient form 

(plant) + (strength)
= experience

Catchphrase

He is using all his strength to hold onto the roots in the cliff. What a dangerous **EXPERIENCE**! **EXPERIENCE** is 历 lì.

Stroke order

脸(臉)FACE liǎn 485
Radical/Component 月 organ/moon

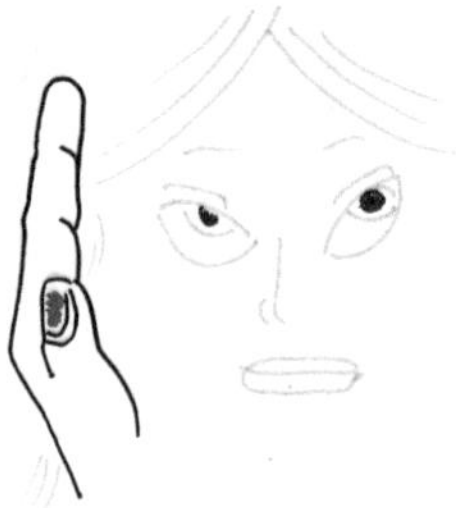

FACE liǎn **脸**

Traditional form 臉

⺼(part of body) ＋僉(five senses)
＝face

Catchphrase

This looks like a woman holding her hand next to her **FACE**. **FACE** is 脸 liǎn.

Stroke order

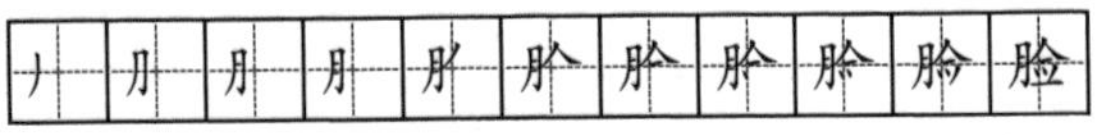

练(練)PRACTICE liàn 486
Radical/Component 纟 silk

PRACTICE liàn **练**

Ancient form 練

Traditional form 練

糸(silk) ＋柬(doing repeatedly)
＝practice

Catchphrase

To make your dance as smooth as silk requires repeated **PRACTICE**. **PRACTICE** is 练 liàn.

Stroke order

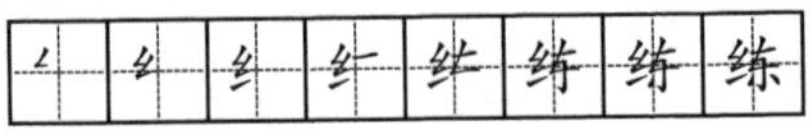

炼(煉)REFINE liàn 487
Radical/Component 火 fire

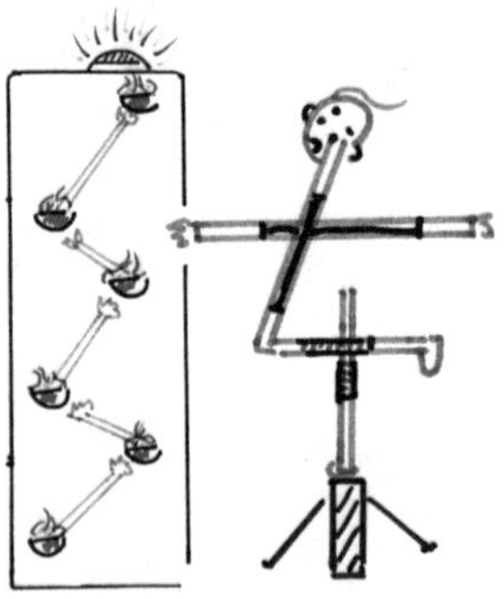

REFINE liàn **炼**

Ancient form 煉

Traditional form 煉

火(flame/fire) ＋柬(doing it repeatedly) ＝ refine

Catchphrase

Climbing this fire wall repeatedly can **REFINE** your mind. **REFINE** is 炼 liàn.

Stroke order

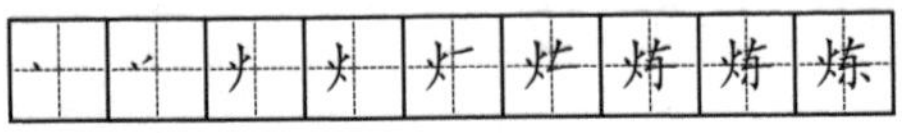

辆(輛)Measure Word for VEHICLES liàng 488
Radical/Component 车 vehicle

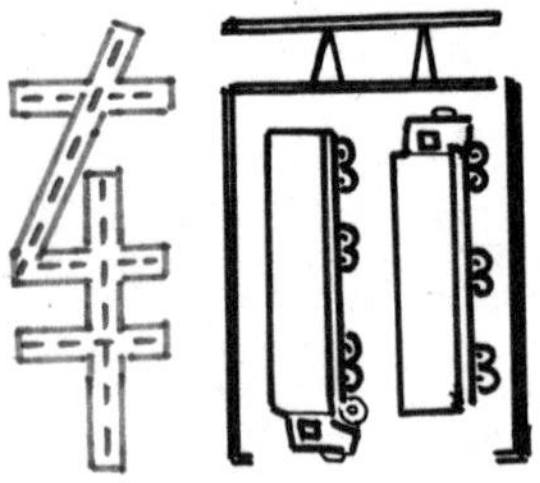

MW for VEHICLES liàng **辆**

Traditional form 輛

車(vehicle) ＋兩(two) ＝ measure word for vehicles

Catchphrase

"Liang" is a **Measure Word** for vehicles. There are two big trucks in this container. **MW** for **VEHICLES** is 辆 liàng.

Stroke order

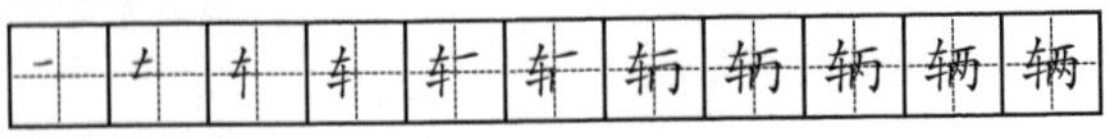

聊 CHAT liáo 489

Radical/Component 耳 ear

CHAT liáo 聊

Ancient form

(ear) + (connecting)

= chat

Catchphrase

Two early birds **CHAT**ted this morning from five to seven. **CHAT** is 聊 liáo.

Stroke order

料 STUFF liào 490

Radical/Component 米 rice

STUFF liào 料

Ancient form

(granary) + (Chinese peck)

= stuff

Catchphrase

The granary supplies a variety of raw food **STUFF** to two local shops. **STUFF** is 料 liào.

Stroke order

邻(鄰) NEIGHBOUR lín 491

Radical/Component 阝 town / city

NEIGHBOUR lín 邻

Ancient form

Traditional form 鄰

(close things) + (town/city)

= neighbour

Catchphrase

NEIGHBOURs are people who live next to you in your town. **NEIGHBOUR** is 邻 lín.

Stroke order

留 STAY liú 492

Radical/Component 田 farmland

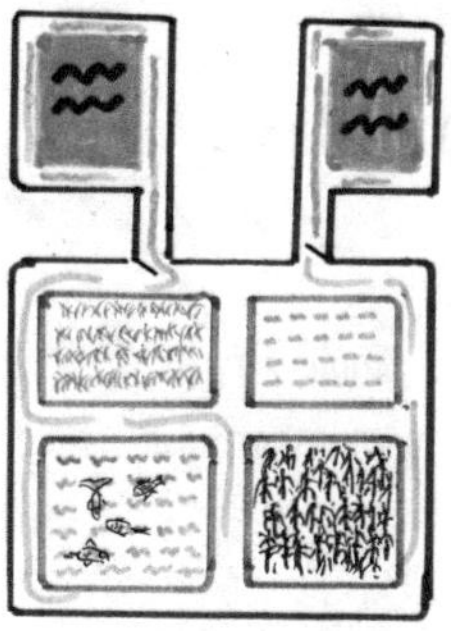

STAY liú 留

Ancient form

(ponds) + (farmland)

= stay

Catchphrase

The two ponds on the outskirts of the farmland must **STAY** there to supply water. **STAY** is 留 liú.

Stroke order

楼(樓) STORIED BUILDING lóu 493

Radical/Component 木 wood

STORIED BUILDING lóu 楼

Ancient form 樓

Traditional form 樓

木(wood) + 婁(storey structure)
= storied building

Catchphrase

This type of **STORIED BUILDING** is a wood storied structure. **STORIED BUILDING** is 楼 lóu.

Stroke order

一	十	才	木	木	木'	木'	木ᐩ	木ᐩ	楼	楼	楼	楼

绿(綠) GREEN lǜ 494

Radical/Component 纟 silk

GREEN lǜ 绿

Ancient form 綠

Traditional form 綠

糸(silk) + 彔(wheel-pulley)
= green

Catchphrase

GREEN silk is made by pulling silk through a top wheel and then setting it in the four dye pools below. **GREEN** is 绿 lǜ.

Stroke order

乙	纟	纟	纟	纟	纟	绿	绿	绿	绿	绿

马(馬) HORSE mǎ 495

Radical/Component 马 horse

HORSE mǎ 马

Ancient form 馬

Traditional form 馬

Catchphrase

This character looks like a **HORSE** head and a powerful big hoof! **HORSE** is 马 mǎ.

Stroke order

㇆	马	马

满 SATISFIED mǎn 496

Radical/Component 氵 water

SATISFIED mǎn 满

Ancient form 滿

氵(water) + 㒼(well balanced)
= satisfied

Catchphrase

We have a room, two flowers, and lots of grass, water and love, so we are very **SATISFIED**. **SATISFIED** is 满 mǎn.

Stroke order

丶	冫	氵	汁	汁	汫	汫	汫	满	满	满	满	满

冒 EVAPORATE mào 497
Radical/Component 冃 headwear

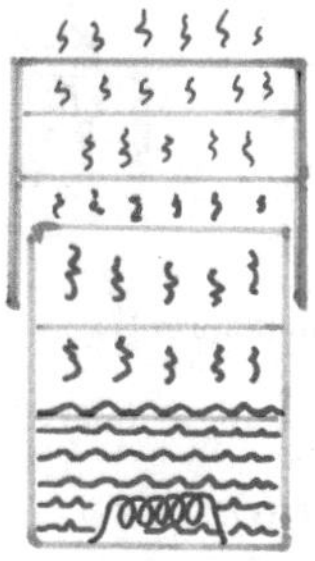

EVAPORATE mào 冒

Ancient form

(the cover) + (head/eye) = evaporate

Catchphrase

The water **EVAPORATE**s through several layers. **EVAPORATE** is 冒 mào.

Stroke order

帽 CAP mào 498
Radical/Component 巾 towel/scarf

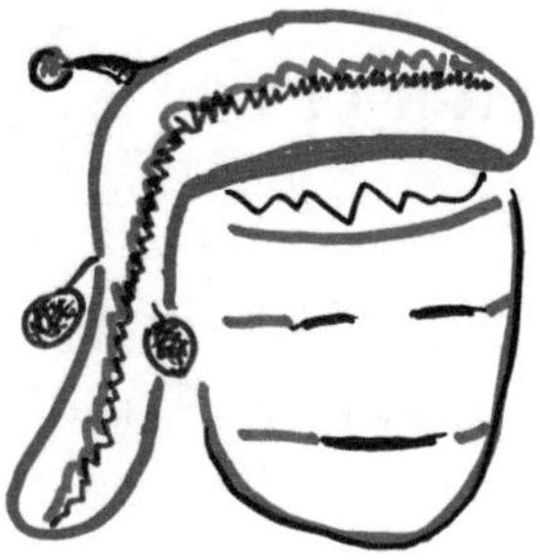

CAP mào 帽

(scarf) + (emit) = cap

Catchphrase

This cloth **CAP** can keep both your head and ears very warm. **CAP** is 帽 mào.

Stroke order

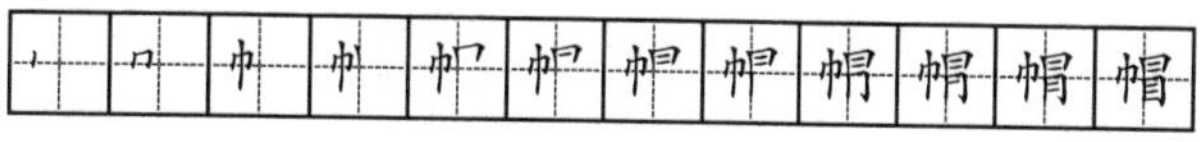

末 END mò 499
Radical/Component 木 wood/tree

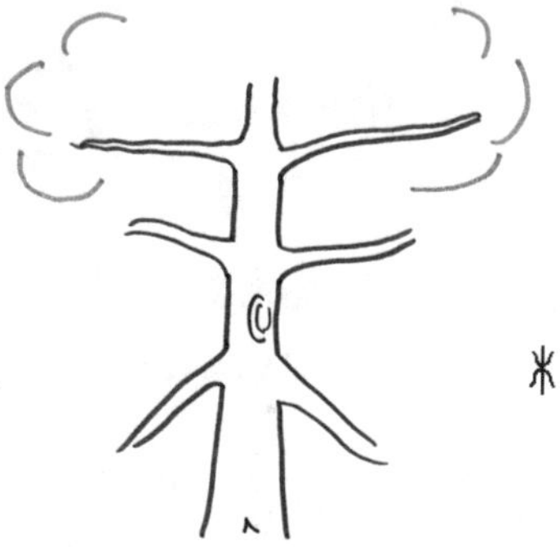

END mò 末

Ancient form

(tree) + 一(the longest branch on the top) = end

Catchphrase

Don't climb out to the **END** of the long tree branch or you will fall! **END** is 末 mò.

Stroke order

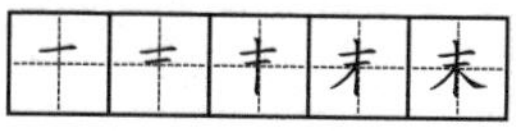

目 EYE mù 500
Radical/Component 目 eye

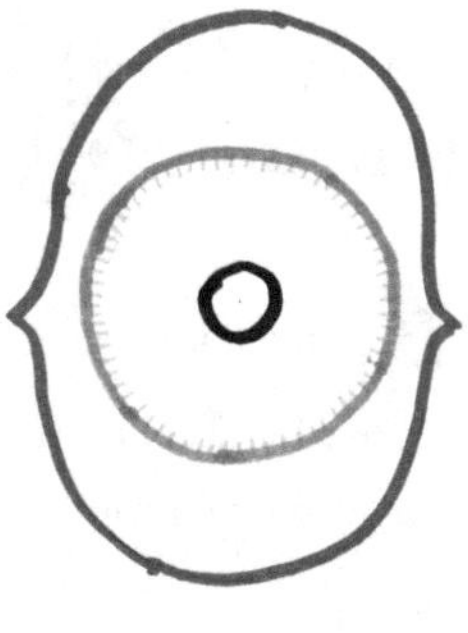

EYE mù 目

Ancient form

Catchphrase

The **EYE** is also called "mu", which is composed of the eye socket, the eyeball, and the pupil. **EYE** is 目 mù.

Stroke order

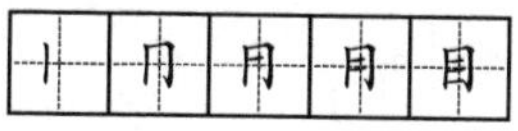

拿 PICK UP ná 501
Radical/Component 手 hand

PICK UP ná 拿

Ancient form

(join together) + (hand) = pick up

Catchphrase

Put your hands together and **PICK UP** your favourite things. **PICK UP** is 拿 ná.

Stroke order

人	个	个	个	合	合	拿	拿	拿	拿

南 SOUTH nán 502
Radical/Component 十 the shape of the strokes/ten

SOUTH nán 南

Ancient form

(the mountain shape) + (trees) = south

Catchphrase

In the northern hemisphere, trees growing on the **SOUTH** of the mountain get more sunshine. **SOUTH** is 南 nán.

Stroke order

一	十	十	冇	冇	冇	南	南	南

难（難）DIFFICULT nán; DISASTER nàn 503
Radical/Component 隹 bird tail

DIFFICULT nán; **DISASTER** nàn 难

Ancient form Traditional form 難

(man made trap) + (bird with long tail) = difficult

Catchphrase

Using a trap to catch a bird with a long tail is very **DIFFICULT**. **DIFFICULT** is 难 nán; **DISASTER** is nàn.

Stroke order

フ	又	对	对	对	对	对	难	难	难

鸟（鳥）BIRD niǎo 504
Radical/Component 鸟 bird

BIRD niǎo 鸟

Ancient form

Traditional form 鳥

Catchphrase

This **BIRD** has a hooked mouth and big wing. **BIRD** is 鸟 niǎo.

Stroke order

ノ	勹	勺	鸟	鸟

努 HARD WORK nǔ — 505
Radical/Component 力 power/strength

HARD WORK nǔ 努

(slave) + (force/strength) = hard work

Catchphrase

Slaves would use all their strength to do **HARD WORK** all day. **HARD WORK** is 努 nǔ.

Stroke order

ㄑ	女	女	如	奴	努	努

爬 CLIMB pá — 506
Radical/Component 爪 paw

CLIMB pá 爬

(paw/creep) + (snake) = climb

Catchphrase

The determined snake slowly **CLIMB**s up the mountain. **CLIMB** is 爬 pá.

Stroke order

丿	厂	爪	爪	爬	爬	爬	爬

怕 AFRAID/FEAR pà — 507
Radical/Component 忄 heart/psychology

AFRAID/FEAR pà 怕

Ancient form

(psychology) + (a white bottle) = afraid/fear

Catchphrase

I am **AFRAID** that this toxic smell came from that broken white bottle! **AFRAID/FEAR** is 怕 pà.

Stroke order

丶	丷	忄	忙	怕	怕	怕	怕

盘(盤) PLATE pán — 508
Radical/Component 皿 container

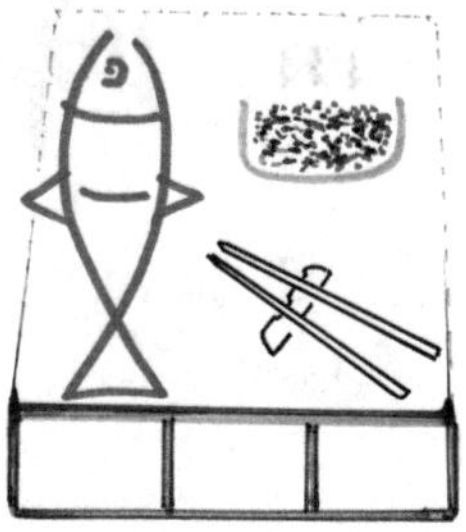

PLATE pán 盘

Ancient form

Traditional form 盤

(boat/fresh meat) + (container/tray) = plate

Catchphrase

The **PLATE** is already set with fish, rice and chopsticks. **PLATE** is 盘 pán.

Stroke order

丿	几	舟	舟	舟	舟	舟	盘	盘	盘	盘

胖 FAT pàng 509

Radical/Component 月 moon/organ

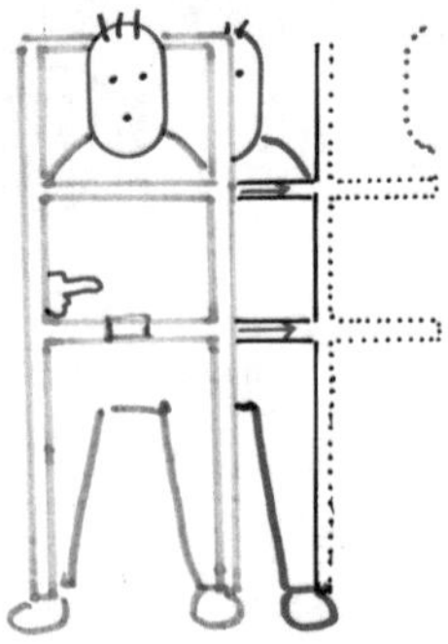

FAT pàng 胖

Ancient form

(body) + (half) = fat

Catchphrase

You're getting **FAT**! Your body is a half width larger than last year! **FAT** is 胖 pàng.

Stroke order

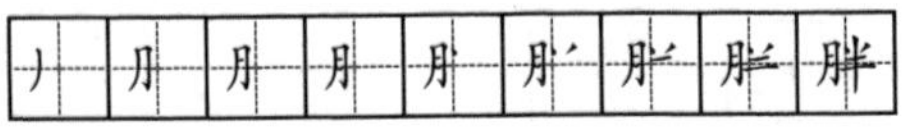

皮 SKIN pí 510

Radical/Component 皮 skin

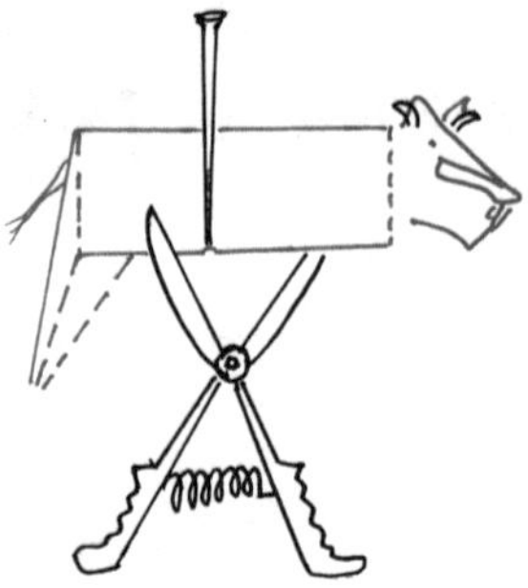

SKIN pí 皮

Ancient form

(animal) + (hand with a tool) = skin

Catchphrase

The **SKIN** of animals like cows is taken off to make clothing and shoes. **SKIN** is 皮 pí.

Stroke order

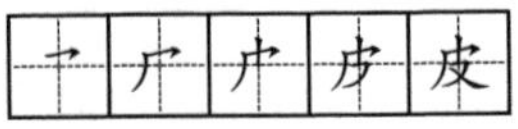

啤 BEER pí 511

Radical/Component 口 mouth

BEER pí 啤

(mouth) + (low value) + (hand) = beer

Catchphrase

BEER feels very undervalued: why is its price so much lower than other alcohol? **BEER** is 啤 pí.

Stroke order

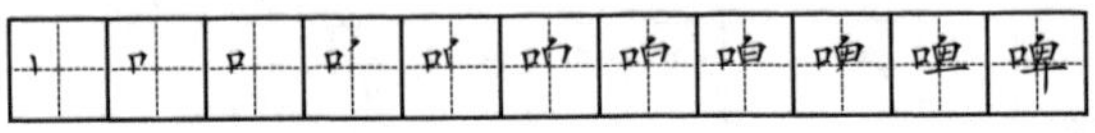

片 PIECE piàn; Orally Rhotic piān(-r) 512

Radical/Component 片 slice

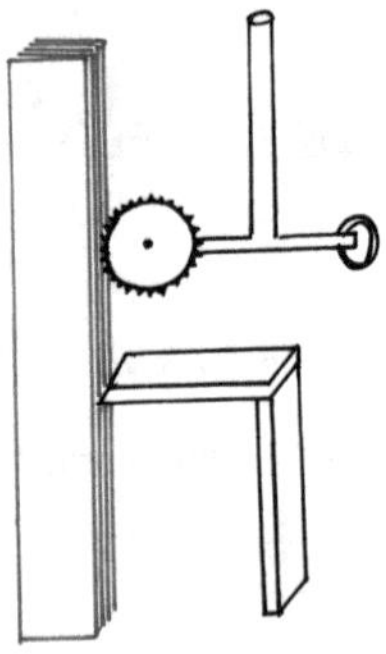

PIECE piàn;
Orally Rhotic piān(-r) 片

Ancient form

Catchphrase

Cutting wood into **PIECE**s requires a special wood saw. **PIECE** is 片 piàn.

Stroke order

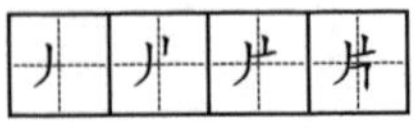

平 FLAT/LEVEL píng 513
Radical/Component 干 dry/do

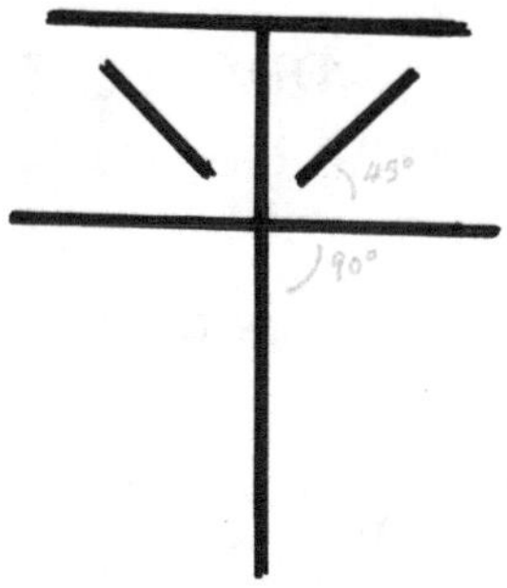

FLAT/LEVEL píng 平

Ancient form

(horizon line) + (balance) = flat

Catchphrase

This structure is very balanced because the horizon line is **FLAT**. **FLAT/LEVEL** is 平 píng.

Stroke order

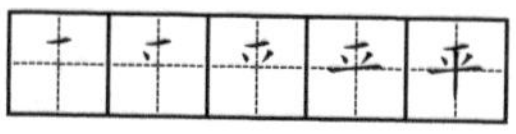

瓶 BOTTLE píng 514
Radical/Component 瓦 tile

BOTTLE píng 瓶

Ancient form

(merge) + (tile/watt) = bottle

Catchphrase

This tall earthenware **BOTTLE** with a handle is handmade. **BOTTLE** is 瓶 píng.

Stroke order

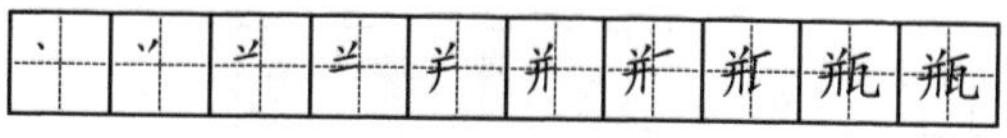

其 IT/THAT qí 515
Radical/Component 八 shape of character eight

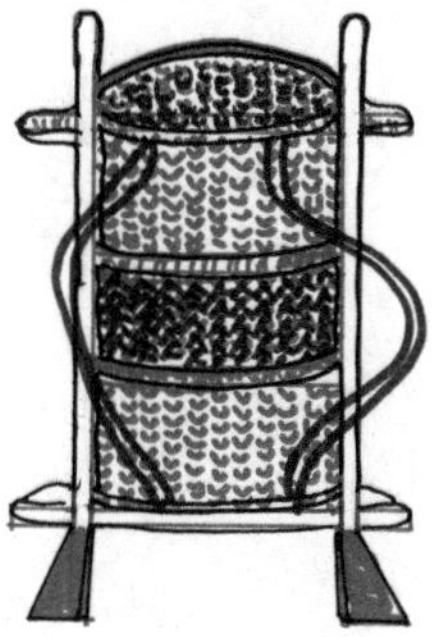

IT/THAT qí 其

Ancient form

(basket) + (legs) = it/that

Catchphrase

This basket with legs is very useful. **IT** can be packed with many things. **IT/THAT** is 其 qí.

Stroke order

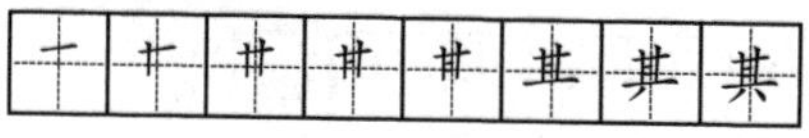

奇 STRANGE qí 516
Radical/Component 大 big

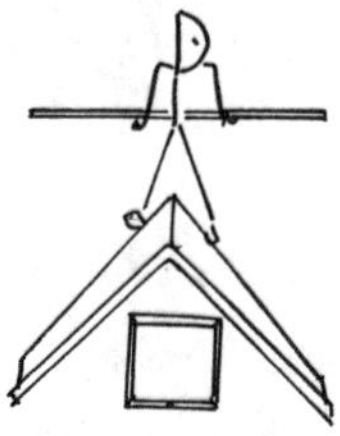

STRANGE qí 奇

Ancient form

(adult) + (a sharp object) = strange

Catchphrase

It's very **STRANGE** to see this adult walking with a pole on this sharp object. **STRANGE** is 奇 qí.

Stroke order

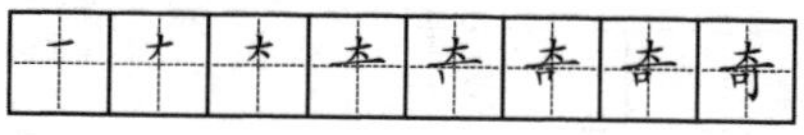

骑（騎）RIDE qí 517
Radical/Component 马 horse

RIDE qí **骑**

Ancient form　Traditional form 騎

(horse) + (strange/rare) = ride

Catchphrase

The man **RIDE**s the horse very strangely. **RIDE** is 骑 qí.

Stroke order

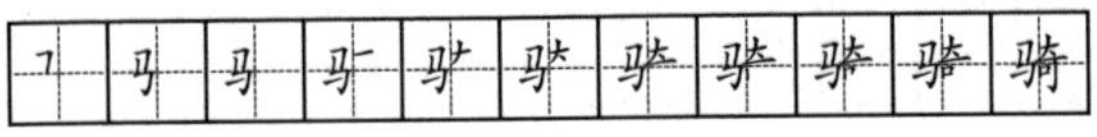

且 ADD/EVEN MORE qiě 518
Radical/Component 一 the first stroke

ADD/ EVEN MORE qiě **且**

Ancient form

Catchphrase

The character for **ADD** looks like a three-step ladder; the sentence is not finished until more words are **ADD**ed. **ADD/ EVEN MORE** is 且 qiě.

Stroke order

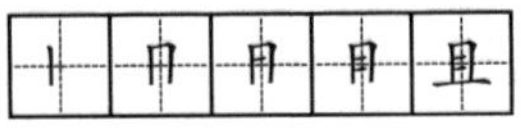

轻（輕）LIGHT qīng 519
Radical/Component 车 vehicle

LIGHT qīng **轻**

Ancient form

Traditional form 輕

(vehicle) + (mountain roads) = light

Catchphrase

To get up the mountain road, our vehicle should be **LIGHT**. **LIGHT** is 轻 qīng.

Stroke order

清 CLEAR qīng 520
Radical/Component 氵 water

CLEAR qīng **清**

Ancient form　/

(water) + (green/tree) = clear

Catchphrase

Trees can grow healthy and tall with clean, **CLEAR** water. **CLEAR** is 清 qīng.

Stroke order

秋 AUTUMN qiū 521
Radical/Component 禾 crop

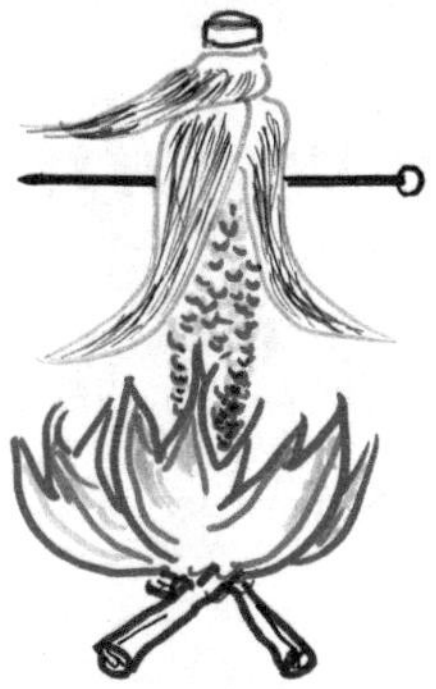

AUTUMN qiū **秋**

Ancient form

(crop) + (fire) = autumn

Catchphrase

AUTUMN is the best time to roast corn on the fire! **AUTUMN** is 秋 qiū.

Stroke order

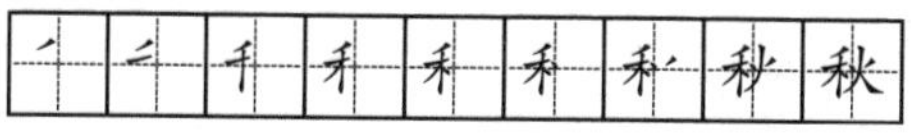

求 ASK FOR qiú 522
Radical/Component 水 water

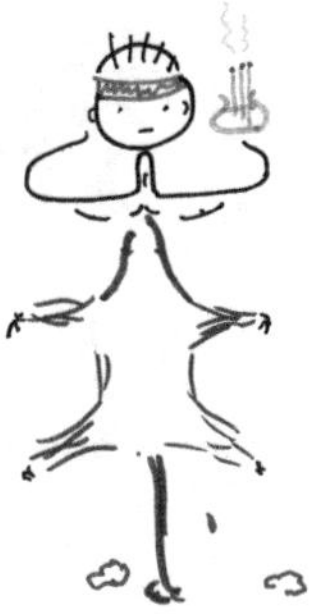

ASK FOR qiú **求**

Ancient form

(hand to hold) + (animal's tail) = ask for

Catchphrase

I had to **ASK FOR** an animal hide to keep me warm last night. **ASK FOR** is 求 qiú.

Stroke order

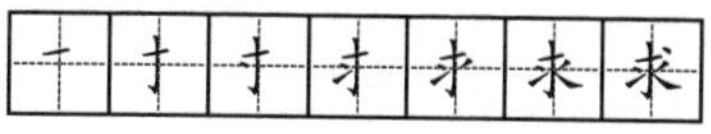

趣 FUN/INTERESTING qù 523
Radical/Component 走 walk

FUN/INTERESTING qù **趣**

Ancient form

(walk) + (hand holds ear) = fun/interesting

Catchphrase

Although it is **FUN** to listen to music while walking, it can be dangerous if you don't pay attention! **FUN/INTERESTING** is 趣 qù.

Stroke order

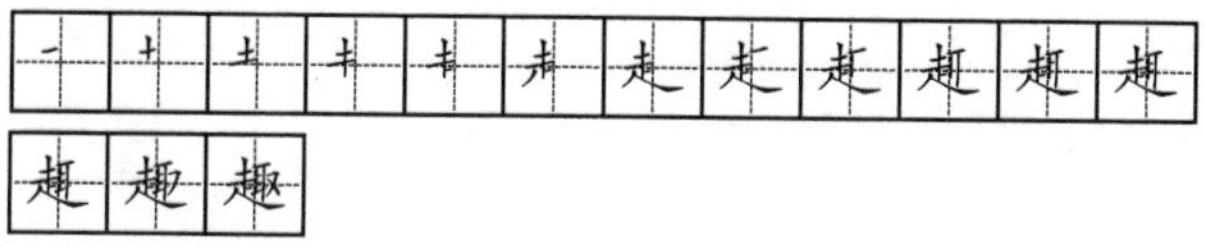

裙 SKIRT qún 524
Radical/Component 衤 cloth/dress

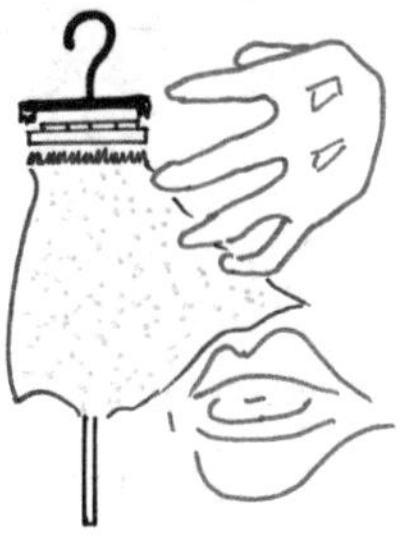

SKIRT qún **裙**

Ancient form

(cloth/dress) + (gentle person) = skirt

Catchphrase

Before buying a **SKIRT**, you should feel the fabric and notice if it has been recommended by word of mouth. **SKIRT** is 裙 qún.

Stroke order

容 ACCOMMODATE róng 525
Radical/Component 宀 roof

ACCOMMODATE róng 容

Ancient form

(roof) + (valley) = accommodate

Catchphrase

Even though the valley is huge and deep, the roof of the heaven can still **ACCOMMODATE** it. **ACCOMMODATE** is 容 róng.

Stroke order

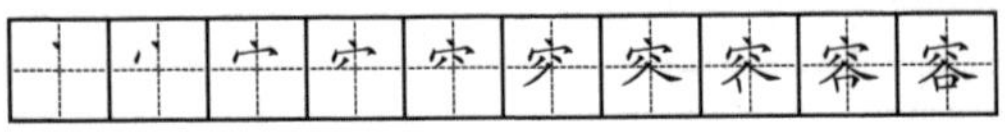

如 SIMILAR rú 526
Radical/Component 女 woman

SIMILAR rú 如

Ancient form

(woman) + (mouth) = similar

Catchphrase

Women have no trouble speaking from the heart. Their words and feelings are often very **SIMILAR**. **SIMILAR** is 如 rú.

Stroke order

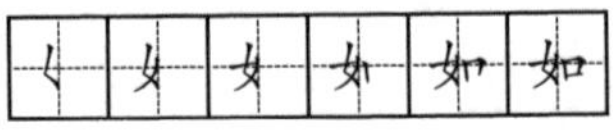

赛(賽)MATCH sài 527
Radical/Component 贝 money/treasury

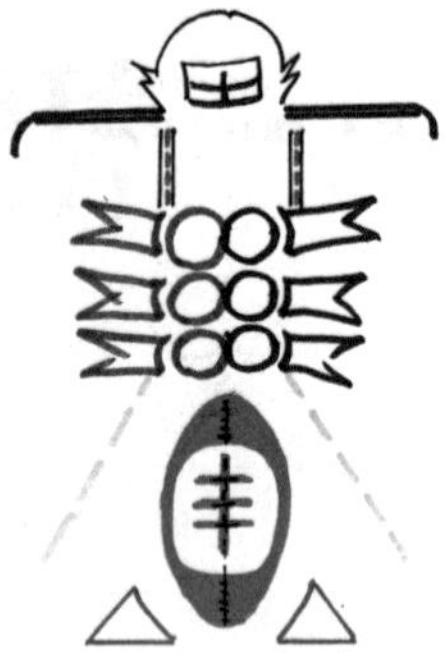

MATCH sài 赛

Ancient form

Traditional form 賽

(compete with each other)

+ (money/treasure) = match

Catchphrase

In a rugby **MATCH**, players compete head-to-head to get the ball which is under them. **MATCH** is 赛 sài.

Stroke order

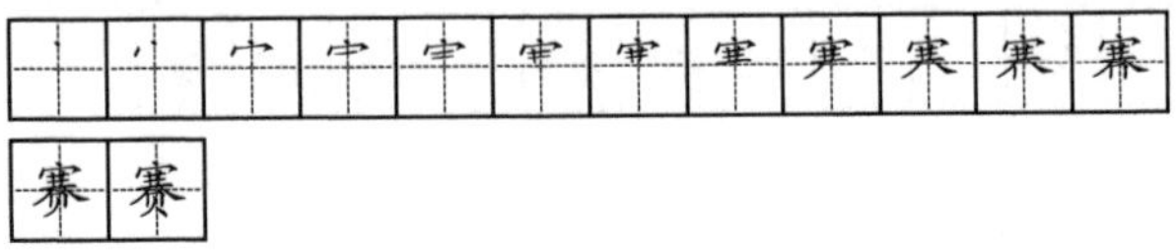

伞(傘)UMBRELLA sǎn 528
Radical/Component 人 people

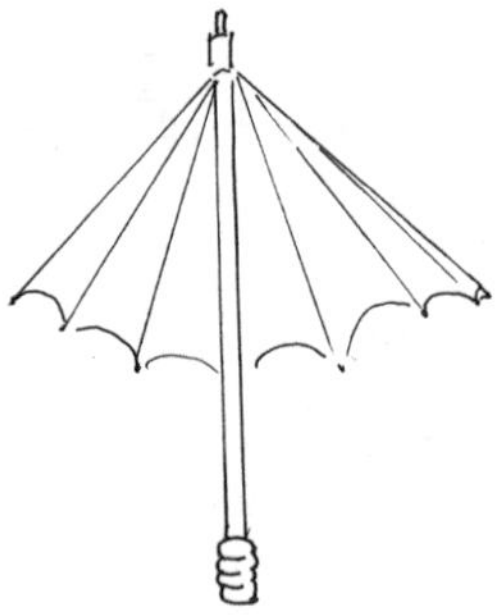

UMBRELLA sǎn 伞

Traditional form 傘

Catchphrase

This character looks just like an **UMBRELLA**. **UMBRELLA** is 伞 sǎn.

Stroke order

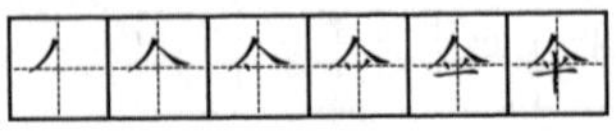

扫(掃) BROOM sào; SWEEP sǎo — 529

Radical/Component 扌 hand

BROOM sào; **SWEEP** sǎo 扫

Traditional form 掃

(hand) + (dustpan) = broom

Catchphrase

Even witches must hold on to their **BROOMs** when whizzing through the air! **BROOM** is 扫 sào; **SWEEP** is sǎo.

Stroke order

山 MOUNTAIN shān — 530

Radical/Component 山 hill/mountain

MOUNTAIN shān 山

Ancient form

Catchphrase

This character looks just like a **MOUNTAIN**. **MOUNTAIN** is 山 shān.

Stroke order

衫 SHIRT shān — 531

Radical/Component 衤 cloth

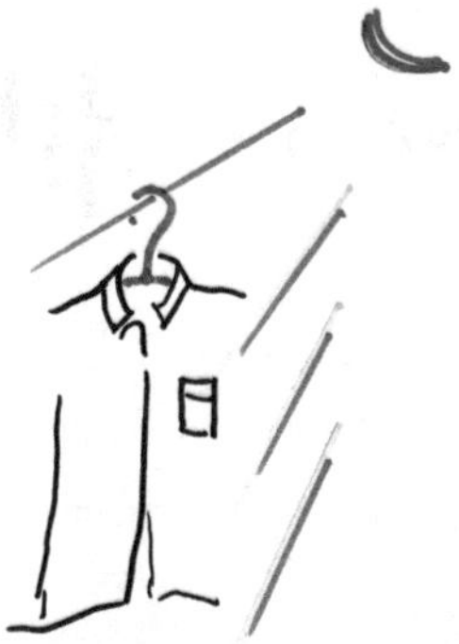

SHIRT shān 衫

Ancient form

(hat & cloth) + (sunny) = shirt

Catchphrase

This looks like a **SHIRT** drying in the sunlight. **SHIRT** is 衫 shān.

Stroke order

烧(燒) BURN shāo — 532

Radical/Component 火 fire

BURN shāo 烧

Ancient form

Traditional form 燒

(fire/burn) + (piling bricks) = fire/burn

Catchphrase

The fire **BURNs** next to the pile of toppling bricks. **BURN** is 烧 shāo.

Stroke order

声(聲)SOUND shēng 533
Radical/Component 士 official staff

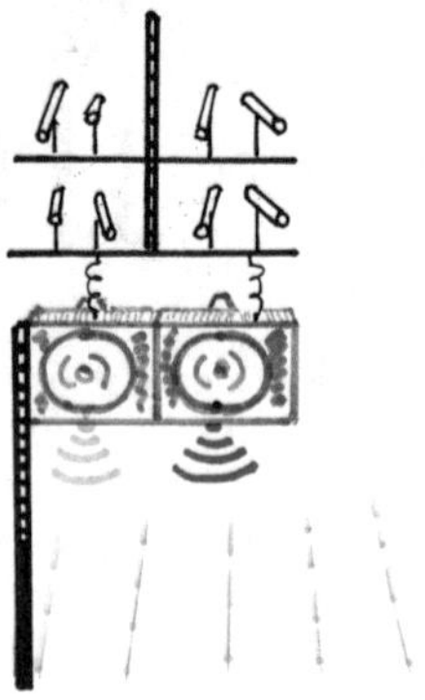

SOUND shēng 声

Ancient form 

Traditional form 聲

(make announcement) + (mouth) = sound

Catchphrase

A **SOUND** should be made when a car speeds by, and cameras can record the violation. **SOUND** is 声 shēng.

Stroke order

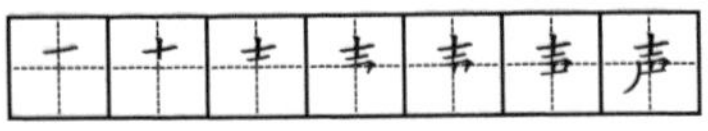

实(實)PRACTICAL shí 534
Radical/Component 宀 roof

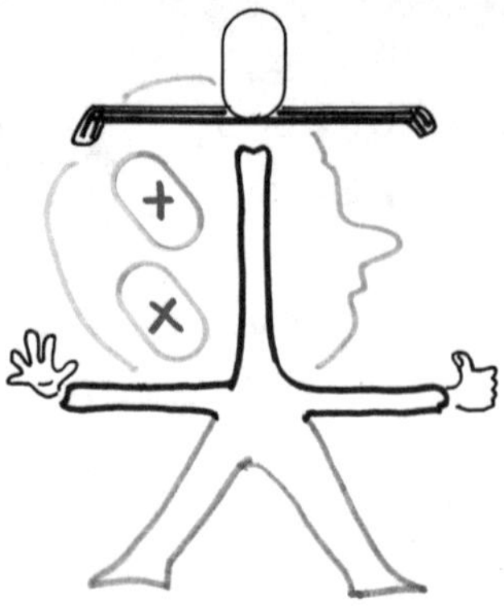

PRACTICAL shí 实

Ancient form 

Traditional form 實

(roof) + (head) = practical

Catchphrase

To worry about getting the roof over your head is a very **PRACTICAL** concern. **PRACTICAL** is 实 shí.

Stroke order

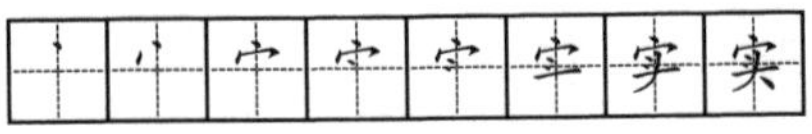

史 HISTORY shǐ 535
Radical/Component 口 mouth

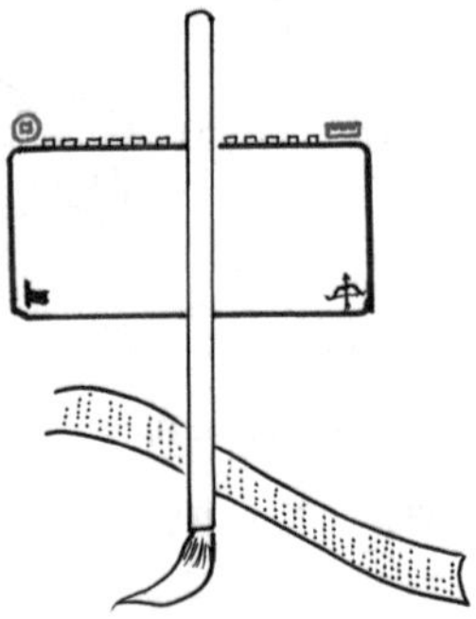

HISTORY shǐ 史

Ancient form 

(brush absorbing ink) + (hand to write) = history

Catchphrase

Ink and a brush are necessary when writing down facts in the **HISTORY** books. **HISTORY** is 史 shǐ.

Stroke order

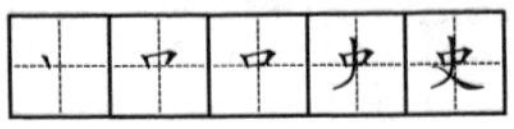

世(卋)CENTURY shì 536
Radical/Component 一 the first stroke

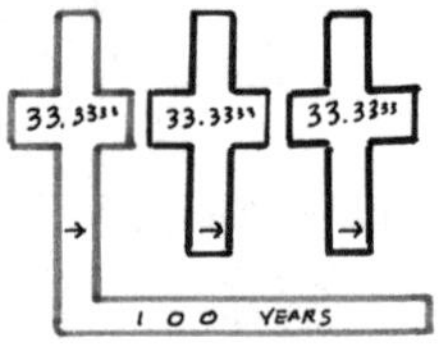

CENTURY shì 世

Ancient form 

Traditional form 丗

(earth/horizon) + (three crosses) = century

Catchphrase

Three generations more or less make a **CENTURY**. **CENTURY** is 世 shì.

Stroke order

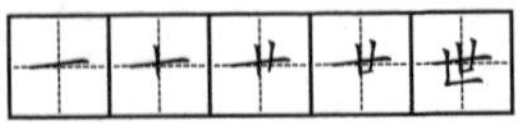

市 MARKET shì 537
Radical/Component 巾 towel

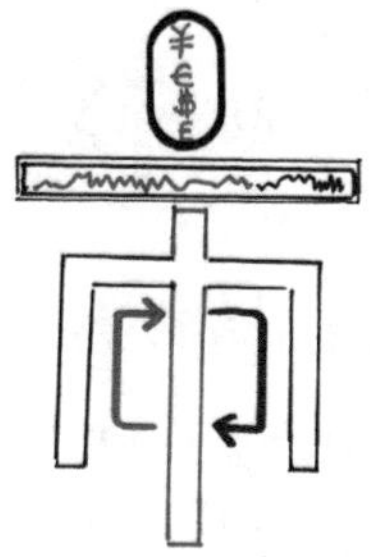

MARKET shì 市

Ancient form

(advertising) + (street) = market

Catchphrase

Stock **MARKET** values are seen on the screens of many computers; they go up and down every day and are extremely difficult to predict. **MARKET** is 市 shì.

Stroke order

瘦 THIN shòu 538
Radical/Component 疒 ill

THIN shòu 瘦

Ancient form

(sickness) + (unhealthy /old body) = thin

Catchphrase

This **THIN** man looks sick wearing a straw hat and supported with a crutch. **THIN** is 瘦 shòu.

Stroke order

叔 UNCLE shū 539
Radical/Component 又 again/arm and hand

UNCLE shū 叔

Ancient form

(above/old generation) + (small/young) + (arm and hand) = uncle

Catchphrase

UNCLEs are in between the younger and older generations. **UNCLE** is 叔 shū.

Stroke order

舒 COMFORTABLE shū 540
Radical/Component 舌 tongue

COMFORTABLE shū 舒

(house) + (giving) = comfortable

Catchphrase

We found a **COMFORTABLE** hotel by searching online. **COMFORTABLE** is 舒 shū.

Stroke order

束 BUNCH shù 541
Radical/Component 木 wood

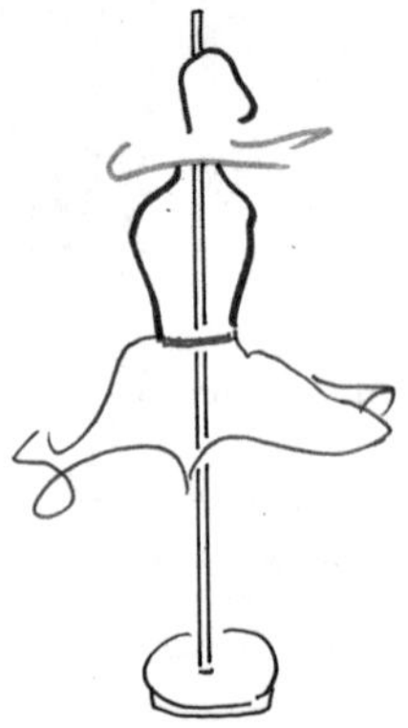

BUNCH shù 束

Ancient form

(wood/tree) + (belt) = bunch

Catchphrase

In a clothing store, a dress with a **BUNCH**ed waist will attract many women. **BUNCH** is 束 shù.

Stroke order

树 TREE shù 542
Radical/Component 木 wood/tree

TREE shù 树

Ancient form /

(seedling) + (repeat) + (measure/inch) = tree

Catchphrase

These **TREE** seedlings were planted too close. **TREE** is 树 shù.

Stroke order

数(數) NUMBER shù; TO COUNT shǔ 543
Radical/Component 攵 tool

NUMBER shù; **TO COUNT** shǔ 数

Ancient form

Traditional form 數

(abacus) + (woman) + (hand with tool) = number

Catchphrase

Our female math teacher's mental arithmetic is so good that she gets the correct **NUMBER** faster than a calculator! **NUMBER** is 数 shù; **TO COUNT** is shǔ.

Stroke order

刷 SCRUB shuā 544
Radical/Component 刂 knife

SCRUB shuā 刷

(window) + (towel) + (engraved) = scrub

Catchphrase

This machine has a **SCRUB** and a rag, and is very effective for wiping windows. **SCRUB** is 刷 shuā.

Stroke order

双(雙)A PAIR shuāng 545

Radical/Component 又 again

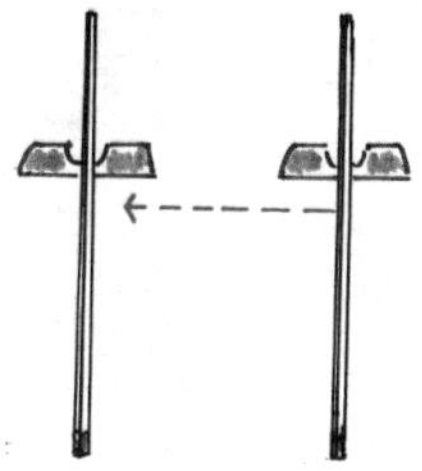

A PAIR shuāng 双

Ancient form 雙

Traditional form 雙

乂(again) + 乂(again) = a pair

Catchphrase

One chopstick plus one chopstick makes **A PAIR**. **A PAIR** is 双 shuāng.

Stroke order

フ	又	双	双

算 CALCULATE suàn 546

Radical/Component ⺮ bamboo

CALCULATE suàn 算

Ancient form 筭

目(eye) + 目(abacus) + 廾(two hands) = calculate

Catchphrase

You need your hands and eyes to **CALCULATE** on an abacus. **CALCULATE** is 算 suàn.

Stroke order

ノ	⺈	⺈	𥫗	𥫗	⺮	竺	笞	笪	笪	笪	筫	筫	算

特 SPECIAL tè 547

Radical/Component 牜 animal

SPECIAL tè 特

Ancient form 特

牛(cow) + 寺/寺(temple) = special

Catchphrase

The word on the left is a cow and on the right is a temple. In ancient times, people believed cows had a **SPECIAL** significance. **SPECIAL** is 特 tè.

Stroke order

ノ	⺧	牛	牜	牛	牪	牪	牸	特	特

疼 PAIN téng 548

Radical/Component 疒 sick

PAIN téng 疼

疒(sickness) + 冬(circle) = pain

Catchphrase

Inflammations in the body can always cause **PAIN**. **PAIN** is 疼 téng.

Stroke order

丶	亠	广	疒	疒	疒	疒	疚	疼	疼

梯 LADDER/STAIRS tī | 549
Radical/Component 木 wood/tree

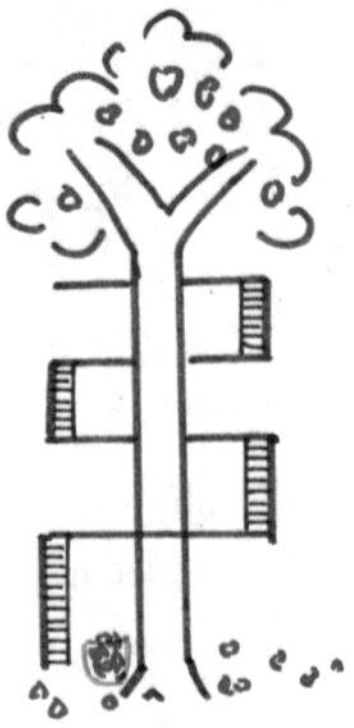

LADDER/STAIRS tī 梯

Ancient form

(tree) + (orderly/young brother) = stairs/ladder

Catchphrase

This character looks like a **LADDER** going up a tree. **LADDER/STAIRS** is 梯 tī.

Stroke order

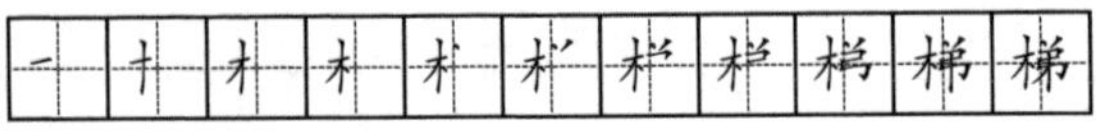

提 CARRY/LIFT tí | 550
Radical/Component 扌 hand

CARRY/LIFT tí 提

Ancient form

(hand) + (correct/right thing) = carry/lift

Catchphrase

Use your hand to **CARRY** or **LIFT** something on the right path under the sun. **CARRY/LIFT** is 提 tí.

Stroke order

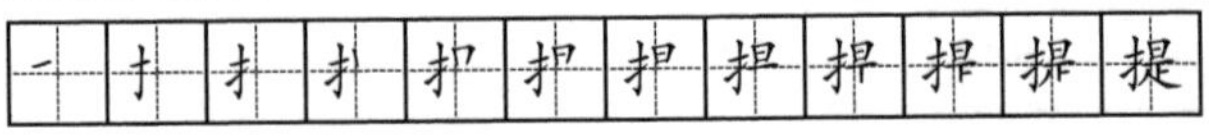

甜 SWEET tián | 551
Radical/Component 舌 tongue

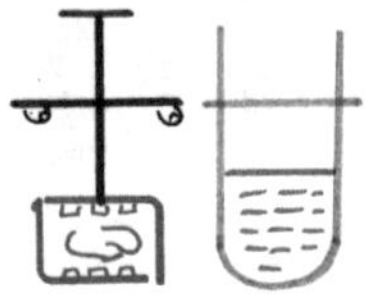

SWEET tián 甜

Ancient form /

(tongue) + (taste) = sweet

Catchphrase

When the tongue tastes sweet water, the result is **SWEET**. **SWEET** is 甜 tián.

Stroke order

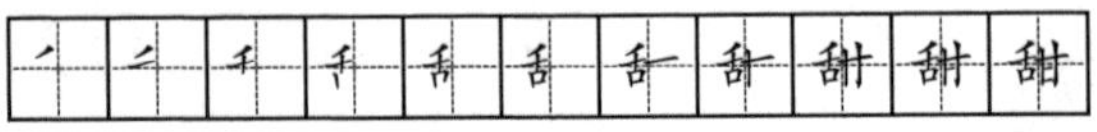

调（調）ADJUST tiáo; ALLOCATE diào | 552
Radical/Component 讠 language

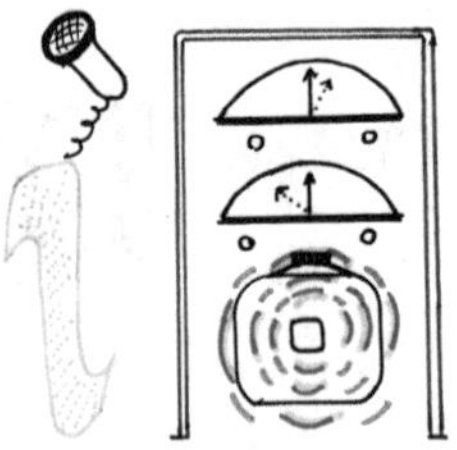

ADJUST tiáo; **ALLOCATE** diào 调

Ancient form

Traditional form 調

(speech) + (comprehensive/all-around) = adjust

Catchphrase

To move people with spoken language, you need to **ADJUST** the sound quality and volume of your voice in a comprehensive way. **ADJUST** is 调 tiáo; **ALLOCATE** is diào.

Stroke order

铁(鐵)IRON tiě 553
Radical/Component 钅 metal/gold

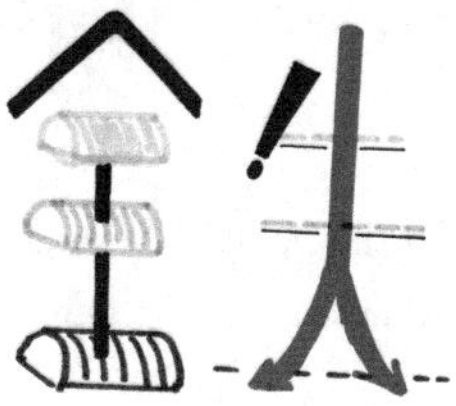

IRON tiě 铁

Ancient form

Traditional form 鐵

金(metal) + 失(miss/lose) = iron

Catchphrase

The radical for this word is metal, and the right side means lost value. Combined, it means a low-priced metal which is **IRON**. **IRON** is 铁 tiě.

Stroke order

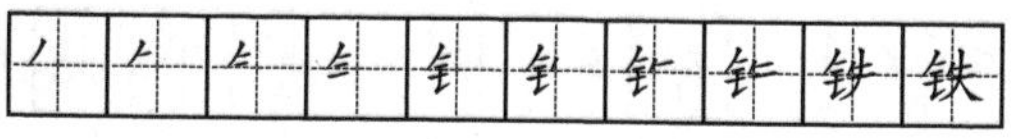

头(頭)HEAD tóu 554
Radical/Component 大 big

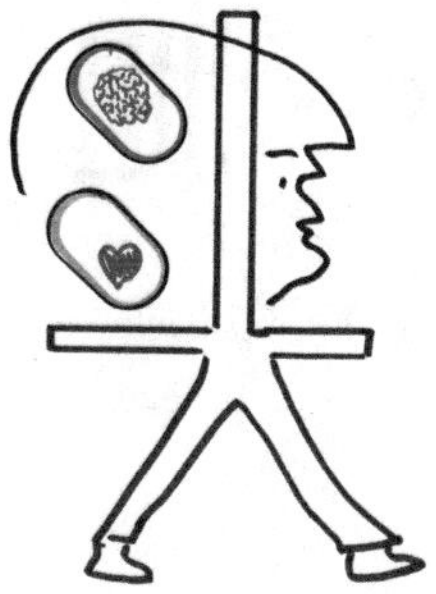

HEAD tóu 头

Ancient form

Traditional form 頭

大(person) + (heart and brain) = head

Catchphrase

The **HEAD** is where a person's brain is located, and is the centre of thought and emotion. **HEAD** is 头 tóu.

Stroke order

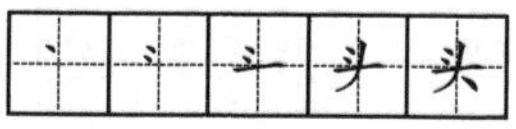

突 SUDDEN tū 555
Radical/Component 穴 cave

SUDDEN tū 突

Ancient form

穴(cave) + 犬(dog) = sudden

Catchphrase

A dog rushed out of a cave and scared me **SUDDEN**ly. **SUDDEN** is 突 tū.

Stroke order

图(圖)PICTURE tú 556
Radical/Component 囗 enclosure

PICTURE tú 图

Ancient form

Traditional form 圖

囗(enclosure) + / (circle / winter) = picture

Catchphrase

This looks like a **PICTURE** of a bird in a winter city. **PICTURE** is 图 tú.

Stroke order

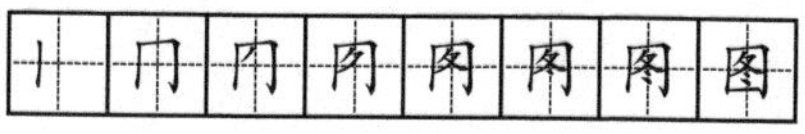

腿 LEG tuǐ 557
Radical/Component 月 part of body

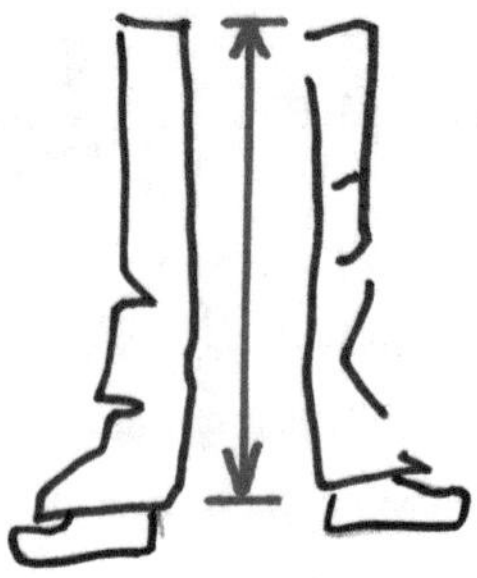

LEG tuǐ 腿

月(part of body) + 退(backward) = leg

Catchphrase

The **LEG**s are parts of the body that can move forwards and backwards. **LEG** is 腿 tuǐ.

Stroke order

碗 BOWL wǎn 558
Radical/Component 石 stone

BOWL wǎn 碗

石(stone) + 宛(the vault of heaven, moon and bent body) = bowl

Catchphrase

Ancient **BOWL**s were made from stone. People used to kneel and be thankful when they had food to eat. **BOWL** is 碗 wǎn.

Stroke order

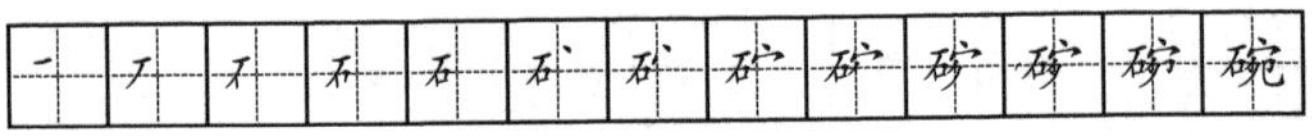

万(萬) TEN THOUSAND wàn 559
Radical/Component 一 the first stroke

TEN THOUSAND wàn 万

Ancient form 萬

Traditional form 萬

Catchphrase

"卍" was an ancient holy symbol of Indian Buddhism which was introduced into China and changed into **TEN THOUSAND**, indicating the large number in the numeral system. **TEN THOUSAND** is 万 wàn.

Stroke order

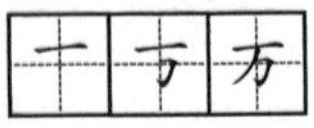

网(網) NET wǎng 560
Radical/Component 冂 frame

NET wǎng 网

Ancient form 网

Traditional form 網

| |(sticks/frame) + XX(net) = net

Catchphrase

This character looks like the **NET** of a football match. **NET** is 网 wǎng.

Stroke order

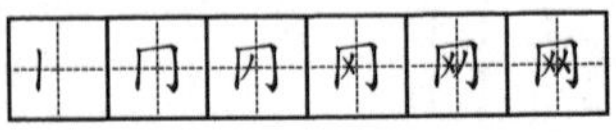

忘 FORGET wàng — 561
Radical/Component 心 heart

FORGET wàng 忘

Ancient form

亡(escape/death) + 心(heart) = forget

Catchphrase

If something escapes from the heart, it can be called **FORGET**-ting. **FORGET** is 忘 wàng

Stroke order

丶 亠 亡 亡 忘 忘 忘

位 POSITION wèi — 562
Radical/Component 亻 man

POSITION wèi 位

Ancient form

亻(man) + 立(stand) = position

Catchphrase

People should show respect to those who have achieved their **POSITION** through ability and hard work. **POSITION** is 位 wèi.

Stroke order

丿 亻 亻 仁 仁 位 位

文 CHARACTER wén — 563
Radical/Component 文 literature / culture

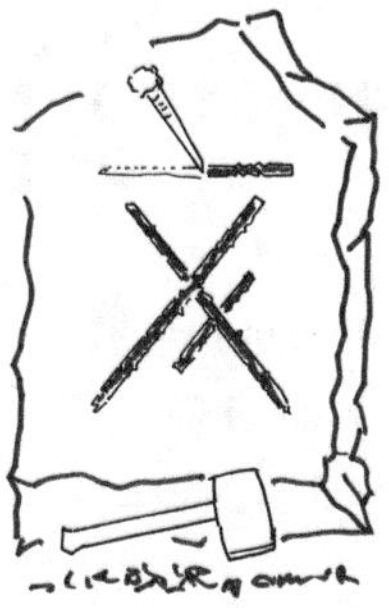

CHARACTER wén 文

Ancient form

Catchphrase

The earliest Chinese **CHARACTER**s were usually engraved on the surface of hard objects, so the strokes were mostly straight lines. **CHARACTER** is 文 wén.

Stroke order

丶 亠 亣 文

闻(聞) HEAR wén — 564
Radical/Component 门 door

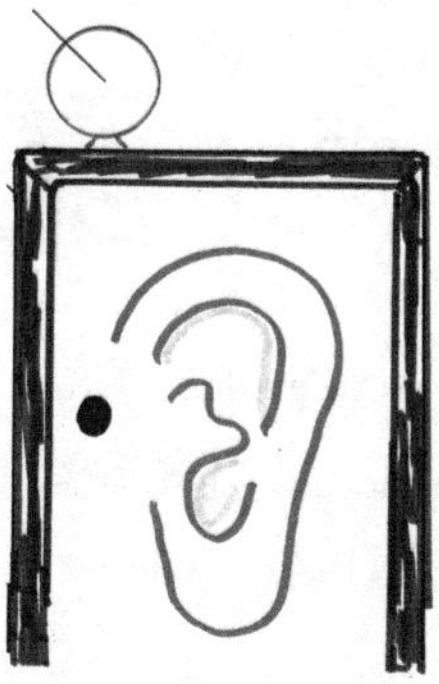

HEAR wén 闻

Ancient form

Traditional form 聞

門(door) + 耳(ear) = hear

Catchphrase

If you put your ear to the door you can **HEAR** what your neighbours are saying. **HEAR** is 闻 wén.

Stroke order

丶 门 门 闩 闩 闻 闻 闻 闻

物 MATTER/THING wù 565
Radical/Component 牛 cow/animal

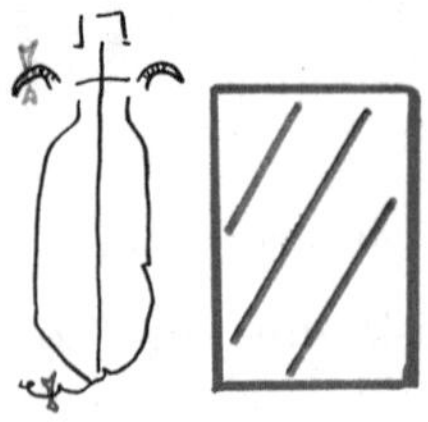

MATTER/THING wù **物**

Ancient form

(cow/life) + (the negative side of natural environment) = matter/thing

Catchphrase

Everything in the world, whether alive or inanimate, is called "**MATTER**". **MATTER/THING** is 物 wù.

Stroke order

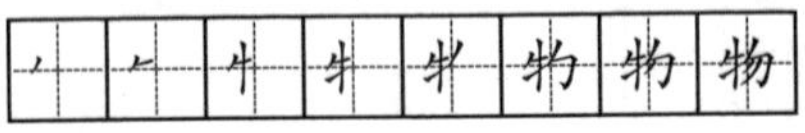

戏(戲) DRAMA xì 566
Radical/Component 戈 dagger/weapon

DRAMA xì **戏**

Ancient form

Traditional form 戲

(plot) + (gong) + (dagger) = drama

Catchphrase

Weapons, painted faces, silk fans and gongs are all necessary things in a Chinese **DRAMA**. **DRAMA** is 戏 xì.

Stroke order

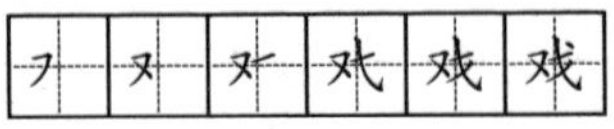

夏 SUMMER xià 567
Radical/Component 夂 arm and leg

SUMMER xià **夏**

Ancient form

(head with cap) + (arms) + (legs) = summer

Catchphrase

On a hot **SUMMER** day, it's best to wear a hat and have something that can cool you down. **SUMMER** is 夏 xià.

Stroke order

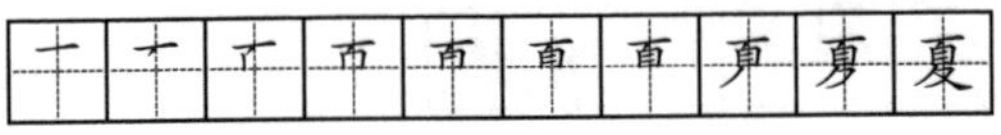

鲜(鮮) FRESH xiān 568
Radical/Component 鱼 fish

FRESH xiān **鲜**

Ancient form

Traditional form 鮮

(fish) + (lamb) = fresh

Catchphrase

A plate of **FRESH** fish and lamb kebabs is really a delicious meal! **FRESH** is 鲜 xiān.

Stroke order

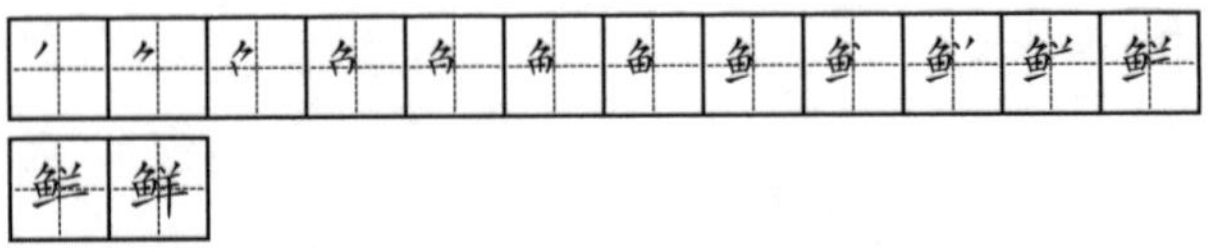

相 SEE/EACH OTHER xiāng; PICTURE xiàng — 569
Radical/Component 木 wood/tree

SEE/EACH OTHER xiāng; **PICTURE** xiàng 相

Ancient form

(tree) + / (eye) = see/each other/picture

Catchphrase

A pair of eyes flashed from inside the tree, **SEE**ing and taking **PICTURES** of the outside world. **SEE/EACH OTHER** is 相 xiāng; **PICTURE** is xiàng.

Stroke order

香 DELICIOUS xiāng — 570
Radical/Component 香 fragrant

DELICIOUS xiāng 香

Ancient form

(crop) + (taste) = delicious

Catchphrase

Making corn into popcorn really tastes **DELICIOUS**! **DELICIOUS** is 香 xiāng.

Stroke order

箱 BOX/CASE xiāng — 571
Radical/Component 竹 bamboo

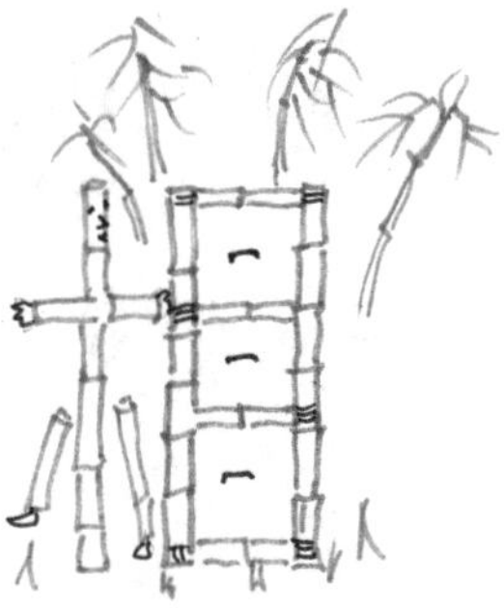

BOX/CASE xiāng 箱

Ancient form

(bamboo) + (see/each other/pictures) = box/case

Catchphrase

See the bamboo **BOX** in the middle of the jungle? **BOX/CASE** is 箱 xiāng.

Stroke order

响(響) SOUND xiǎng — 572
Radical/Component 口 mouth

SOUND xiǎng 响

Ancient form

Traditional form 響

(mouth) + (direction) = sound

Catchphrase

My neighbour and I yelled at one another with a loud **SOUND**. **SOUND** is 响 xiǎng.

Stroke order

向 TOWARDS xiàng 573
Radical/Component 口 mouth

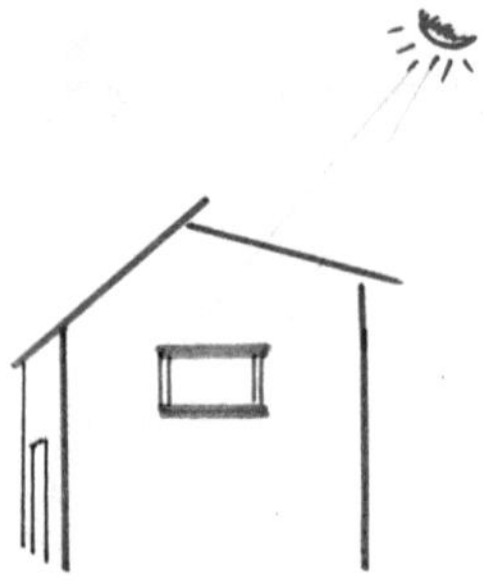

TOWARDS xiàng 向

Ancient form

(building) + (mouth/window) = towards

Catchphrase

This building is very warm because the windows face **TOWARDS** the sun. **TOWARDS** is 向 xiàng.

Stroke order

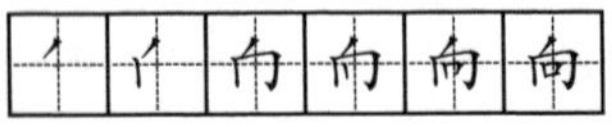

像 IMAGE xiàng 574
Radical/Component 亻 man

IMAGE xiàng 像

Ancient form

(man) + ((elephant) = image

Catchphrase

A man finds some buried bones which assemble into the **IMAGE** of an ancient elephant. **IMAGE** is 像 xiàng.

Stroke order

鞋 SHOE xié 575
Radical/Component 革 leather/cut

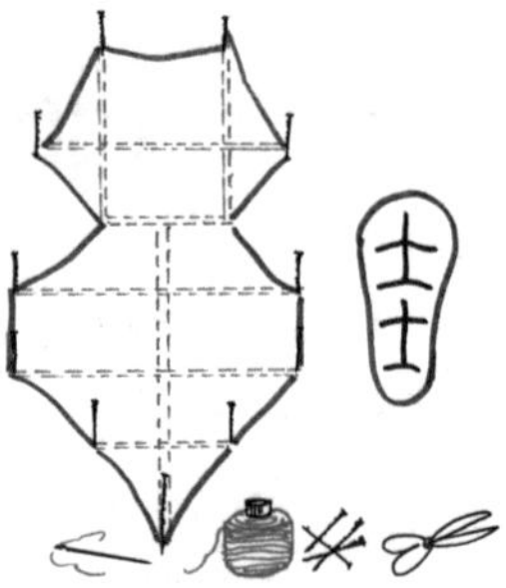

SHOE xié 鞋

(leather/cutting) + (stone) + (stone) = shoe

Catchphrase

Ancient people would use stones to cut leather to make simple **SHOE**s. **SHOE** is 鞋 xié.

Stroke order

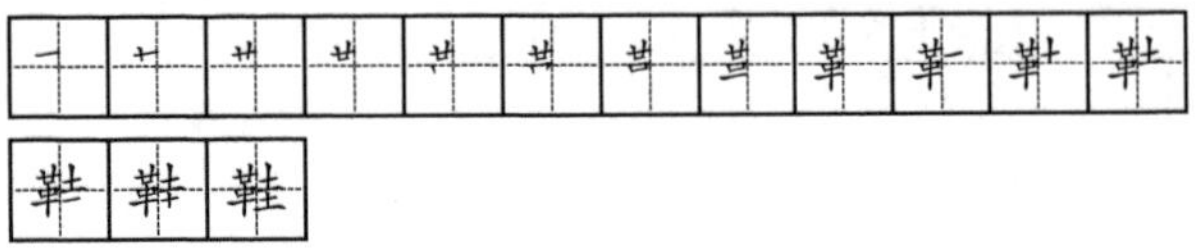

心 HEART xīn 576
Radical/Component 心 heart

HEART xīn 心

Ancient form /

Catchphrase

The character for heart looks like an actual **HEART**. **HEART** is 心 xīn.

Stroke order

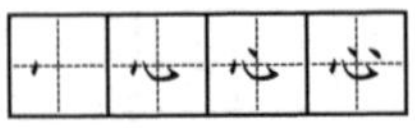

信 TRUST xìn 577
Radical/Component 亻 man

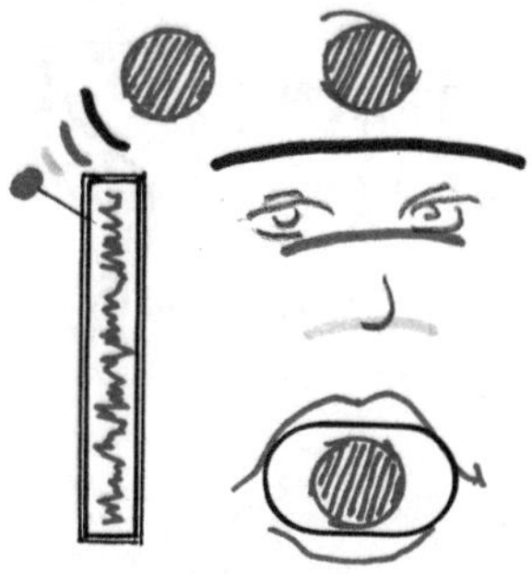

TRUST xìn 信

Ancient form

(man) + (language) = trust

Catchphrase

Once language is recorded, it becomes a testimony of **TRUST**. **TRUST** is 信 xìn.

Stroke order

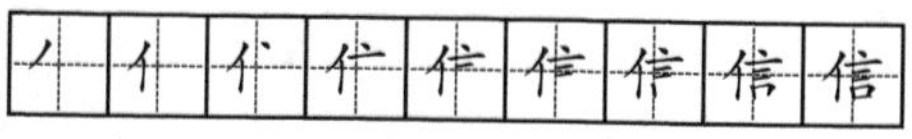

熊 BEAR xióng 578
Radical/Component 灬 four claws/fire

BEAR xióng 熊

Ancient form

(head) + (body) + (claws) = bear

Catchphrase

The combined characters of head, body and claws form the character for **BEAR**. **BEAR** is 熊 xióng.

Stroke order

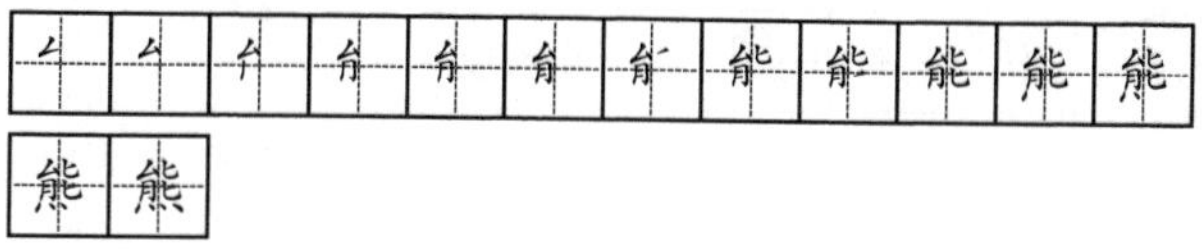

须 BEARD xū 579
Radical/Component 页 face/page

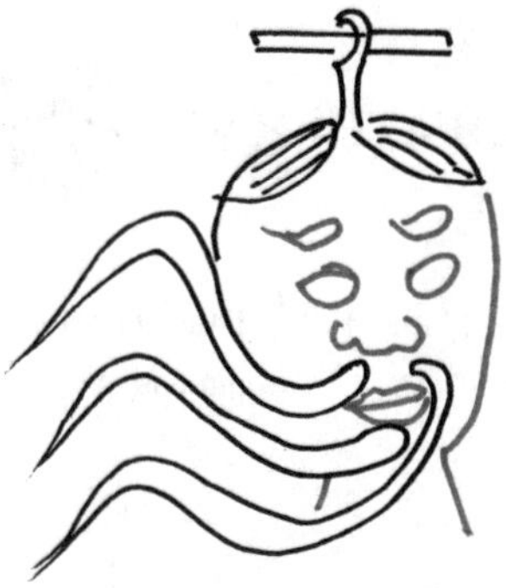

BEARD xū 须

Ancient form

(beard) + (face) = beard

Catchphrase

The wind blows this man's long **BEARD** from his face. **BEARD** is 须 xū.

Stroke order

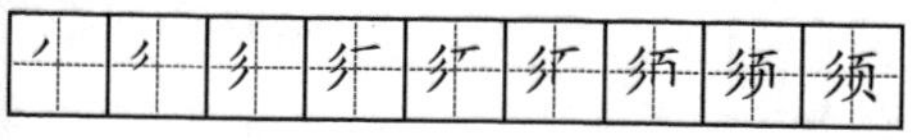

需 NEED xū 580
Radical/Component 雨 rain

NEED xū 需

Ancient form

(rain) + (beard person) = need

Catchphrase

The people living in this desert house really **NEED** some rain. **NEED** is 需 xū.

Stroke order

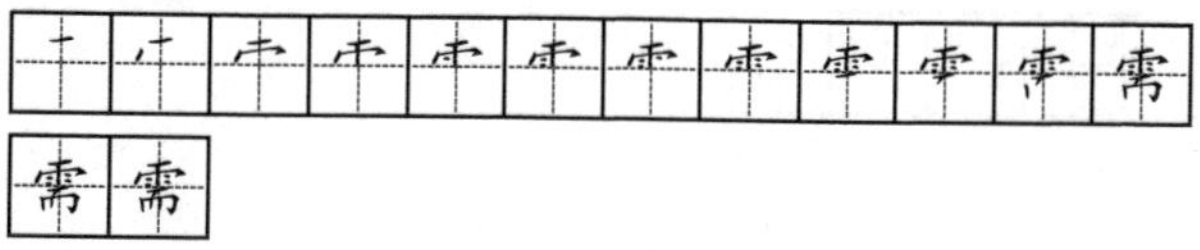

选(選)SELECT xuǎn 581
Radical/Component 辶 walk

SELECT xuǎn 选

Ancient form

Traditional form 選

辵(walk/run) + 先(first) = select

Catchphrase

This runner was the first to cross the finish line and was **SELECT**ed for the finals. **SELECT** is 选 xuǎn.

Stroke order

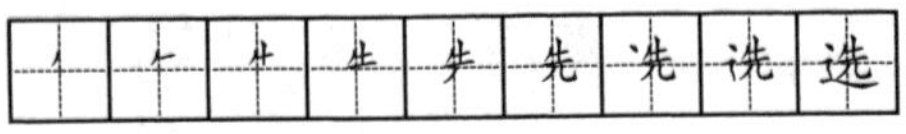

牙 TEETH yá 582
Radical/Component 牙 teeth

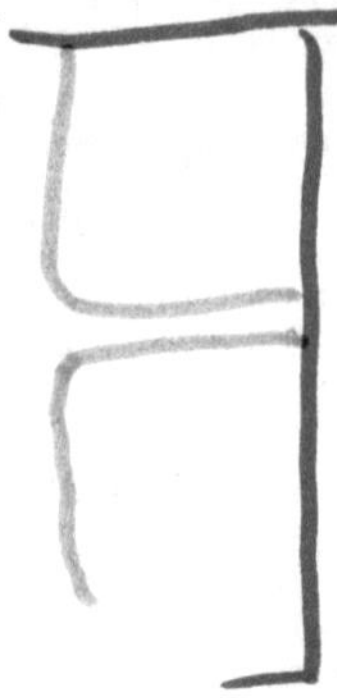

TEETH yá 牙

Ancient form

Catchphrase

The gaps between **TEETH** need to be brushed frequently to keep healthy. **TEETH** is 牙 yá.

Stroke order

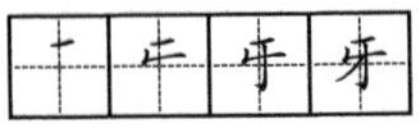

阳(陽)SUN yáng 583
Radical/Component 阝 cliff

SUN yáng 阳

Ancient form

Traditional form 陽

阜(cliff) + 昜(sun at 12 pm) = sun

Catchphrase

The hot **SUN** shines brightly on the cliff. **SUN** is 阳 yáng.

Stroke order

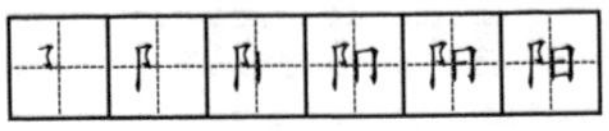

爷 GRANDFATHER yé 584
Radical/Component 父 father

GRANDFATHER yé 爷

父(father) + 卩(father bow to) = grandfather

Catchphrase

In this picture, father below bows to his father above, my **GRANDFATHER**. **GRANDFATHER** is 爷 yé.

Stroke order

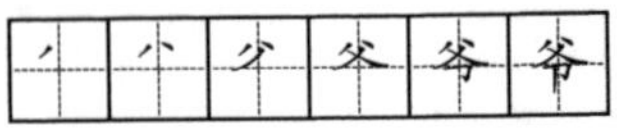

业(業) LINE OF BUSINESS yè 585
Radical/Component 一 the first stroke

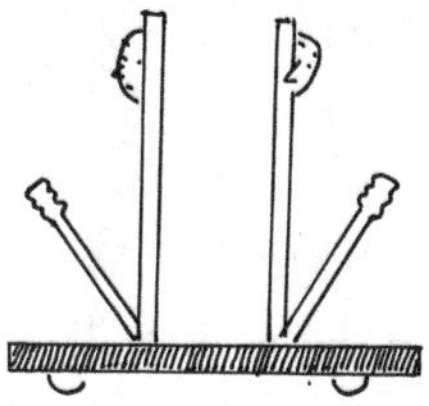

LINE OF BUSINESS yè 业

Ancient form
Traditional form 業
(worker one) + (worker two)
= line of business

Catchphrase

This character for **LINE OF BUSINESS** shows two workers together. It is mostly used as a suffix element of business/industry/occupation. **LINE OF BUSINESS** is 业 yè.

Stroke order

姨 AUNT yí 586
Radical/Component 女 female

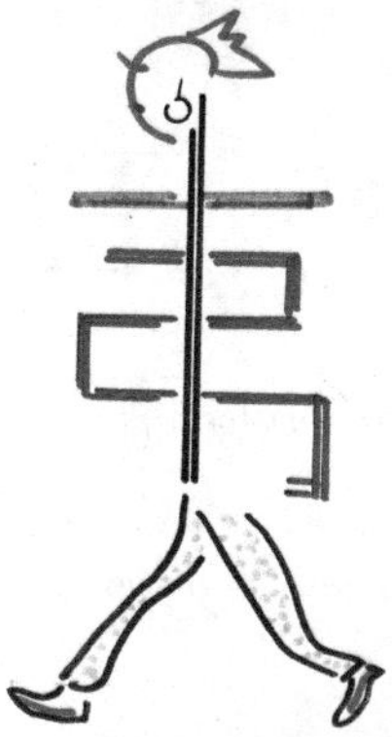

AUNT yí 姨

Ancient form
(woman) + (foreigner) = aunt

Catchphrase

My **AUNT** loves to wear funny styles of clothing. **AUNT** is 姨 yí.

Stroke order

议(議) DISCUSS yì 587
Radical/Component 讠 language

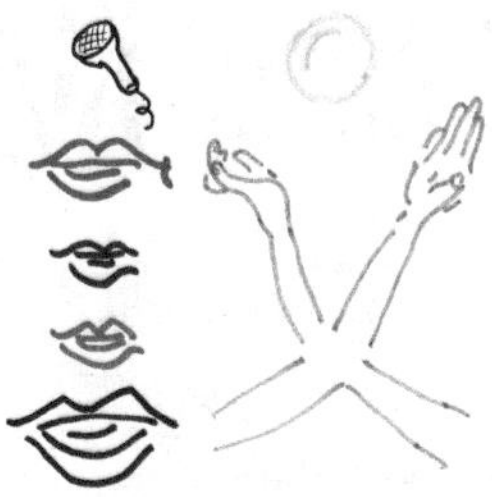

DISCUSS yì 议

Ancient form
Traditional form 議
(language) + 丶(proposal) +
乂(hand/arm) = discuss

Catchphrase

Many people must **DISCUSS** an idea before raising their hands for a final vote. **DISCUSS** is 议 yì.

Stroke order

易 CHANGE yì 588
Radical/Component 日 sun

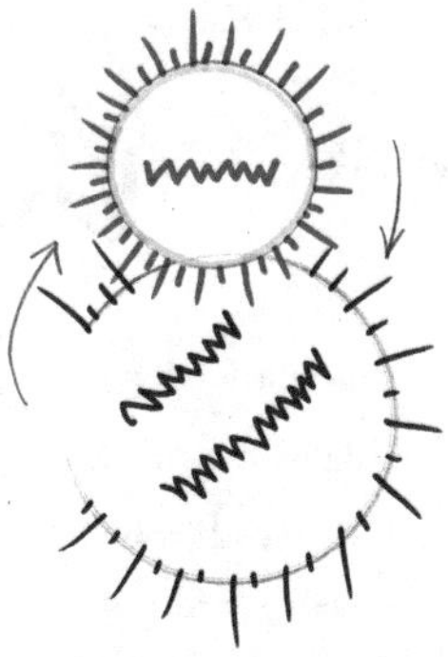

CHANGE yì 易

Ancient form
(sun/positive) + (shadow/negative) = change

Catchphrase

The character for **CHANGE** shows the positive sun atop the negative shadow in a continuous cycle. **CHANGE** is 易 yì.

Stroke order

音 MUSIC yīn 589
Radical/Component 音 music

MUSIC yīn 音

Ancient form

(standing/come out) + (heart or mouth) = music

Catchphrase

MUSIC begins from the heart below and comes out through expression. **MUSIC** is 音 yīn.

Stroke order

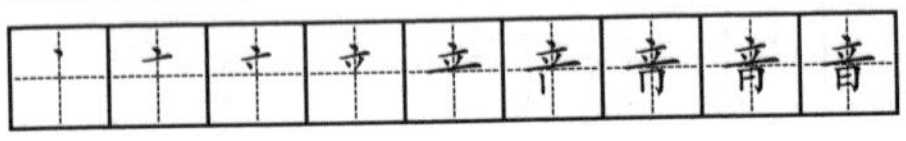

银(銀) SILVER yín 590
Radical/Component 钅 metal/gold

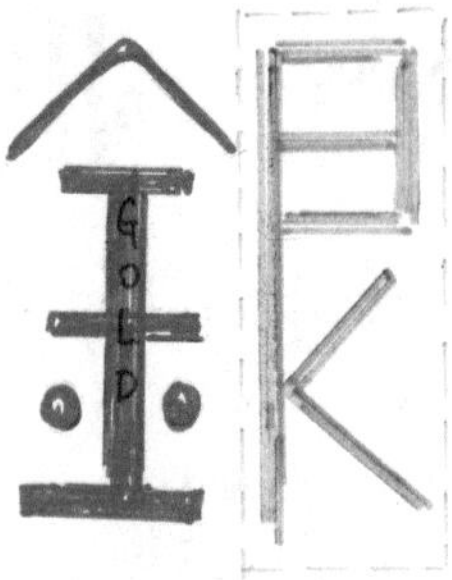

SILVER yín 银

Ancient form

Traditional form 銀

(gold) + (relative to the gold) = silver

Catchphrase

Gold and **SILVER** are both precious metals, but silver is not as valuable as gold. **SILVER** is 银 yín.

Stroke order

饮(飲) DRINK yǐn 591
Radical/Component 饣 food/eat

DRINK yǐn 饮

Ancient form

Traditional form 飲

(food and wine) + (stretched body) = drink

Catchphrase

This thin man examines all his food and wine, looking for something to **DRINK**. **DRINK** is 饮 yǐn.

Stroke order

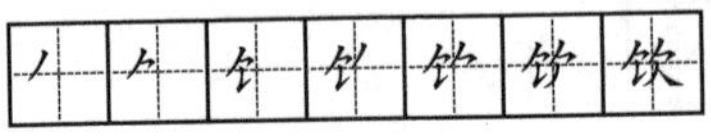

应(應) SHOULD yīng; RESPOND yìng 592
Radical/Component 广 wide/broad

SHOULD yīng; **RESPOND** yìng 应

Ancient form

Traditional form 應

(wide) + (bird) = respond /should

Catchphrase

The tiny bird on the rooftop calls out to his three friends across the street but they do not **RESPOND**. **SHOULD** is 应 yīng; **RESPOND** is yìng.

Stroke order

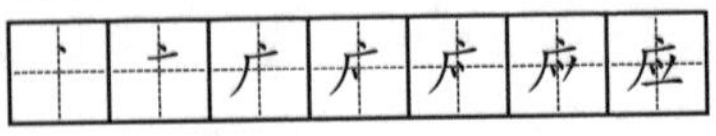

迎 WELCOME yíng 593
Radical/Component 辶 walk

WELCOME yíng 迎

Ancient form

(walk) + (person looks up) = welcome

Catchphrase

When people walk into your home, the tradition is to be polite and cordially **WELCOME** them. **WELCOME** is 迎 yíng.

Stroke order

丿	𠂉	卬	卬	迎	迎	迎

用 USE yòng 594
Radical/Component 用 use

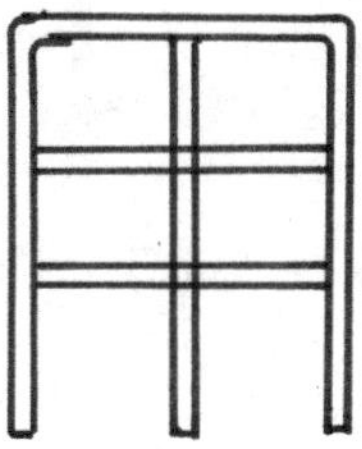

USE yòng 用

Ancient form

Catchphrase

A shelf unit with partitions is very **USE**ful! **USE** is 用 yòng.

Stroke order

丿	月	月	用	用

邮 POST yóu 595
Radical/Component 阝 town/city

POST yóu 邮

Ancient form

(pass through) + (town/city) = post

Catchphrase

POSTal mail can pass through cities, towns, and the countryside. **POST** is 邮 yóu.

Stroke order

丨	冂	日	由	由	由阝	邮

又 AGAIN yòu 596
Radical/Component 又 again

AGAIN yòu 又

Ancient form

Catchphrase

The picture shows three fingers, which means that number one is odd, number two is even, and number three **AGAIN** is also odd. **AGAIN** is 又 yòu.

Stroke order

乛	又

于 AT yú 597
Radical/Component 二 two

AT yú 于

Ancient form

Catchphrase

I am neither **AT** the T-junction nor at the crossroads. I am at the bottom of this vertical line. **AT** is 于 yú.

Stroke order

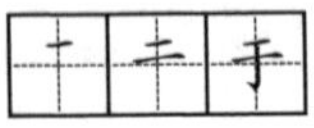

育 RAISE yù 598
Radical/Component 月 part of body/moon

RAISE yù 育

Ancient form

(baby) + (breast) = raise

Catchphrase

A mother must do her best to **RAISE** her baby. **RAISE** is 育 yù.

Stroke order

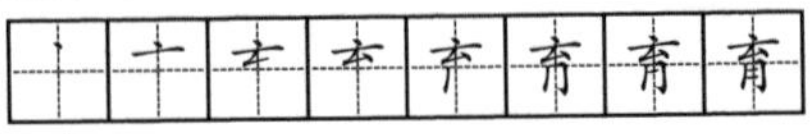

遇 MEET yù 599
Radical/Component 辶 walk

MEET yù 遇

Ancient form /

(road) + (farmland) + (stop) = meet

Catchphrase

Two people stop and **MEET** on a farmland road. **MEET** is 遇 yù.

Stroke order

元 ORIGIN yuán 600
Radical/Component 二 two

ORIGIN yuán 元

Ancient form

(father and mother) + (child) = origin

Catchphrase

Combining the characters for father and mother on top, and child beneath, we create the word for **ORIGIN**. **ORIGIN** is 元 yuán.

Stroke order

园(園) GARDEN/PARK yuán — 601
Radical/Component 囗 enclosure

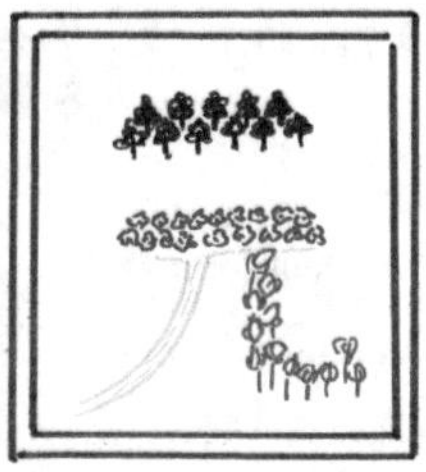

GARDEN/ PARK yuán 园

Ancient form

Traditional form 園

囗 (four-side walls) + 元 (unit) = garden/park

Catchphrase

A **PARK** is a unit of land with trees, flowers, paths, and all the elements of life surrounded by walls. **GARDEN/PARK** is 园 yuán.

Stroke order

丨	冂	冃	冃	冃	园	园

愿 WISH yuàn — 602
Radical/Component 心 heart

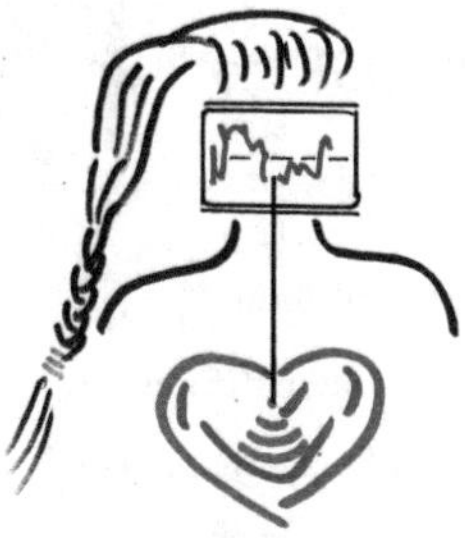

WISH yuàn 愿

Ancient form

原 (original) + 心 (heart) = wish

Catchphrase

A **WISH** has its origin in the heart before it is expressed. **WISH** is 愿 yuàn.

Stroke order

一	厂	厂	厂	厅	盾	盾	盾	厡	原	原	愿
愿	愿										

越 SURPASS yuè — 603
Radical/Component 走 walk

SURPASS yuè 越

Ancient form

走 (walk) + 戉 (tools and dagger) = surpass

Catchphrase

This climber is well-prepared with all of his tools. He will surely **SURPASS** all the others. **SURPASS** is 越 yuè.

Stroke order

一	十	土	牛	丰	走	走	赴	走	越	越	越

澡 BATH zǎo — 604
Radical/Component 氵 water

BATH zǎo 澡

Ancient form

氵 (water) + 喿 (bubble) = bath

Catchphrase

This tree is having a bubble **BATH** in the rainwater. **BATH** is 澡 zǎo.

Stroke order

丶	冫	氵	氵	沪	沪	沪	沪	沪	泀	淂	淂
澡	澡	澡	澡								

择(擇)CHOOSE zé 605

Radical/Component 扌 hand

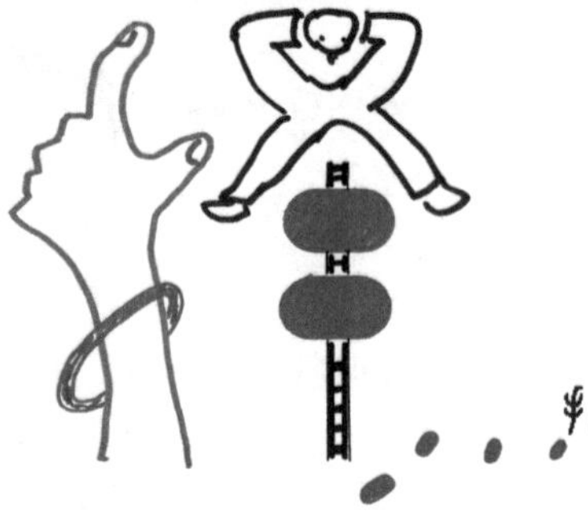

CHOOSE zé 择

Ancient form

Traditional form 擇

(hand) + (positive energy) = choose

Catchphrase

First you must **CHOOSE** with your mind, and then select with your hand. **CHOOSE** is 择 zé.

Stroke order

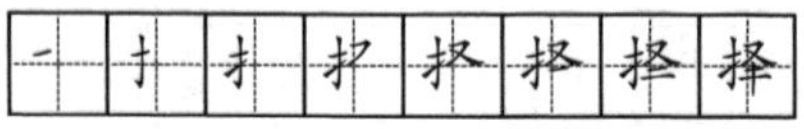

张(張)BE OPENED zhāng 606

Radical/Component 弓 bow

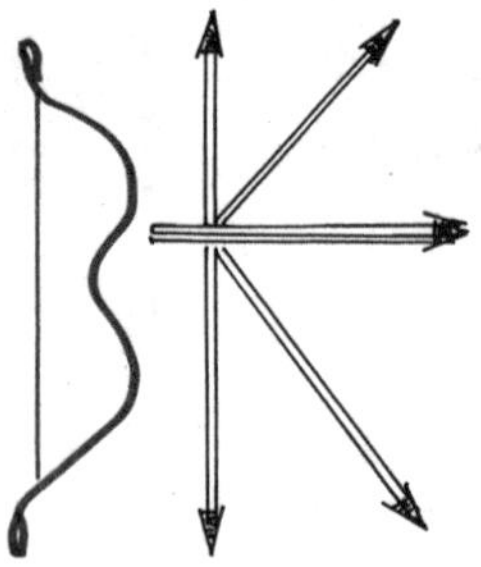

BE OPENED zhāng 张

Ancient form

Traditional form 張

(bow) + (stretch) = be opened

Catchphrase

This bow can **BE OPENED** so far that it can unleash five arrows at a time. **BE OPENED** is 张 zhāng.

Stroke order

照 ILLUMINATE zhào 607

Radical/Component 灬 fire

ILLUMINATE zhào 照

Ancient form

(torch) (hand holds) + (calling and shouting) = illuminate

Catchphrase

When entering a dangerous place, you need to **ILLUMINATE** the area with a torch and hold a weapon for self-defense. **ILLUMINATE** is 照 zhào.

Stroke order

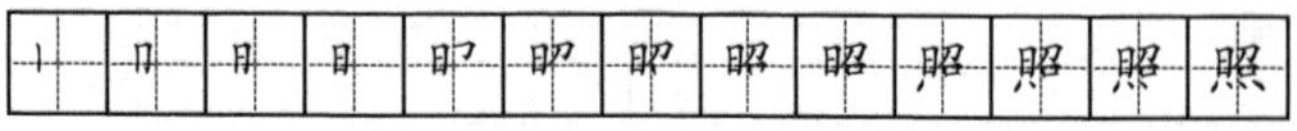

者 PERSON zhě 608

Radical/Component 耂 old person

PERSON zhě 者

Ancient form

(pattern) + (lips and mouth) = (aged) person

Catchphrase

Behind this painted Peking opera mask is the **PERSON**. **PERSON** is 者 zhě. * "ZHE" means person(s), it is also a suffix of a word which can't be used by itself and must preceded by another word.

Stroke order

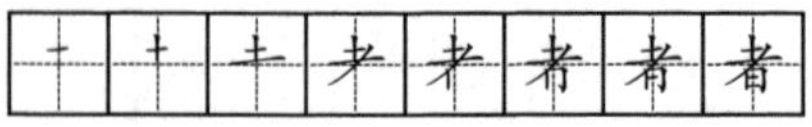

直 STRAIGHT zhí 609
Radical/Component 目 eye

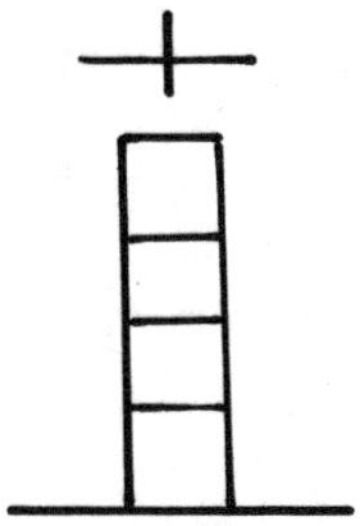

STRAIGHT zhí 直

Ancient form

乚(base) +十(vertical) +目(eye) = straight

Catchphrase

This is a four-storey building that goes **STRAIGHT** up and down. **STRAIGHT** is 直 zhí.

Stroke order

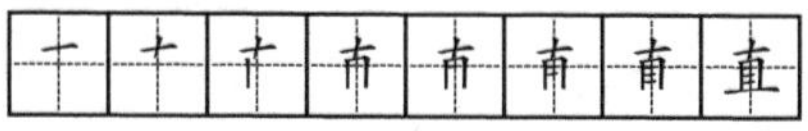

终(終)BE OVER zhōng 610
Radical/Component 纟 silk

BE OVER zhōng 终

Ancient form

Traditional form 終

糸(silk) +冬(end of) = is over

Catchphrase

It's a pity that just as I finished sewing my woolly hat, winter **WAS OVER**. **BE OVER** is 终 zhōng.

Stroke order

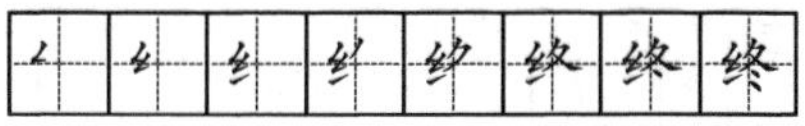

种(種)SEED zhǒng; PLANT zhòng 611
Radical/Component 禾 crop

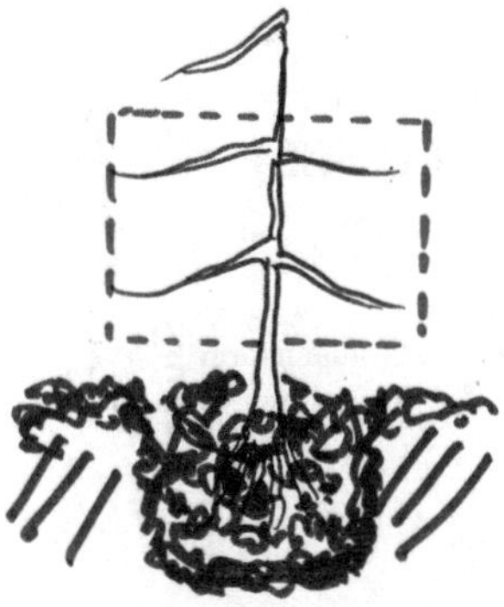

SEED zhǒng;
PLANT zhòng 种

Ancient form Traditional form 種

禾(crop) +中(at the middle) = seed/plant

Catchphrase

SEEDs should be **PLANT**ed in the middle of the hole. **SEED** is 种 zhǒng; **PLANT** is zhòng.

Stroke order

重 HEAVY zhòng; REPEAT chóng 612
Radical/Component 里 inside/mile

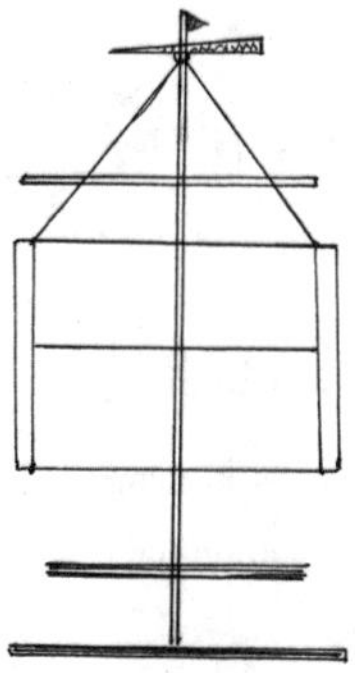

HEAVY zhòng;
REPEAT chóng 重

Ancient form

(stuffs) +東(machine) +土(land) = heavy

Catchphrase

This rectangular billboard is very **HEAVY** and needs to be firmly fixed both at its top and its bottom. **HEAVY** is 重 zhòng; **REPEAT** is chóng.

Stroke order

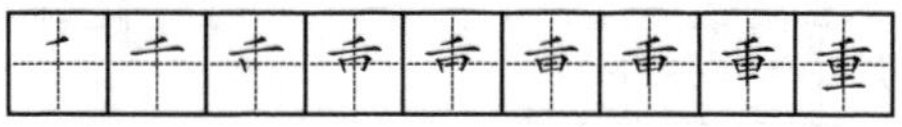

周 SURROUNDING zhōu 613
Radical/Component 口 well/mouth

SURROUNDING zhōu 周

Ancient form

(farm field) + (well)
= surrounding

Catchphrase

The well below supplies water to the **SURROUNDING** farmland and vegetable fields. **SURROUNDING** is 周 zhōu.

Stroke order

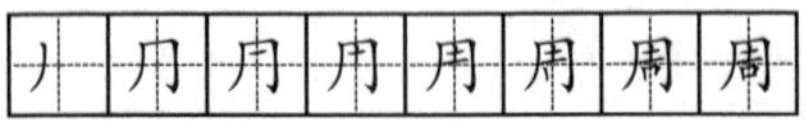

主 MAIN/MASTER zhǔ 614
Radical/Component 丶 drop

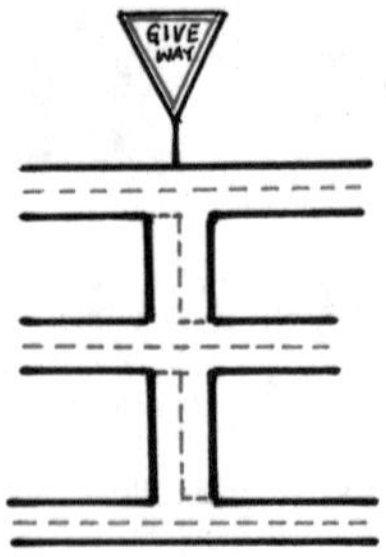

MAIN/MASTER zhǔ 主

Ancient form

Catchphrase

Cars on secondary roads should give way to cars on the **MAIN** road. **MAIN/MASTER** is 主 zhǔ.

Stroke order

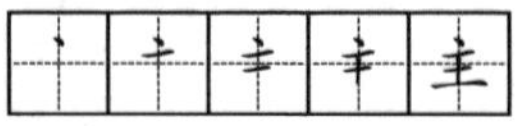

注 ATTENTION zhù 615
Radical/Component 氵 water

ATTENTION zhù 注

Ancient form

(water) + (main)
= attention

Catchphrase

Pay **ATTENTION** and watch out for crocodiles which inhabit the main waters around here. **ATTENTION** is 注 zhù.

Stroke order

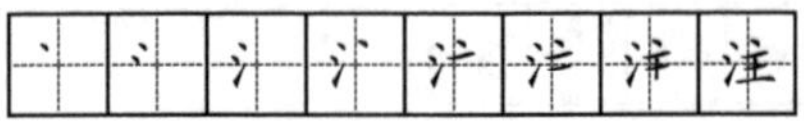

自 ONESELF zì 616
Radical/Component 自 oneself

ONESELF zì 自

Ancient form /

Catchphrase

This character represents a nose. Chinese people often point to their nose when referring to **THEMSELVES**. **ONESELF** is 自 zì.

Stroke order

总(總)SUM UP zǒng 617

Radical/Component 心 heart

SUM UP zǒng 总

Ancient form

Traditional form 總

(the top being the brain and the base being the heart) = sum up

Catchphrase

To **SUM UP** my results into a decision, I must consider the thoughts of my brain and the feelings from my heart. **SUM UP** is 总 zǒng.

Stroke order

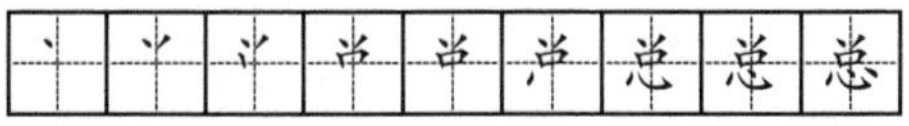

嘴 MOUTH zuǐ 618

Radical/Component 口 mouth

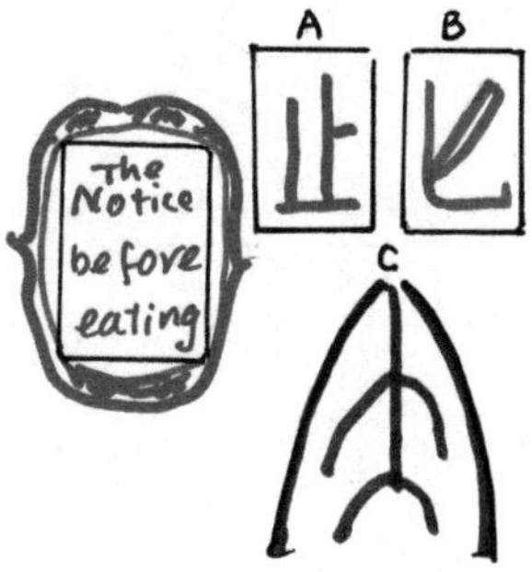

MOUTH zuǐ 嘴

Ancient form

(mouth) + (stop; sharp object) + (bones) = mouth

Catchphrase

Your **MOUTH** will quickly alert you if there is something hard or sharp in what you are about to eat. **MOUTH** is 嘴 zuǐ.

Stroke order

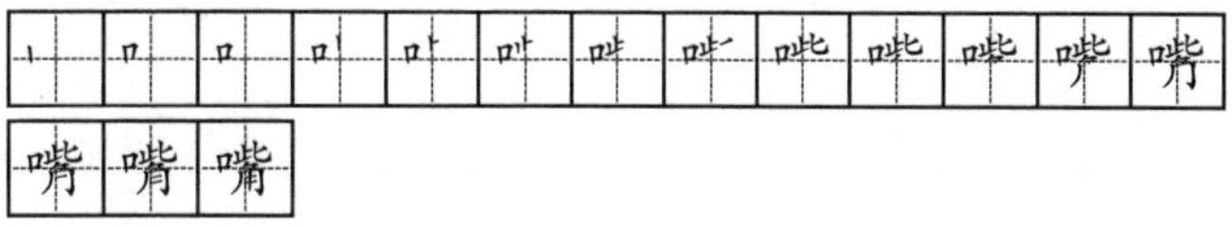

词句篇

Grammatical Codes & Notes

As in Elementary Chinese, it will be necessary to learn the grammatical function of certain characters before understanding how they are used in the sentences. These grammar structures involve the characters: 把 bǎ (353), 被 bèi (361), 除 chú (378), and 地 de (390).

B 353 把 (the grammatical code) bǎ

请(你)把门关好!	Please (you) close the door properly!
请(你)把灯打开!	Please (you) switch on the light!

As BA(把) sentences do not exist in the English language, so we provide a detailed guide below:

If you want to change the status of an object into a new situation through an action, two verbs are required: the first one is the verb of "BA: handle/hold/grasp", the second is the verb of action, and a word of outcome is placed to the second verb which indicates the new status. In general, the "outcome" to the latter verb is an adjective, or a verb, or even a clause. With regards to people's daily lives, the changing status of objects happens often, therefore the BA Sentence is a very useful sentence pattern.

The formulation of a BA sentence is:

Subject + BA (the first verb) + object + the second verb with the outcome.

For example:

In Chinese: 请(你)把门关好(了)!

Please (you) close the door properly!

请 你(please you) 把 BA(hold or handle: Verb One)+ 门(door: Object)+ 关(close: Verb Two)+ 好(了)(properly: the outcome to the second verb). 关 - 好(了)~ here the verb-adjective outcome combination shows a new outcome: Close it properly.

More examples:

1. 她一进门就把 (v1) 门关 (v2)- 上 (outcome) 了 (outcome of the actions)，可能是怕冷。

She closed the door properly as soon as she came in because she is afraid of the cold.

2. 我今天不去学校，请把 (v1) 这本书交给 (v2 a joined verb means Give To) 老师 (outcome of the actions)。

I won' t go to the school today; will you deliver this book to the teacher please?

3. 小李，请把 (v1) 椅子搬到 (v2 a joined verb means Move To) 楼上去吧 (outcome of the actions)。它太重了，我搬不动。

Young Li, could you take this chair and move it upstairs? It is so heavy that I cannot move it.

4. 你别把 (v1) 你的手机当成 (v2 a joined verb means Regard As) 字典 (outcome of the actions)，因为手机里的字典常常有错!

Don't use your mobile phone as a dictionary, because the phone's dictionary is often wrong!

In summary, the BA sentence is a double verb pattern, using two verbs plus an adjective/verb/clause outcome to complete a status change.

被 (the grammatical code) bèi 361 B

The Chinese language often utilises the passive pattern for unexpected situations or things. From the Chinese point of view, it is within the responsibility of, say, a postman to deliver mail, so there is no need to emphasise an action which is within a person's normal responsibility. For the same reason, cleaners cleaning, doctors healing, teachers teaching, and even a mother cooking for her family etc., in the Chinese point of view are all social divisions of labour for each profession.

If something unusual happens, however, e.g., a letter opened, a suitcase stolen, a house damaged, or a friend detained, we shall have to add something called the passive.

被打	be beaten
被爱	be loved
被开除	was kicked out

Here are some examples:

(English) My suitcase was stolen.

(Chinese) My suitcase BEI stolen.

BUT,

(English) The office has been cleaned.

(Chinese) The office cleaned.

More examples:

1. 我弟弟昨天被他的同学打了。

My younger brother was beaten by his classmate yesterday.

2. 今天来打扫教室的工人觉得很奇怪，因为教室已经被学生们扫得干干净净了。

When the cleaner came to clean the classroom today she was surprised because the classroom had already been fully cleaned by the students.

除 (the grammatical code) chú 378 C

The pattern 除了……以外 can be used in three ways:

One: apart from (the verb) A, also (the same verb as used for A) B.

我除了喜欢北京以外 (omittable)，也喜欢东北。	Apart from liking Beijing, I also like the northeast.

Two: except not doing A, do all others.

我除了不喜欢北京以外 (omittable)，其他的地方都喜欢。	Apart from not liking Beijing, I like all other places.
我除了喜欢北京以外 (omittable)，其他的地方都不喜欢。	Apart from liking Beijing, I don't like all the other places.

Three: apart from doing A, in addition do B

我去北京除了要见朋友以外 (omittable)，还得参加汉语水平考试。	I go to Beijing where besides needing to meet friends, I also have to take the HSK test.

D 390 地 (the grammatical code) de

This code character 地 is always situated in between an adjective and a verb to indicate in what manner the action is done. For example:

他很快地吃完了饭，然后就走了。	He quickly finished the food, then left.
小李高兴地对我说，他明天要去法国旅游了。	Young Li happily told me that he will travel to France tomorrow.

In a word, 地 plays the same role as the adverbial suffix-ly in English.

阿 prefix of name/pet/family relatives ā; ē 349 A

Chinese	English	Character codes
阿 + 姨 = 阿姨	prefix + aunt = aunt/aunty	349/586
阿哥	elder brother	349/218
阿三	the third child (some regions in South China)	349/106
阿门	Amen	349/257
阿李	Young Li	349/481

Example Sentences

1/179	我阿姨不在家，她在公司。 My aunt is not at home. She is at the company.
2/349	我阿姨住在北京。 My aunt lives in Beijing.
3/349	我的阿姨是中文老师。 My aunt is a Chinese teacher.
4/349	A: 你阿姨在家吗？ B: 不在，她去公园了。 A: Is your aunt at home? B: No, she went to the park.
5/349	A: 你有几个阿姨？她们都在哪儿呢？ B: 我有三个阿姨，一个在中国，一个在西班牙，一个在法国。 A: How many aunts do you have? Where are they? B: I have three aunts; one is in China, one in Spain, and another in France.

A 350 啊 interjection or particle(expressing, surprise, etc)/used in enumerating items ā; á; ǎ; à

Chinese	English	Character codes
好 + 热 + 啊 = 好热啊！	very + hot + wow =Wow, the weather is so hot!	039/103/350
怎么回事啊？	What's going on?	165/077/048/281/350
东北啊、西北啊……	northeast China, northwest China...	019/005/350/135/005/350
"啊"什么？	What's the surprise for?	350/111/077
听话，好好吃啊！	Behave, and eat properly!	129/046/039/039/011/350
吃啊、喝啊……	eating, drinking...	011/350/041/350

Example Sentences

1/350	天气好热啊，把空调打开吧！ It's too hot, please switch on the air-conditioning!
2/350	你怎么这么喜欢中国茶啊？ How come you like Chinese tea so much?
3/350	天气好冷啊，外面都结冰了！ The weather is so cold, it's freezing outside!
4/350	这是一个多么好的工作机会啊，希望我能得到这个工作。 What a great work opportunity! I hope I could get the job.
5/350	A: 你为什么这么喜欢北京呢？ B: 因为北京是一个非常有生气的城市啊！ A: Why do you like Beijing so much? B: Because Beijing is such a dynamic and vigorous city.

矮 short (in height)/low ǎi 351 A

Chinese	English	Character codes
矮 + 个 + 子 = 矮个子	short + stature + person = short person	351/031/172
矮小	small	351/143
矮床	low bed	351/199
矮桌子	low table	351/171/172
不高不矮	good size	007/378/007/351
高矮胖瘦	(people) in different sizes	378/351/509/538

Example Sentences

1/351	有些树天生矮小，长不高。 Some trees are naturally small and cannot grow tall.
2/351	一般来说，人老的时候会比年轻的时候矮一些。 In general, people are a little shorter in old age than when they were young.
3/351	她不高不矮，不胖不瘦，看上去很舒服。 Everything in her appearance is in the right proportions, so she is very pleasing to look at.
4/351	足球明星里有一些个子矮的人，这些人往往跑得很快，踢得很出色。 Some football stars are quite short, but they often run faster and play really well.
5/351	世界上的人千差*万别，样子不同不说，就是同一个人种的人，高矮胖瘦也不一样。 The people in the world are very diverse, not only different in appearance but within each race the height, weight, and size are also different.

注释 Note

* 差 chā=different

A 352 安 peaceful/at ease/set at ease/rest content/safe/set up/install… ān

Chinese	English	Character codes
安 + 静 = 安静	peace + calm = quiet	352/461
安心	feel at ease	352/576
安于	be content	352/597
没安好心	have an evil intention	078/352/039/576
不安	worry; unease	007/352
安定	stable	352/392
天安门	Tiananmen	128/352/257
安上门	to fix a door	352/108/257
平平安安	very safe and sound	513/513/352/352
心安理得	free from worry or guilt	576/352/070/207
安居乐业	live and work in peace and contentment	352/466/246/585

Example Sentences

1/352	老师要讲课了，请大家安静。 Be quiet please, our teacher will start the lesson soon.
2/352	她把杯子打坏了，心里很不安。 She has broken the glass and is very worried about it.
3/352	你要安心地学习，不要想别的事情。 You have to study with peace of mind and not think about other things.
4/352	我希望阿姨去西安一路平安。 I hope Aunt will have a safe journey to Xi'an.
5/352	我们的老师一进教室，大家马上就安静下来了。 As soon as our teacher came into the classroom, everyone immediately quietened down.

把 hold/grasp/handle/MW... bǎ 353 B

Chinese	English	Character codes
把 + 关 = 把关	hold + mountain pass = check/final control	353/034
手把手	step by step	284/353/284
总把……	always take...	617/353
把手	handle	284/353
一把手	top leader; boss	152/284/353
把不住	cannot control	353/007/170
一大把……	a lot of something	152/014/353
把灯打开	switch on the light	353/389/013/061

Example Sentences

1/353	她一进门就把门关上了，可能是怕冷吧。 She closed the door as soon as she came in. Perhaps she was afraid of the cold.
2/353	我今天不去学校，请把这本书还给周老师。 I won't go to school today. Will you bring this book and return it to Teacher Zhou please?
3/353	小李，请把椅子搬到楼上去吧，太重了，我搬不动。 Xiao Li, could you take this chair and move it upstairs? It is so heavy that I can't move it.
4/353	这个球进得太漂亮了，大门没把住。 That shot was so beautiful that the goalkeeper couldn't stop it.
5/353	你别把你的手机当成字典，因为手机里的字典常常有错！ Don't use your mobile phone as a dictionary, because the phone's dictionary is often wrong!

B | 354 般 type/same as/just like bān

Chinese	English	Character codes
一 + 般 = 一般	one + kind = general	152/354
一般见识	common knowledge	152/354/054/115
一般来说	generally speaking	152/354/065/122
这般 / 那般	same as; such as	165/354/085/354
百般	in every possible way	181/354
万般	everything; in every possible way	559/354

Example Sentences

1/354	她的中文很一般。 Her Chinese is so-so.
2/354	一般来说，人到十八九岁时上大学；可是楚春阳十四岁就学完大学以前的课考进大学了。 Generally, students start university aged 18 or 19, but at the age of 14, Chu Chunyang had finished high school and was entering university.
3/354	她的歌声像小鸟唱歌般动听。 Her song is so pleasant to listen to, like a bird singing.
4/354	经过百般地说服，他终于同意我的意见了。 After trying every possible way to persuade him, he finally agreed with me.
5/354	因为他一年来像黄牛般地工作，所以成绩很突出。 His performance was outstanding because he worked like an ox all year.

搬 move/remove/take away… bān 355 B

Chinese	English	Character codes
搬 + 家 = 搬家	move + home = to move home	355/053
搬家公司	the removals company	355/053/221/285
搬运	handle; move	355/333
搬不动	cannot move	355/007/212
搬运工人	porter	355/333/032/104
搬来搬去	often moving	355/065/355/102
照搬	to copy	607/355

Example Sentences

1/355	请你把椅子搬到教室里去。 Please move this chair into the classroom.
2/355	他是搬运工。 He is a porter.
3/355	请你把这张桌子搬到楼上去。 Please move this table upstairs.
4/355	A: 你需要我帮你搬家吗？ B: 谢谢，不用了，搬运工已经帮我把家搬好了。 A: Do you need any help moving home? B: No, thanks. The porters have helped me move already.
5/355	答题时不要照搬书本上的，要写自己的想法。 When you answer the questions, please don't copy everything from the textbook, and you need to write your own opinion.

B 356 板 board/plank/shutter/stiff bǎn

Chinese	English	Character codes
黑 + 板 = 黑板	black + board = blackboard	228/356
板子	board	356/172
白板	whiteboard	180/356
老板	boss	066/356
地 * 板	floorboard	390/356
天花板	ceiling	128/426/356
刻板	inflexible	473/356
板球	cricket	356/272
有板有眼	rhythmical; orderly	158/356/158/316
一板一眼	(do things) follow the rules	152/356/152/316
纸板	cardboard	342/356

Note

* 地 dì=earth; land; ground

Example Sentences

1/356	老师今天在黑板上写了一百多个汉字。 The teacher has written more than 100 Chinese characters on the blackboard.
2/356	他不喜欢别人叫他老板。 He does not like others calling him “Boss”.
3/356	谁把我的名字写在这个纸板上了？ Who has written my name on the piece of cardboard?
4/356	在英国，老师以前都是在黑板上写字，现在在白板上写了。 In the UK, teachers used to write characters on the blackboard, now they write them on a whiteboard.
5/356	他把学生的名字都写在黑板上了。 He wrote all the students’ names on the blackboard.

办 deal/do/manage/set up/run… bàn 357 B

Chinese	English	Character codes
办 + 法 = 办法	do/deal + method = method	357/402
办公室	office	357/221/283
办得到	can be done	357/207/205
办不到	cannot do	357/007/205
办公	do business	357/221
办公会议	business meeting	357/221/049
办好	do well	357/039
办公桌	desk	357/221/171
办理	do/deal	357/482
包办	take care of everything	359/357
办学	to run a school	357/150
主办	sponsor	614/357

Example Sentences

1/357	我有办法解决这个问题。 I have a method to solve this problem.
2/357	家和办公室，他更喜欢在家里办公。 Between the home and the office, he prefers working from home.
3/357	办公室在里面，请去那里办理业务。 The office is inside, please go there to conduct your business.
4/357	我虽然有不少关系，可是我不是超人，很多事情我一个人办不了。 Although I have good contacts, I am not a superman and cannot deal with a lot of things on my own.
5/357	这两年，他把中文学校办得很好，人们都在向他学习办学的方法。 He has been running a Chinese school very well for a couple of years, so people like to learn from him how to run schools.

B 358 半 half/semi/in the middle/partly/very little... bàn

Chinese	English	Character codes
一＋半＝一半	one + half = a half	152/358
半个月	a half month	358/031/162
半大不小	(age or size) in between adults (large) and children (small)	358/014/007/143
下半场	the second half	139/358/196
多半	more than a half	023/358
一人一半	a half each	152/104/152/358
上半年	the first half of the year	108/358/090

Example Sentences

1/358	这个苹果你们两人一人吃一半。 You two can each have a half of this apple.
2/358	他只用了半个月就把一多半的工作做完了。 It only took him half a month to finish most of his work.
3/358	我哥哥是在足球比赛的下半场才进来的。 My older brother came in the second half of the football match.
4/358	真有意思，他是上半年开始学中文的，他爸爸是下半年开始学中文的。 It's very interesting that he started learning Chinese in the first half of the year and his father started learning Chinese in the second half of the year.
5/358	中学生都半大不小，他们多半认为自己什么都懂。 A lot of secondary school students that are teenagers think they know everything.

包 wrap/bag/bundle/include/guarantee/hire/charter/MW… bāo 359 B

Chinese	English	Character codes
面 + 包 = 面包	flour + bun = bread	081/359
书包	school bag	119/359
钱包	wallet	100/359
包车	hire a car for a period	359/010
包子	steamed stuffed bun	359/172
打包	take away	013/359
红包	red envelope	229/359
包办	manage everything; run the whole show	359/357
一包衣服	a pack of clothes	152/359/153/029

Example Sentences

1/359	他喜欢吃包子，不喜欢吃面包。 He likes to eat steamed stuffed buns, but doesn't like to eat bread.
2/359	我不怎么喜欢用大钱包。 I really don't very much like to use big wallets.
3/359	请把书包给我。 Please pass me the school bag.
4/359	A: 你的钱包在哪里？ B: 我的钱包在我的手提包里。 A: Where is your wallet? B: My wallet is in my handbag.
5/359	他每天都坐出租车去学校，是长包的车，他的早点常常在路上吃，最常吃的是他妈妈做的包子。 He goes to school by taxi every day. It's a long-term cab hire, and he often eats breakfast on the way. His favourite food is the buns made by his mum.

B 360 饱 be full/have eaten enough/full/satisfy… bǎo

Chinese	English	Character codes
饱 + 满 = 饱满	full + satisfied = full; plump	360/496
饱了	have eaten enough/full	360/067
饱学	scholarly	360/150
饱和	saturation	360/042
饱读经书	scholarly in classics	360/021/237/119
酒足饭饱	have drunk and eaten a lot	464/346/026/360

Example Sentences

1/360	你们吃吧，我真的吃饱了，不能再吃了。 You carry on eating. I am really full. I can't eat anymore!
2/360	你们吃饱了吗？ Have you eaten enough?
3/360	我刚才吃了很多包子，我很饱了。 I ate many steamed stuffed buns just now. I am really full.
4/360	虽然张先生长期住在西班牙，但是谁都知道，他是位饱读中国历史和文学书的学者，很了不起。 Although Mr. Zhang has lived in Spain for a long time, everyone knows he is a well-read scholar of Chinese history and literature, and he is very impressive.
5/360	今天的青菜都是刚刚从市场买来的新鲜菜，吃饱一点儿吧。吃饱了再上船，晚上睡一觉，第二天就到了。 Today's greens are all freshly bought from the market. Go on, eat your fill, then get back on the boat, get a good night's sleep and you will arrive the next day.

被 Grammatical Code/quilt/cover by bèi 361 B

Chinese	English	Character codes
被 + 打 = 被打	by + beat = be beaten	361/013
被爱	be loved	361/001
被害人	victim	361/421/104
被开除	be dismissed	361/061/378
被告	defendant	361/217
被动	passive (position)	361/212
被子	quilt	361/172
被单	bed sheet	361/386

Example Sentences

1/361	你如果不好好学习，考试就会很被动。 If you don't study hard, you will not master the contents of the exam.
2/361	教室居然 * 被我们校长打扫得干干净净！ Surprisingly, our classroom was cleaned spotless by our headteacher!
3/361	我弟弟昨天被他的同学打了。 My younger brother was beaten up by his classmate yesterday.
4/361	A: 报纸上说那两人中一定有一个是被害者。 B: 那么谁是被害者呢？ A: Out of these two people, one must be the victim, the newspaper said. B: Well, which one is it?
5/361	A: 你喜欢爱人，还是被人爱？ B: 我喜欢爱，也喜欢被爱。你呢？ A: Do you like to love, or being loved? B: I like to love and also being loved. How about you?

注释 Note

* 居然，surprisingly; unexpectedly

B | 362 鼻 nose bí

Chinese	English	Character codes
鼻 + 子 = 鼻子	nose + suffix = nose	362/172
鼻子眼儿	nostril	362/172/316/024
鼻息	breath	362/308
鼻音	nasal sound	362/589
大鼻子	big nose	014/362/172

Example Sentences

1/362	她的鼻子很漂亮。 Her nose is pretty.
2/362	西方人都是大鼻子吗？ Do Western people all have big noses?
3/362	高年级的那个总穿着蓝上衣的男生说起话来鼻音很重。 The senior male student who is always in a blue shirt speaks with heavy nasal sound.
4/362	我最近得了重感冒，不但身体感觉不舒服，鼻子也疼了好几天了。 I recently had a bad cold. Not only did my body feel uncomfortable, but also my nose was sore for days.
5/362	一般来说，动物的鼻子比人的有用，特别是狗的鼻子，能很快地闻出几百米以外的东西是什么。 In general, an animal's nose is more useful than a human's, especially a dog's nose which can immediately smell something hundreds of meters away.

必 must/certainly/surely/have to bì 363 B

Chinese	English	Character codes
必 + 须 = 必须	must + need = must	363/579
必定	certainly	363/392
必要	necessary; essential; indispensable; required	363/319
不必	no need; don't have to	007/363
必然	inevitable; certain	363/273
必需	essential; basic	363/580
必不可少	must have	363/007/242/109
大可不必	no need at all	014/242/007/363

Example Sentences

1/363	我听说，当今中国的小学生必须学英语。 I heard that today's Chinese primary school students must learn English.
2/363	这个问题解决了，你今天不必来我家了。 You don't have to come to my house today, as the issue has been sorted out.
3/363	学好（中国）语文是中国的中学生考上大学必不可少的一个条件。 Learning Chinese language well is an essential condition for Chinese middle school students to get into university.
4/363	你们知道"必须"和"必需"有什么不同吗？让我来告诉你们："必须"是一定要做，"必需"是一定要有。 Do you know what the difference is between 必须 and 必需？Let me tell you: 必须 means must do, 必需 means must have.
5/363	A: 请问，我有必要学中文吗？ B: 如果你要去中国工作，学中文就很有必要。 A: Do I have to learn Chinese? B: Since you want to go to China to work, learning Chinese is indispensable.

B | 364 变 become different/change/change into/transform/hanged biàn

Chinese	English	Character codes
变 + 化 = 变化	change + melt = change	364/427
变更 *	change; alter; modify	364/414
不变	no change; stable	007/364
变心	cease to be faithful	364/576
变动	alteration	364/212
事变	incident	281/364
千变万化	many changes	268/364/559/427
一成不变	unchangeable; never change	152/375/007/364
变成	change to	364/375
变为 (wéi)	change into	364/303

Example Sentences

1/364	他今年变化很大。 He has changed a lot this year.
2/364	你变了，他没变。 You have changed, but he hasn't.
3/364	我爱你的心不变。 I love you, my heart will not change.
4/364	这十年我们公司变化很大，变成了全世界数一数二 ** 的大公司。 In the past ten years, our company has changed a lot and become one of the very best companies in the world.
5/364	人和人很不一样。有的人喜欢千变万化，有的人喜欢一成不变。 People are very different. Some people like constant changes and some people like to stay the same.

注释 Note

* 更 gēng=change

** 数一数二 shǔyī-shǔ'èr=one of the best; the number one or two

冰 ice/put on the ice/feel cold bīng 365 B

Chinese	English	Character codes
冰 + 箱 = 冰箱	ice + box = refrigerator	365/571
冰冷	ice-cold	365/068
冰水	ice water	365/121
冰块儿	ice cube	365/412
冰球	ice ball	365/272
冰场	ice stadium	365/196
冰山	iceberg	365/530
冰灯	ice lantern	365/389
结冰	to freeze	455/365
冰天雪地 *	a world of ice and snow	365/128/314/390

Example Sentences

1/365	他把冰箱搬进来了，我们现在可以把啤酒冰上了。 He has moved the refrigerator in. We can now have iced beer.
2/365	我买的冰水都被他们喝了。 The iced water I bought has been drunk by them.
3/365	外面结冰了，天气越来越冷了。 It's freezing outside. The weather is getting colder.
4/365	很多中国人夏天的时候不喜欢喝冰水，因为他们觉得热天喝冰冷的水对身体不好。 Many Chinese don't like to drink ice water in the summer because they feel that drinking cold water on a hot day is not good for their health.
5/365	当中国的东北冬天结冰的季节，我们可以在冰河上看到五颜六色 ** 的冰灯。 In northeast China during its freezing winter season, we can watch the multi-coloured ice lanterns on the frozen river.

注释 Note

* 地 dì=earth; land; ground

** 五颜六色 colourful

C 366 才 only/capability/talent/a moment ago/not until/just cái

Chinese	English	Character codes
刚 + 才 = 刚才	just + until = just now; just about	411/366
才来	just come	366/065
天才	genius	128/366
才能	ability; capability; talent	366/088
才气	literary or artistic talent	366/098
真才实学	real ability and knowledge	338/366/534/150

Example Sentences

1/366	你怎么才来？刚才张老师来找你，你去哪儿了？ Why didn't you come until now? Teacher Zhang came looking for you just now. Where have you been?
2/366	她不但很聪明很努力，而且也很有才能。 Not only is she smart and diligent, but also very talented.
3/366	就算是一个天才也需要努力才能有成就。 Even a genius needs to work hard to succeed.
4/366	在学外语方面他很有才气。比方说，他会说法语，也会说日语、西班牙语什么的 *。 He has real talents. He can speak French, as well as other foreign languages, such as Japanese, Spanish and so on ...
5/366	他的小儿子是个音乐天才，才六岁就会写歌了。 His youngest son is a musical prodigy, who is only 6 years old yet, can compose songs.

注释 Note

才, one of its usages is in an assertion or contradiction, emphasizing what comes next; usually with 呢 at the end of the sentence. For example, 这才贵呢！Now this is really expensive! 那本才是我想买的书呢！Now that book is what I wanted to buy!

* 什么的 and so on...(used after a series of items)

参 join/enter/refer/consult/participate cān 367 C

Chinese	English	Character codes
参 + 加 = 参加	participate + add/join = join; participate	367/442
参天	reach high to the sky; of great height; towering	367/128
参见	see; refer	367/054
参考	reference; consult	367/241
参半	half-and-half	367/358
参照	consult and follow	367/607

Example Sentences

1/367	她今天会来参加会议。 She will attend the meeting today.
2/367	在这个特别的公园里有很多参天 * 的大树。 There are many towering trees in this special park.
3/367	如果你想看到更多中文句子，请参见附件。 If you want to read more Chinese sentences please refer to the attached files.
4/367	昨天来参会的人员有一百多人，老师和学生参半。 Over a hundred people joined the meeting yesterday, half were teachers and half were students.
5/367	你放心吧，我下个月一定会参加你们的会议，因为这是我最喜欢的工作。 Don't worry. I will definitely attend your meeting next month, because this is my favourite job.

注释 Note

* 参天 reach to sky

C 368 草 grass/straw/careless/rough cǎo

Chinese	English	Character codes
草 + 地 *= 草地 *	grass + land = lawn; meadow; turf	368/390
种 ** 草	planting grass	611/368
花草	plants and flowers	426/368
绿草	green grass	494/368
草草	carelessly; hastily	368/368
草字头	grass radical (in Chinese character)	368/173/554
草房	thatched cottage	368/213
草书	(Chinese calligraphy) cursive script	368/119
草草了事	get the work done carelessly; rush through the work	368/368/067/281
中草药	Chinese herbal medicine	168/368/318

Example Sentences

1/368	我家门前有一大片草地 *。 There is a large lawn in front of my house
2/368	她草草地 *** 吃完饭就出去了。 She ate her meal hastily and went out.
3/368	“茶”和“花”两个汉字都有草字头。 The Chinese characters for “tea” and “flower” both have the grass radical.
4/368	这个开了几家法国饭馆的老板非常喜欢种 ** 花草，她家的花五颜六色，草地 * 也大得望不到边。 The owner of several French restaurants really likes gardening. The flowers at her house are very colourful and the lawn stretches as far as the eye can see.
5/368	中国的中草药有千百种，北方和南方的草药也很不一样，而且每一种都有自己特别的、有意思的名字。 There are thousands of Chinese herbal medicines in China. The herbs in north and south China are also very different, and each of them has its own special and interesting name.

Note

* 地 dì=earth; land; ground

** 种 zhòng=plant; farm

*** 地 de=grammatical code

层 storey/floor/layer/level/one on top of another/MW céng 369 C

Chinese	English	Character codes
上 + 层 = 上层	above + floor = upper class	108/369
一层	one layer; the ground floor	152/369
层层	one on top of another	369/369
几层	several floors	052/369
楼层	floor; storey	493/369
层次	level	369/200
层次分明	well structured	369/200/028/082
下层	lower class	139/369

Example Sentences

1/369	他家的楼层比我家的楼层高。 His home is on a higher floor than mine.
2/369	我家住五层，他家住二层。 My family lives on the fifth floor, his on the second floor.
3/369	他的作文层次分明，水平很高。 His compositions are well structured and of high standard.
4/369	A: 图书馆在哪儿？教室呢？ B: 图书馆在五层，教室在一层。 A: Where is the library? And what about the classroom? B: The library is on the fifth floor and the classroom is on the first floor.
5/369	我家住在七楼，我的男朋友住在二楼。每次我们见面时，他都需要爬五层楼，因为我们的大楼没有电梯。 My family lives on the seventh floor and my boyfriend lives on the second floor. Each time we meet, he needs to climb five floors as our building has no lift.

C | 370 查 check/examine/look into/look up/consult chá

Chinese	English	Character codes
检 + 查 = 检查	check + investigation = examine; inspect	444/370
检查身体	body check; check-up	444/370/279/294
调 * 查	investigate; investigation	552/370
查对	check up	370/022
查找	to search for; to look up	370/336

Example Sentences

1/370	你把作业再检查一下，别又错了。 Check the homework one more time. Don't get it wrong again.
2/370	你可以在成语字典上查找这个成语。 You can look up this idiom in the Idioms Dictionary.
3/370	我听说经理让他去调 * 查这件事。 I heard that our manager asked him to investigate into this matter.
4/370	我最近老是觉得很累，我想去医院检查一下身体，看看是怎么回事。希望不是什么大问题。 I have always felt very tired of late. I want to go to the hospital for a check-up and see what is going on. I hope it's nothing serious.
5/370	这几个星期，我们总公司的经理正在调 * 查在公司里是不是有人做了些有害于公司运作的事情。 In the past few weeks, our head office manager has been investigating whether someone in the company has done something harmful to the company's operations.

注释 Note

* 调 (diào) 查 =investigate

差 difference chā; fall short of/be less than/poor/not up to standard chà 371 C

Chinese	English	Character codes
很 + 差 = 很差	very + no good = very poor	043/371
不差	not bad; quite good	007/371
差点儿	not good enough; not quite up to the mark	371/016/024
差不多	about the same	371/007/023
走差了	walk in a wrong direction	345/371/067
差（chā）别	difference	371/190

Example Sentences

1/371	他好久没有上中文课了，所以他的中文越来越差。 He hasn't attended Chinese class for a while, so his Chinese is getting worse.
2/371	我们班虽然有四十个学生，但是大家的水平都差不多，没什么差（chā）别。 Although there are 40 students in our class, everyone's level is similar, and there is little difference.
3/371	他问的那个问题太难了，我差点儿没 * 回答上来。 The question he asked was so difficult I almost failed to answer it.
4/371	我爸爸过去是大学的老师，他六十岁离了休。从我爸爸离休到现在差不多有十五年了。 My father used to be a teacher at a university, but he retired at 60. It has been almost 15 years since his retirement.
5/371	我总是听别人介绍说这家饭馆的菜不但好吃，而且便宜。可是今天一尝，比他们说的差多了。下次我再也不去了。 I always hear other people saying that this restaurant is not only good but also cheap. But today I tried it and it's a lot worse than they said. I won't go again.

注释 Note

* 差点儿没，almost miss; just get it. For example: 上课我差点儿没迟到：I almost missed the class.

C | 372 尝 taste/try the flavour/be aware of/experience chǎng

Chinese	English	Character codes
尝 + 尝 = 尝尝	try + try = try the flavour	372/372
尝鲜	have a taste of a delicacy	372/568
尝试	try; attempt	372/282
尝新	have a taste of what is just in season	372/311
尝到甜头	come to know the good of...	372/205/551/554

Example Sentences

1/372	你们是第一次来中国吧？来，请坐，请尝尝我们的北京菜。 Is this your first time in China? Come, please sit down and try our Beijing dishes.
2/372	我学中文快半年了，今天是我第一次尝试用中文介绍自己。 I have been learning Chinese for almost half a year. Today is the first time I have tried to introduce myself in Chinese.
3/372	我哥哥是一个小发明家，他总是和别人想法不一样，而且总是喜欢尝试新的东西。 My brother is a young inventor. He always thinks differently from others, and always likes to try new things.
4/372	很多中国人都知道什么季节应该吃什么菜，这个想法在中文里叫作“尝鲜”，意思是要吃最新鲜的菜。 Many Chinese people know what foods should be eaten in each season. This idea is called “early taste” in Chinese, which means eating the freshest foods.
5/372	如果一个人总是怕事，那么结果就是他什么事也做不成；所以应该先去尝试一下，然后再决定是不是做下去。 If a person is always afraid of things, the result is that he can’t do anything; so you should try things first, then decide if you want to do them or not.

超 exceed/overtake/surpass/transcend/pass chāo 373 C

Chinese	English	Character codes
超 + 市 = 超市	super +market = supermarket	373/537
高超	excellent; superb; superlative	030/373
超车	overtake (a vehicle)	373/010
超过	overtake; exceed; surpass	373/225
超人	superhuman	373/104
超前	take the lead; advanced; be ahead of one's time	373/099
超然	aloof; detached	373/273

Example Sentences

1/373	我很喜欢在超市买东西。 I really like to buy things in the supermarket.
2/373	他非常有本事，我们都觉得他像是一个超人。 He has exceptional talent. We all think he is like a superman.
3/373	我们数学老师不但很聪明，而且他的思路很超前，所以大家都很爱上他的课。 Our maths teacher is not only very smart, but also ahead of his time, so everyone really loves his class.
4/373	在公共道路上开车一定不能像赛车一样，因为超车不是好玩儿的，出一点点错都可能会带来事故。 Driving on public roads must not be like racing a car, because overtaking other cars is not a game, and a tiny mistake may cause an accident.
5/373	习阿姨是那种经常把病人视为自己家人的医生，加上她能力高超，难怪大家都说她是这家医院里数一数二*的好人、好大夫。 Aunty Xi is the kind of doctor who often regards patients as her own family, plus her ability is superb. No wonder everyone says she is one of the very best people in this hospital and a great doctor.

注释 Note

* 数一数二 shǔyī-shǔ'èr=one of the best; the number one or two

C 374 衬 inner lining/liner/set off/underneath chèn

Chinese	English	Character codes
衬 + 衫 = 衬衫	lining + shirt = shirt	374/531
衬衣	underclothes; shirt	374/153
衬着	provide a background for	374/337
帮衬	help; support	183/374
衬里	lining	374/070
相衬	to go well with	569/374

Example Sentences

1/374	我一会儿去超市买一两件衬衫。 I will go to the supermarket to buy one or two shirts later.
2/374	这件红色的和那件黄的衬衫，我认为红的更漂亮些，你的感觉呢？ Look at this red shirt and that yellow one. I think the red one is nicer. How do you feel about it?
3/374	我的爸爸妈妈很喜欢我的女朋友，认为我们两个都可以帮衬对方。 My mum and dad really like my girlfriend and they think the two of us can help each other.
4/374	看，河边的红花有白雪衬着，就像一张画儿一样，好漂亮啊！ Look, the red flowers by the river are contrasted by the white snow, it's just like a painting, really beautiful!
5/374	这件衬衫便宜是便宜，但是颜色不理想；不过，我觉得理想的那一件又太贵了，我买不起。 Sure, this shirt is cheap, but the colour is unsatisfactory; however, I think the ideal one is too expensive. I can't afford it.

成 accomplish/succeed/become/turn into/achievement/fully grown/ready-made/able chéng 375 | C

Chinese	English	Character codes
成 + 绩 = 成绩	achieve + record = achievement; grades	375/441
成人	adult	375/104
成名	become famous	375/083
成为 (wéi)	become (as)	375/303
成语	idiom, proverb	375/159
成长 (zhǎng)	to grow; growth	375/194

Example Sentences

1/375	一般来说，学习的成绩和努力的多少成正比。 In general, the grades achieved in people's studies are directly proportional to the amount of effort they put in.
2/375	现在很多孩子在电脑上玩儿成人的游戏，这是很不应该的。 Nowadays, many children play adult games on their computers, which is not a good thing.
3/375	他说话的时候喜欢用成语。 He likes to use idioms when he speaks
4/375	他是我们大学最年轻的讲师，从助教成为讲师才用了两年。 He was the youngest lecturer at our university. It only took him two years to progress from teaching assistant to a lecturer.
5/375	我在电视上看到一些国家的孩子没有上学的机会，这让我非常难过 *。我真的希望有一天，世界上所有的孩子都上大学，都能健康地成长。 I saw on TV that in some countries children don't have opportunities to go to school. This made me very sad. I really hope that one day all the children in the world will be able to go to college and grow up healthily.

注释 Note

* 难过 nánguò=feel bad; feel sorry; be sad

C | 376 城 town/city/city wall chéng

Chinese	English	Character codes
城 + 市 = 城市	city wall + market = city	376/537
城里	inside the city; downtown	376/070
城外	outside the city	376/297
城门	city gate	376/257
城楼	a tower over the city gate	376/493
城里人	townspeople	376/070/104
大城市	big city	014/376/537
小城市	small city	143/376/537
城市化	urbanisation	376/537/427

Example Sentences

1/376	年轻人大多喜欢住在城市里。 Most young people like to live in the city.
2/376	你喜欢住在城里还是住在城外? Do you like to live in the city or outside of it?
3/376	中国城市化的步子很快。 China's pace of urbanisation is very fast.
4/376	如果房子在城里都很便宜，那么城外就会更便宜一些了。 If houses are cheap in the city, they will be a bit cheaper outside.
5/376	现在很多西方国家的城里人都愿意搬到城外住，一来是空气新鲜，二来是现在有了电脑，可以在家里上班。 Nowadays many people in Western countries are willing to move out of the city. Firstly, the air is fresh, and secondly computers allow them to work from home.

迟 slow/tardy/late chí 377 C

Chinese	English	Character codes
迟 + 到 = 迟到	late + arrival = be late	377/205
迟迟	slow; tardy	377/377
迟早	sooner or later	377/334
迟于	later than	377/597
说时迟那时快	in an instant	122/116/377/084/116/244

Example Sentences

1/377	在我看来 *，经常迟到的学生一定不是好学生。 In my opinion, students who are often late are definitely not good students.
2/377	没有人喜欢经常迟到的人。 No one likes people who are often late.
3/377	火车平常都很准时，今天不知道怎么回事，一直迟迟不来。 The trains are usually very punctual, so I don't know what happened today and why it is not coming.
4/377	汉语在世界上越来越重要，只要想学习，什么时候都不算迟。 The Chinese language is becoming more and more important in the world. As long as you want to learn, it will never be too late.
5/377	看到火车的门马上就要关了，说时迟那时快，他一下子就跳上了车。 When he saw the door of the train is about to shut, he instantly jumped into the carriage.

注释 Note

* 在我看来 , in my opinion, from my point of view... In this phrase, 我 can be replaced by any people. For example, 在我妈妈看来 , from my mum's point of view; 在那些记者看来 , in those journalists' view....

C 378 除 remove/rid of/eliminate/divide/except/besides chú

Chinese	English	Character codes
除 + 了 = 除了	except + suffix =except; besides; apart from; in addition to	378/067
除号	division sign (math.)	378/040
除以	divide by	378/323
除法	division (math.)	378/402
除去	get rid of; eliminate; besides; apart from; except; except for	378/102
除非	only if; only when; ...unless	378/214
除根	dig up the roots; cure once and for all	378/413
除旧更 * 新	replace the old with the new	378/465/415/311

注释 Note

* 更 gēng=change; replace

** 什么都 : whatever; all. The question word 什么 is used to refer to something indefinite.

Example Sentences

1/378	除了咖啡，我什么都 ** 喝。 I drink everything except coffee.
2/378	一千除以十等于一百。 One thousand divided by ten equals one hundred.
3/378	刚刚出生的孩子，一天二十四小时，除了吃就是睡。 Apart from eating, a new-born baby just sleeps all day long.
4/378	他妈妈已经病了很多年了，要想除根，不容易。 His mother has been ill for many years, and it is not easy to find a permanent cure for her disease.
5/378	这星期的天气，除了刮风就是下雨，真的很不舒服！ The weather this week was either windy or rainy — very uncomfortable.

楚 clear/neat/delicate/miserable chǔ 379 C

Chinese	English	Character codes
清 + 楚 = 清楚	clean + clear = clear	520/379
清清楚楚	very clear; distinct	520/520/379/379
不清不楚	not clear and confused	007/520/007/379
一清二楚	crystal clear	152/520/025/379
楚楚动人	delicate and charming	379/379/212/104

Example Sentences

1/379	这个法国人的汉语说得很清楚。 This Frenchman speaks Chinese very clearly.
2/379	她不是很漂亮，但是样子楚楚动人。 She is not that pretty, but her appearance is attractive and delicate.
3/379	请大点儿声，我听不清楚。 Please speak louder, I can't hear you clearly.
4/379	A: 请问，去图书馆怎么走？ B: 你去问问门房，他清楚，我们不清楚。 A: Excuse me, how can I get to the library? B: Go and ask the concierge, he knows, we don't.
5/379	他是一个超好的老师，可以把很难的问题用很短的时间讲得一清二楚。 He is a super good teacher and can make a difficult problem crystal clear in a very short time.

C | 380 船 boat/ship chuán

Chinese	English	Character codes
船 + 员 = 船员	boat + staff = ship's crew	380/331
船位	accommodation on the ship	380/562
坐船	go by boat	177/380
船票	boat ticket	380/265
船期	shipping date	380/096
船运	shipping; transport by ship	380/333
船长 (zhǎng)	captain	380/194
船主	the owner of a ship	380/614

Example Sentences

1/380	这是秋季，船期比夏季要迟三天。 This is autumn, and the sailing time is three days longer than in summer.
2/380	这个船公司的总经理被换了，因为生意越做越差。 The general manager of this shipping company was replaced because business was getting worse.
3/380	我下个月打算跟我女朋友坐船去外国旅游。 I have planned to travel abroad by ship with my girlfriend next month.
4/380	船运在中国有重要的地*位，不过相比起来，中国北方不如南方。北方主要的黄河在有些季节水位不高，所以只能让一些不大的船只运行。 Shipping has an important place in China, but in comparison, north China is not as good as south China. The water level of the Yellow River in north China is not high in some seasons, so it can only be used by some small vessels.
5/380	我们先坐飞机，然后在法国换坐船，最后再坐法国的高铁回国。 We will take the plane first, then switch to the ship in France, and finally take the French high-speed rail to come back to our country.

注释 Note

* 地 dì=position; place

春 spring/joyful/youthful/life/vitality/love chūn 381 C

Chinese	English	Character codes
春 + 天 = 春天	spring + sky = spring; springtime	381/128
春季	spring; spring season	381/440
新春	the beginning of spring	311/381
春节	Chinese New Year	381/454
春色	colour of spring; spring scenery	381/277
春意	springtime in air	381/324
春风得意	flushed with success; proud of one's success; as pleased as punch	381/405/207/324
春夏秋冬	spring, summer, autumn, winter	381/567/521/393

Example Sentences

1/381	中国很多地 * 方，春季往往很短。 In many places of China, spring is usually very short.
2/381	北方不比南方，春天老刮风。 North China, unlike south China, is windy in spring.
3/381	我最不喜欢南方的春季，因为雨水太多！ I enjoy spring in the south the least because there is lots of rain!
4/381	春天来的时候，天气越来越好，花儿也越开越多。 When the spring comes, the weather gradually becomes better, and more flowers are blooming.
5/381	因为季风的影响，这儿四季如春，春夏秋冬一点儿都不分明。 Here it enjoys a mild climate year-round because of the monsoon. The seasons of spring, summer, autumn and winter are not so distinct.

注释 Note

* 地 dì=place; earth; land; ground

C | 382 词 word/term/speech/statement/poetry cí

Chinese	English	Character codes
词 + 典 = 词典	words+ classics books = dictionary	382/391
成语词典	idioms dictionary	375/159/382/391
单词	word	385/382
生词	new words	112/382
词句	sentences; phrases	382/467
歌词	lyrics	219/382
解说词	commentary	456/122/382
用词	wording; diction; usage of a term	594/382
词法	morphology	382/402

Example Sentences

1/382	老师要求所有学习中文的学生，一定要买一本好的汉语词典。 The teacher asks that all students studying Chinese must buy a good Chinese dictionary.
2/382	我很喜欢西班牙的歌，那些歌词往往很动听。 I really like Spanish songs. Their lyrics are often very pleasant.
3/382	这个教学片的解说词非常好，你要认真看！ The commentary of this teaching video is really good, and you should watch it carefully.
4/382	汉字已有几千年的历史，所以在汉语词典里有很多有意思的词语。 The Chinese character has thousands of years of history, so there are many interesting words in Chinese dictionaries.
5/382	中国词典里的成语有成百上千个，其中，有很多成语都来自于典故。 There are hundreds upon hundreds of idioms in Chinese dictionaries, many of which come from classical allusions.

聪 faculty of hearing/quick at hearing/wise/clever cōng 383 C

Chinese	English	Character codes
聪 + 明 = 聪明	accurate hearing + bright = intelligent; clever	383/082
小聪明	cleverness in trivial matters; petty trick; sly; sharp but petty-minded; too clever by half	143/383/082
聪明能干 *	clever and able	383/082/088/409
聪明过人	cleverer than the average	383/082/225/104
冰雪聪明	exceptionally intelligent	365/314/383/082
自作聪明	to think oneself clever	616/176/383/082

注释 Note

* 干 gàn=do; strike; main part

** 同行 tóngháng=people of the same trade, profession or occupation

Example Sentences

1/383	大家都知道，很多事情坏在小聪明上。 Everyone knows that a lot of things are ruined by petty cleverness.
2/383	聪明过人的学生常常不努力。 Smart students often don't work hard.
3/383	中国人认为，一个人聪明是好事，可是过于聪明就是小聪明了。 The Chinese believe that being smart is a good thing, but being too smart can turn into being too clever by half and petty.
4/383	人人都觉得她冰雪聪明，只是她自已不那么觉得，反而她工作很努力，所以她的成绩远远超过她的同行 **。 Everyone thinks she is very smart, but she doesn't think so. Instead she works hard, so her performance can far exceed her peers.
5/383	我们不喜欢小聪明，我们喜欢又聪明又正直的人。 We don't like petty cleverness. We like people who are smart and honest.

D 384 答 agree/promise dā; answer/reply/respond/return dá

Chinese	English	Character codes
回 + 答 = 回答	return + answer = reply; respond; to answer	048/384
答应 *	promise; agree	384/592
答题	answer the questions (on a test paper); questions on exam	384/293
问答	question and answer	304/384
一问一答	one asking and the other answering; questions and answers	152/304/152/384
答复	answer; respond; reply	176/384
所答非所问	to answer beside the point; give an irrelevant answer; sidestep a question	290/384/214/290/304

注释 Note

* 答应 dāying=agree; promise

Example Sentences

1/384	请回答我的问题。 Please answer my questions.
2/384	太好了，他答应 * 我去中国了！ He has promised me he will go to China, that's great!
3/384	请别现在打我的手机，我在考试，在答题呢。 Please don't call my mobile phone now. I am in an exam, answering questions.
4/384	在新闻节目里，我最喜欢看的是那些名人和记者的一问一答，因为那些人常常所答非所问，很可笑。 In the news programmes, my favourite thing is to watch questions and answers featuring celebrities and journalists, because those people often answer beside the point and are ridiculous.
5/384	今年的期中考试真难，有一道数学题，我差不多思考了二十分钟，最后总算回答出来了。 This year's midterm exam was really difficult. There was a maths question which I thought about for almost twenty minutes before I finally worked out the answer.

带 bring/take with/carry/lead/head/look after/attached/belt/tape/ribbon/band dài 385 D

Chinese	English	Character codes
带 + 路 = 带路	bring + road = lead the way; to show the way	385/250
带头	take the lead; be the first	385/554
带来	bring in	385/065
带上	to take along with	385/108
一带	area; region; district	152/385
一带一路	Belt and Road Initiative	152/385/152/250

Example Sentences

1/385	天这么黑，路灯又坏了，没有人带路，我们找不到那个门啊！ It is so dark. The street lights are broken. There is no one to lead the way. We can't find the door!
2/385	我听一个朋友说，这一带要变成商业街了，所以现在所有的住家都必须搬走，是吗？ I heard a friend say that this area will become commercial streets, so all the current residents must move out. Is that true?
3/385	今天是你三十岁的生日，我带来的礼物是一瓶也已经三十年的法国红酒。 Today is your 30th birthday. The gift I brought is a bottle of French red wine which is also already 30 years old.
4/385	我去中国旅游不懂中文没有关系，我女儿懂，也会说，我们带她一起去就没有问题了。 It doesn't matter if I travel to China and don't understand Chinese. My daughter understands it and can also speak it, so if we bring her with us, there won't be any problems.
5/385	我们的中文课本一红一黑两大本，太重了，每次上课带来带去很不方便，所以我的解决办法是用手机上的照相 * 机把要学的课文照下来。 Our Chinese textbooks, one red and one black, are too big and heavy, so it is very inconvenient to bring them to class each time. My solution is to use the mobile phone camera to photograph the text needed for the lesson.

注释 Note

* 相 xiàng=appearance of a person or object; looks; posture

D | 386 单 list/single/odd/only/unlined dān

Chinese	English	Character codes
菜 + 单 = 菜单	dish + list = menu	008/386
简单	simple; not complicated	445/386
名单	list (of names)	083/386
单一	single; only; sole	386/152
单个	single; alone; individually; an odd one	386/031
单调 (diào)	dull; drab; monotonous	386/552
不单	not the only; not simply; not merely	007/386
单方	unilateral; one-sided	386/403
单身	unmarried; single	386/279
清单	list of items	520/386
床单	bed sheet	199/386
买单	to pay the restaurant bill	075/386
单位	unit (group of people as a whole); work unit (place of employment)	386/562

Example Sentences

1/386	让我们来看看今天的菜单上都有些什么菜。 Let's see what's on the menu today.
2/386	这个颜色的单人床单已经卖完了。 Single bedsheets in this colour are sold out.
3/386	图书馆所有新书的清单都可以在网上查到。 The library's list of new books can be found online.
4/386	自从他妻子去世后，他一个人已经单身好几年了。 He has been single since his wife passed away.
5/386	请你把参加者的名单发到我的邮箱里。 Please email me the list of participants.

担 to undertake/carry on a shoulder dān; burden dàn 387 D

Chinese	English	Character codes
担 + 心 = 担心	to undertake + heart = anxious; worried; uneasy; to worry	387/576
担当	take upon oneself; to assume; take on	387/388
分担	to share (a burden, a cost, a responsibility)	028/387
重担 *	heavy burden; difficult task; great responsibility	612/387
担 * 子	carrying pole and the loads on it; burden; task; responsibility	387/172

注释 Note

* 担 dàn=burden; load (All other examples are pronounced as dān.)

Example Sentences

1/387	奶奶身体不好，让我们十分担心。 We are worried about Grandma's poor health.
2/387	别为我担心，我很好。 Don't worry about me. I'm very well.
3/387	他决定担起照顾弟弟妹妹的重担 *。 He decided to take on the heavy burden of looking after his younger siblings.
4/387	别担心，我会跟你一起分担租车的钱。 Don't worry. I'll share the cost of the car hire with you.
5/387	如果出了事，我怎么担当得起呢？ How could I bear for anything to happen?

D 388 当 be/when/act as/during/just at/deserve/ought to/clang dāng; proper/appropriate/right/be equal to/pawn dàng

Chinese	English	Character codes
当 + 然 = 当然	to be + so = only natural; as it should be; certainly; of course; without doubt	388/273
相当	equivalent to; appropriate; considerably; to a certain extent; fairly; quite	569/388
当时	then; at that time; while	388/116
当心	to take care; to look out	388/576
得 (dé) 当 (dàng)	appropriate; suitable	207/388
正当	timely; just (when needed); just the time for; just as	339/388
正当 (dàng)	legitimate; proper; correct	339/388
响当当	resounding; loud; well known; famous	572/387/388
家当 (dàng)	familial property; belongings; possessions	053/388
当家	in charge of family	388/053
上当 (dàng)	taken in (by sb's deceit); to be fooled; to be duped	108/388
当面	to sb's face; in sb's presence	388/081
当前	current; today's; modern; present	388/099
理所当然	as it should be by right (idiom); proper and to be expected as a matter of course; inevitable and right	482/290/388/273

Example Sentences

1/388	好吧，只要你喜欢，你当然可以去。 Well, if you'd like to go, of course you can go.
2/388	帮助自己的朋友对她来说是理所当然的。 Helping her friends comes naturally to her.
3/388	你得（dé）了这个病，得（děi）护理得当（dédàng）才行（xíng）。 He has such a disease and needs proper nursing.
4/388	那辆汽车虽然很旧了，可还能开得相当的快。 Even though that car is very old, it can still travel quite fast.
5/388	当时这本书是我当面给他的，他怎么可能说他没有呢？ At that time, I gave this book to him personally. How come he doesn't have it?

灯 light/lamp/lantern dēng 389 D

Chinese	English	Character codes
电 + 灯 = 电灯	electric + light = electric light	017/389
街灯	streetlight	453/389
花灯	coloured lantern (used at Lantern Festival)	426/389
灯火	lights	389/050
开灯	to turn on the light	061/389
灯红酒绿	feasting and pleasure-seeking; debauched and corrupt environment	389/229/464/494

Example Sentences

1/389	你知道谁是电灯的发明者吗？ Do you know who the inventor of the electric bulb is?
2/389	我们从飞机上的窗口可以看到下面城市的万家灯火。 We can see the city lights from the airplane's window.
3/389	因为场地 * 上没有电灯，所以那场比赛会在白天进行。 Since there are no lights on the pitch, the game will be played during daylight.
4/389	我被那个坏了的电灯开关电了一下。 I got an electric shock from that faulty light switch.
5/389	大家离开房间的时候，请把灯关上。 Everyone, please remember to turn off the light when you leave the room.

注释 Note

* 地 dì=earth; land; ground

D 390 地 earth/land/soil/ground de; grammatical code dì

Chinese	English	Character codes
……地 *	grammatical code	390
地 + 图 = 地图	earth + map = map	390/616
地方	area; place; space; room; territory; region; local	390/402
地球	the earth	390/272
地位	position; status; place	390/618
地点	place; site; venue	390/016
本地	local; this locality	006/390
所在地	location; site	290/163/390
心地	character; moral nature	576/390
地面	floor; ground; surface	390/081
地铁	underground train; metro; underground	390/553
天长地久；地久天长	enduring while the world lasts (idiom); eternal	128/194/390/463；390/463/128/194

注释 Note

* 地 de=grammatical code (All other examples are pronounced as dì.)

Example Sentences

1/390	你是什么地方人？ Where are you from?
2/390	我不知道钱都花到什么地方去了。 I don't know where my money goes!
3/390	我家离地铁站很近。 My house is close to the underground station.
4/390	每到一个新的城市，我爸爸都会很快地 * 买一张当地的地图。 Dad buys a local map right away every time he is in a new city.
5/390	请问，能把你的地图借给我看看吗？ Excuse me, can you lend your map to me so that I can have a look?

典 standard/canon/allusion/literary quotation/classic/pawn diǎn 391 D

Chinese	English	Character codes
字 + 典 = 字典	character + standard = dictionary; character dictionary	173/391
词典	dictionary (of Chinese compound words)	382/391
成语词典	idioms dictionary	375/159/173/391
法汉词典	French-Chinese dictionary	402/038/173/391
经典	the classics; scriptures; classical	237/391
典故	allusion (to classic story or saying); classical quotation; parable	391/416
典礼	celebration; ceremony	391/480
典当 (dàng)	to pawn; pawnshop	391/388

Example Sentences

1/391	她买了一本新词典。 She bought a new dictionary.
2/391	你用哪一本字典查汉字? Which dictionary do you use for checking Chinese characters?
3/391	明天是开学典礼，所有学生都要参加。 Tomorrow is the opening ceremony, which all students have to attend.
4/391	这本字典对我来说再好不过了。 For me there is no dictionary better than this one.
5/391	你可以从学校的图书馆借到这本词典。 You can borrow this dictionary from the school’s library.

D | 392 定 to set/to fix/calm/stable/to book/surely dìng

Chinese	English	Character codes
决 + 定 = 决定	decide + to set = to decide; to do something; to resolve; decision	469/392
一定	surely; certainly; necessarily; given; a certain (extent etc) particular; must	152/392
特定	special; specific; designated	547/392
一定要	must	152/392/319
不一定	not necessarily; maybe; not sure	007/152/392
定期	at set dates; at regular intervals; periodic; fixed term	392/096
安定	stable; quiet; settled; maintained	352/392
定居	to settle; to take up residence (in some city, country etc)	392/466
商定	to agree; to decide after consultation; to come to a compromise	107/392
定位	to orientate; to position; to categorise (as)	392/562

Example Sentences

1/392	让我想想再决定吧。 Let me think it over before making the decision.
2/392	别担心，六点以前，我一定会到家。 Don’t worry! I shall definitely be home before six o’clock.
3/392	他要不定期地在这里住下去。 He will stay here on an irregular basis.
4/392	你最好别把我算进去，我去不去还不一定呢。 You’d better reckon without me, as I am not sure if I will go or not.
5/392	因为工钱给得不公平，员工们对公司不加钱的决定很不满意。 Because the salaries given were not fair, the employees were not happy with the company’s decision not to increase pay.

冬 WINTER dōng 393 D

Chinese	English	Character codes
冬 + 季 = 冬季	winter + season = winter	393/440
冬天	winter (time)	393/128
过冬	to get through the winter	225/393
越冬	to pass the winter	603/393
冬泳	winter swimming	393/327

Example Sentences

1/393	今年冬天来得比以往都早。 Winter has come earlier than in the past this year.
2/393	每到冬季他就会参加冬泳。 He does winter swimming every winter.
3/393	因为怕冷所以她不喜欢冬天。 She doesn't like winter because of the cold.
4/393	在中国最北的地 * 方，冬天的时候，下午四点，天就会黑下来。 During the winter in northern most China, the sky is dark by four o'clock.
5/393	哪怕就是在最冷的冬季，孩子们在冰天雪地 * 里一样可以得到很大的乐趣。 Even during the coldest days of winter, children can find great joy in the ice and snow.

注释 Note

* 地 dì=earth; land; ground

D 394 短 short (for length)/brief/lack/weak point duǎn

Chinese	English	Character codes
短 + 信 = 短信	brief + letter = text message; SMS	394/577
短片 *	short film; video clip	394/512
发 ** 短信	to text; to send SMS message	401/394/512
短期	short term; short-term	394/096
简短	brief; short-duration	445/394
短发 ***	short hair	394/401
长短	length; duration; accident; right or wrong; good and bad; long or short	194/394
短路	short circuit	394/250
短语	phrase; clause (grammar)	394/159
短裤	shorts; short trousers	394/477
短跑	sprint (race)	394/263
护短	to shield (one's shortcoming); to cover up (errors)	425/394

注释 Note

* 片 piān=film; video

** 发 fā=distribute; to send out; rise

*** 发 fà=hair

Example Sentences

1/394	开车的时候不能用手机发短信，因为可能会出事。 You can't use your mobile phone to send messages while driving, because it's dangerous.
2/394	他的讲话虽然简短，可是非常有意思。 His speech was brief but quite interesting.
3/394	万一他有个（三）长（两）短，怎么办? What if anything should happen to him?
4/394	自从学会了怎么用手机发 ** 短信，妈妈每天都给我发 ** 一条短信。 Mum has sent me a text every day since she learnt how to send text messages on mobile phone.
5/394	那位平时很喜欢穿短裙的法语老师让同学们每节课都听写五句短句。 The French teacher who usually likes to wear short skirts dictated five phrases to the class during every lesson.

段 section/part/period/a length/paragraph duàn 395 D

Chinese	English	Character codes
片 + 段 = 片段	piece + section = fragment (of speech etc); extract (from book etc); episode (of story etc)	512/395
手段	method; means (of doing sth); strategy; trick	284/395
前段	first part; front end; forepart; the preceding section	099/395
中段	middle section; middle period; mid-	168/395
末段	final segment; last stage	499/395
身段	a woman's physique; figure; posture of stage	279/395
地 * 段	section of a town; district; area	390/395
时段	time interval; work shift; time slot	116/395
非常手段	an emergency measure	214/195/284/395

Example Sentences

1/395	哥哥租的房子是在城市的中心地 * 段。 The flat my brother rents is in the downtown part of the city.
2/395	你的这所房子真好，地 * 段也不错。 What a fine house you have! It is a great location as well.
3/395	我很不喜欢那句“非常时刻需要非常手段”的话！ I really don't like the expression “Desperate times call for desperate measures”!
4/395	这家酒吧的“快乐时段”是每天下午三点到五点。 In this pub Happy Hour is from three to five in the afternoon every day.
5/395	我当然记得，前一段时间你和你的妻子一起来过我们的饭店吃饭。 Of course I remember, you and your wife have been to our restaurant for dinner on previous occasions.

注释 Note

* 地 dì=earth; land; ground

D 396 锻 forge/to discipline duàn

Chinese	English	Character codes
锻 + 炼 = 锻炼	to discipline + to refine = to engage in physical exercise; to work out	396/487
体育锻炼	physical exercise	294/598/396/487
锻炼身体	take exercise; to work out	396/487/279/294
经常锻炼	often exercise	237/195/396/487
不锻炼	not to do exercise	007/396/487

Example Sentences

1/396	每天早上姐姐都去公园跑步，锻炼身体。 Every morning my sister runs in the park to keep fit.
2/396	李叔叔多年来一直在锻炼身体。 Uncle Li has kept up exercising all these years.
3/396	有时候很难找到时间去锻炼身体。 Sometimes it can be difficult to find time to exercise.
4/396	因为他把锻炼身体当一回事 *，所以他每天都锻炼，结果是他看上去很年轻。 Because he treats physical exercise as a serious matter, he does it every day, and as a result it makes him look younger.
5/396	你锻炼身体吗？多长时间锻炼一次？ Do you work out? How often do you exercise?

注释 Note

* 当一回事，taken something as a serious matter

朵 MW for flower or cloud/a suffix of ear or flower duǒ 397 D

Chinese	English	Character codes
耳 + 朵 = 耳朵 (duo)	ear + earlobe = ear	400/397
花朵	flower	426/397
一朵朵	flower by flower	152/397/397
鲜花朵朵开	in full blossoms	568/426/397/397/061
左耳朵进右耳朵出	go in one ear and out the other	348/400/397/235/329/400/397/012

Example Sentences

1/397	这句话在他的耳朵里回响了很久。 The words echoed in his ears for long time.
2/397	爷爷老了，耳朵也听不清楚了。 Granddad is getting old and his hearing is not good.
3/397	奶奶的耳朵不太好，所以她说话的声音常常很大。 Grandma's hearing is bad, so she often speaks very loudly.
4/397	街道两旁开满了五颜六色的花朵，空气中都是花香。 The streets were strewn with flowers of all different colours, and the air was full of their fragrance.
5/397	妈妈生日时，妹妹做了一朵大红花送给她做生日礼物。 My sister made a big red (paper) flower for mum's birthday gift.

E | 398 饿 hungry è

Chinese	English	Character codes
饿 + 坏了 = 饿坏了	hungry + bad = terribly hungry	398/429/067
饿极了	starving	398/436/067
饿得不行	extremely hungry	398/207/007/422
好饿	famished	039/398
解饿	to relieve hunger	456/398

Example Sentences

1/398	晚饭吃什么？我饿极了！ What's for dinner? I'm starving!
2/398	我不太饿，来点儿小吃就行了。 I'm not very hungry, a small snack is fine for me.
3/398	你走了那么长的路，一定饿了吧。 You must be hungry after such a long walk.
4/398	我在床上一个多小时了，又累又饿，怎么也睡不着。 I have been in bed over an hour, tired, hungry, and unable to sleep.
5/398	我又冷又饿，只想快快回到家，吃上一碗妈妈做的热面。 I'm cold and hungry. I just want to get home quickly and eat one bowl of hot noodles mum cooks.

而 and/as well as/but/and yet/and also/but also/to ér 399 E

Chinese	English	Character codes
而 + 且 = 而且	as well as + and = (not only...) but also; moreover; in addition; furthermore	399/518
而是	rather	399/117
从而	thus; thereby	201/399
然而	however; yet; but	273/399
而已	that's all; nothing more	399/322
因而	therefore; as a result; thus; and as a result	325/399
故而	therefore	416/399
而今	now; at the present (time)	399/058
而后	after that; then	399/044
自然而然	involuntary; automatically	616/273/399/273
视而不见	to turn a blind eye to; to ignore	282/399/007/054

Example Sentences

1/399	小奇会说法语，而且说得很好。 Xiaoqi can speak French and she speaks very well.
2/399	爸爸烧的菜不但好看而且非常好吃。 The dishes my dad cooked look good, and they are also very tasty.
3/399	我弟弟跑得快，因而早到了五分钟。 My brother ran fast, that's why he got there five minutes early.
4/399	她每天来咖啡店不是为了喝咖啡而是为了找人聊天。 She came to the coffee shop every day, not to drink coffee but to find someone to chat with.
5/399	秋季不冷不热，自然而然地成为一年中最好的旅游时段，也是我最喜爱的季节。 It's not hot or cold in the fall, it is naturally the best time of the year to travel, and it's also my favourite season.

E 400 耳 ear/ear like ěr

Chinese	English	Character codes
耳 + 朵 = 耳朵	ear + earlobe = ear	400/397
耳目	eyes and ears	400/500
耳环	earring	400/430
耳闻	to hear of; to hear about	400/564
耳语	to whisper in sb's ear; a whisper	400/159
耳机	headphones; earphones; telephone receiver	400/051
耳聪目明	sharp ears and keen eyes; keen and alert	400/382/496/082

Example Sentences

1/400	天真冷，冷得我耳朵发 * 疼。 It's so cold that my ears hurt.
2/400	这件事我早有耳闻，就是不知道是不是真的。 I have heard about this matter, but I don't know if it is true or not.
3/400	姐姐说话的声音越来越轻，最后成了耳语。 My sister's voice became softer and softer until it trailed off to a whisper.
4/400	因为小时候的一场大病，她的一只耳朵几乎听不见了。 The hearing in one of her ears is almost gone because of a serious illness she had when she was little.
5/400	她把所有的耳环都放在一个小包里了，然后就给忘了，直到昨天才突然想起来。 She had put all her earrings in a small bag and forgotten about them until yesterday when she suddenly remembered about them.

注释 Note

* 发 fā=feel; distribute; to send out; rise

发 launch/distribute/to send out/rise fā; hair fà 401 F

Chinese	English	Character codes
发 + 生 = 发生	to develop + produce = to happen; to occur; to take place; to break out	401/112
发现	to find; to discover	401/141
发表	to issue; to publish	401/189
开发	to exploit (a resource); to open up (for development); to develop	061/401
发送	to transmit; to dispatch; to issue (an official document or credential)	401/287
发给	to issue; to grant; to distribute	401/220
出发	to set off; to start (on a journey)	012/401
出发点	starting point; (fig) basis; motive	012/401/016
发出	to issue (an order, decree etc)	401/012
发行 *	to publish; to issue (stocks, currency etc); to release; to distribute (a film)	401/422
发病	onset; outbreak (of a disease)	401/192
头发 **	hair	554/401
结发 ** 夫妻	husband and wife by the first marriage	455/401/216/266
白发 **	white hair; hoary	180/401
理发 ** 店	the hairdresser's	482/401/018

Example Sentences

1/401	这位作家说，这个故事发生在 1971 年的夏天。 This writer said this story was set in the summer of 1971.
2/401	这条十字路口经常有事故发生。 Accidents often happen at this intersection.
3/401	我发现这段历史很有意思，请接着讲下去。 I found this section of history you talked about was very interesting, please carry on.
4/401	当他往下一坐，椅子就发出了响声，说明这把椅子该换新的了。 The chair gave a groan as he sat down, indicating the chair should be replaced with a new one.
5/401	当我们出发时，天已经黑了，还下着小雨，道路很难行 * 走。 It was already dark and drizzling when we set out, and the road was very difficult to walk on.

注释 Note

* 行 xíng

** 发 fà, all other examples are pronounced as fā.

F 402 法 law/method fǎ; method fá

Chinese	English	Character codes
方 + 法 = 方法	square + method = method; way; means	403/402
办法	means; methods; way (of doing sth)	357/402
没办法	there is nothing to be done; one can't do anything about it	078/357/402
法 * 子	way; method	402/172
没法 * 子	at a loss; unable to do anything about it; to have no choice	078/402
想法	way of thinking; opinion; notion; to think of a way (to do sth)	142/402
说法	way of speaking; wording; formulation; one's version (of events)	122/402
看法	way of looking at a thing; view; opinion	062/402
手法	technique; trick; skill	284/402
不法	lawless; illegal; unlawful	007/402
法国	France	402/036
法文	French language	402/563
法办	punish by law; bring to justice	402/357

Example Sentences

1/402	你的这个方法能行吗？ Will your method work?
2/402	你有解决这个问题的办法吗？ Do you have a way to solve this problem?
3/402	我实在没法 * 子让这些孩子安静下来，请你帮帮我。 I'm at my wits' end to keep these children quiet, please help me.
4/402	康经理让我们每个人都谈谈对这件事的看法。 Manager Kang askes every of us to state the opinion on the issue.
5/402	对上个月发生的那个事件，请大家谈谈个人看法。 Regarding the incident that happened last month, everyone, please talk about your personal opinion.

注释 Note

* 法 fá, 法子 = way, method, (colloquial) (All other examples are pronounced as fǎ.)

方 square/direction/place/side/method/just/still fāng 403 F

Chinese	English	Character codes
地 * + 方 = 地 * 方	earth + square = area; place; space; room; territory	390/403
方面	aspect; side; field; in the area of	403/081
方向	direction; orientation; path to follow	403/573
一方面	on the one hand	152/403/081
一方	a party (in a contract or legal case); one side; area; region	152/403
第三方	third party	210/106/403
双方	bilateral; both side; both parties involved	545/403
下方	underneath; below the underside; world of mortals	139/403
方位	direction; points of compass; bearing; position; azimuth	403/562
对方	counterpart; other person involved; opposite side; other side; receiving party	022/403
方方面面	all sides; all aspects; multi-faceted	403/403/081/081
四面八方	in all directions; all around; far and near	123/081/002/403

注释 Note

* 地 dì=earth; land; ground

Example Sentences

1/403	周老师是北方人。 Teacher Zhou comes from the north.
2/403	我很快就会有机会去南方工作了。 I will very soon have a chance to go to the south to work.
3/403	在这么高的地 * 方，雪终年都不化。 At this high altitude, snow never melts.
4/403	这两辆公共汽车都是开往市中心方向的，但是一个终点站是火车站，一个终点站是市图书馆。 These two buses are all going to the city centre. One bus terminal is the rail station, the other is the city library.
5/403	在画画儿方面，他很有才能，这么年轻就已经是一个知名画家了。 As far as painting is concerned, he is very talented and at such a young age he is already a well-known painter.

F 404 放 to put/release/set free/lay aside/put out fàng

Chinese	English	Character codes
放 + 心 = 放心	to put + heart = to feel relieved; to feel reassured; to be at ease	404/576
开放	to bloom; to open; to be open (to the public); to be open-minded; unrestrained by convention; unconstrained in one's sexuality	061/404
放大	to enlarge; to magnify	404/014
发放	to provide; to give; to grant	401/404
放送	to broadcast; to announce over loudspeakers	404/287
解放	to liberate; to emancipate; liberation	456/404
下放	to delegate; to decentralise	139/404
放下	to put down; to let go; to set aside	404/139
放水	to turn on the water; to let water out; to throw a game (sports)	404/121
放手	to let go one's hold; to give up; to have a free hand	404/284
安放	to lay; to place; to put in a certain place	352/404
放学	classes are over	404/150

Example Sentences

1/404	（你们）放心吧，不会出事的。 Don't worry, nothing will go wrong.
2/404	因为一直出错，老板对他越来越不放心。 The boss doesn't trust him anymore because of all the mistakes he made.
3/404	多好的照片啊！你怎么不把它放大呢？ What a lovely picture! Why don't you have it blown up?
4/404	小李把会议需要的文件又检查了一次，这才放心地离开了会议室。 Young Li checked the documents for the meeting once more, then left the conference room with confidence.
5/404	我家附近那所小学的学生们，常常在放学回家的半路上就玩儿起来了。 After school the children from my neighbouring primary school would stop to play on their way home.

风 wind/news/attitude/style/tendence/bearing fēng 405 F

Chinese	English	Character codes
刮 + 风 = 刮风	to blow + wind = to be windy	418/405
风情	mien; bearing; grace; amorous feelings; flirtation expressions	405/270
学风	style of study; academic atmosphere; school discipline; school traditions	105/405
作风	style; style of work; way	176/405
风气	general mood; atmosphere; common practice	405/098
风趣	humour; wit; charm	405/523
新风	new trend; new custom	311/405
中 * 风	to suffer a paralysing stroke	168/405
风化	decency; public morals; to weather (rocks); wind erosion	405/427

注释 Note

* 中 zhòng=be hit by

Example Sentences

1/405	今天刮风了，出门时你多穿（一）点儿衣服吧。 It's windy today. Wear more clothes when you go out.
2/405	打火机在风中很难打着 (zháo)。 The lighter was hard to get going in the wind.
3/405	顾择秋说起话来聪明又风趣，大家都喜欢他。 Gu Zeqiu is a smart and witty talker. Everyone likes him.
4/405	这几天因为刮风加上下大雪，火车和飞机都不准点了。 In the last few days the trains and planes have all been delayed because of the wind and heavy snow.
5/405	雪花在满天飞舞着，天气虽然冷，但是大雪中的校园别有一种风情。 Snowflakes are dancing in the air. The weather is cold, but the school looks different in the snow.

F | 406 附 to add/be near/attach/get closed to/enclose/affiliate fù

Chinese	English	Character codes
附 + 近 = 附近	to be close to + near (in the) vicinity; nearby; neighbouring; next to	406/236
附件	enclosure; attachment (of email); appendix	406/232
附着 *	adhere to; stick to	406/337
附加	additional; annex	406/442
附和 (hè)	to agree; to go along with; to echo (what sb says)	406/042
附上	attached; included here with	406/108

注释 Note

* 着 zhuó=touch; contact

Example Sentences

1/406	我哥哥买的房子在车站附近。 The house my brother bought is close to the station.
2/406	那家超市现在算是附近最大的了。 That supermarket is now regarded as the biggest in the vicinity.
3/406	他一般都在报告的正文后附上一个或几个附件。 He usually has one or more files attached at the end of the main report.
4/406	我儿子学校的附近有一个很大的飞机场，飞机飞过上空的时候，声音大得不得了。 There is a big airfield near my son's school. Once the airplane flies over, it makes huge noises!
5/406	请再查一下吧，我已经把所有的文件和它们的附件都发到你的邮箱里了。 Please check again, I've already sent all the documents and the attachments to your email box.

复 to repeat/return/recover fù 407 F

Chinese	English	Character codes
重*+复=重*复	repeat + again = to repeat; to duplicate; overlap	612/407
回复	to reply; to recover; to return (to a previous condition)	048/407
复查	rechecking; re-inspection; re-examination	407/370
复习	review; revision	407/136
康复	rehabilitate; recover from illness; to convalesce	471/407
平复	to pacify; to calm down; to be healed	513/407
复出	to come out of retirement; to get involved again after having withdrawn	407/012
报复	to make reprisals; to retaliate; revenge; retaliation	184/407
复发	to recur (of a disease); to reappear; to relapse (into a former bad state)	407/401
周而复始	move in circles	613/399/407/280

注释 Note

* 重 chóng=repeat; again; overlap; layer

Example Sentences

1/407	可能是年岁大了，爷爷近来总是重*复同样的话。 Grandpa recently always repeats the same words, perhaps he is old.
2/407	校长每天都有不少信件要回复。 The headmaster has many letters to reply to every day.
3/407	我哥哥有个很好的学习习惯，每天除了完成老师要求的作业外，他还会把上课的笔记复习一下。 My older brother has very good study habits. Not only does he finish the homework set by the teacher but he also goes over the lesson notes every day.
4/407	我把这个问题重*复了几次，他终于明白了。 I explained the problem to him for several times, and he finally understood.
5/407	我姐姐以前得过这种病，不过已经好了十几年了，可是今年一月又复发了。 This type of illness my elder sister had before was already cured for more than a decade, but it has come back again in January this year.

G 408 该 should/ought to/be sb.'s turn/deserve/owe/the said gāi

Chinese	English	Character codes
应 + 该 = 应该	to respond + should = ought to; should; must	592/408
不该	should not; to owe nothing	007/408
该人	that above-mentioned person	408/104
应该说	it should be mentioned but...	592/408/122

Example Sentences

1/408	一个大学生应该学会思考。 A university student should learn to think.
2/408	你已然不是孩子了，就不该让他影响你。 You are not a teenager anymore. You shouldn't let him affect you.
3/408	我应该怎样理解这句话的意思呢？ How should I understand the meaning of that remark?
4/408	你不该把钱借给那个你刚刚认识两天的人。 You shouldn't lend him any money as you just met him a couple of days ago.
5/408	你认为我该不该去参加前女友的婚礼呢？ Do you think I should attend my ex-girlfriend's wedding?

干 dry/be implicate in/futilely gān; do/strike/main part gàn 409 G

Chinese	English	Character codes
干 + 净 = 干净	dry + clean = clean; neat	409/460
相干	relevant; to have to do with; coherent	569/409
干杯	to drink a toast; cheers; bottoms up; here's to you	409/004
主干 *	trunk; main force; mainstay	614/409
实干 *	to work industriously; to get things done	534/409
才干 *	ability; competence	366/409
能干 *	capable; competence	088/409
干 * 练	capable and experienced	409/486
干 * 事	administrator; executive secretary	409/281
树干 *	tree trunk	542/409
干 * 道	arterial road; main road; main watercourse	409/206

注释 Note

* 干 gàn=do; strike; main part (All other examples are pronounced as gān.)

Example Sentences

1/409	你的手不干净，去洗洗吧。 Your hands are not clean, go and wash them.
2/409	他回家后换了一身干净的衣服以后又出门了。 He went home and changed into some clean clothes, then went out again.
3/409	她不但长得漂亮，而且很有才干 *。 She is not just beautiful, but also very talented.
4/409	周末的时候，姐姐不但帮妈妈把衣服都洗了，而且把房间也都打扫干净了。 Elder sister helped Mum did the laundry and as well cleaned the rooms at the weekend.
5/409	弟弟学会了洗衣服，他把自己的衬衫洗得干干净净。 My brother has learnt to do the laundry and his shirts came out really clean.

G | 410 感 to feel/to sense/emotion/affect/feeling gǎn

Chinese	English	Character codes
感 + 冒 = 感冒	to feel + to emit = to catch cold; (common) cold	410/497
感觉 (jué)	to feel; to become aware of; feeling; sense; perception	410/056
感兴趣	be interested	410/149/523
感谢	(express) thanks; gratitude; grateful; thankful; thanks	410/147
情感	feeling; emotion; to move; emotionally	270/410
感情	feeling; emotion; sensation; likes and dislikes; deep affection for sb or sth; relationship	410/270
感到	to feel; to sense; to have the feeling that; to think	410/205
感想	impressions; reflections; thoughts	410/142
感动	to move (sb); to touch (sb emotionally); moving	410/212
直感	intuition; direct feeling or understanding	609/410
同感	(have the) same feeling; similar impression; common feeling	130/410

Example Sentences

1/410	妹妹对写作很感兴趣，她想当一名作家。 My sister is interested in writing and wants to be a writer.
2/410	我爬山回来后，感到非常的累。 I felt exhausted when I came back from hiking.
3/410	哥哥不爱吃甜的，对糕点一点儿都不感兴趣。 My brother doesn't like sweet things. He is not interested in cakes and pastries at all.
4/410	我的感冒已经好得差不多了，明天就可以去上班了。 My cold is much better now. I can go back to work tomorrow.
5/410	这本书写的是关于学习动力的，我第一次读到它时就很有同感。 This book is about study motivation. I fully agreed with it when I first read it.

刚 just/hard gāng 411 G

Chinese	English	Character codes
刚 + 才 = 刚才	just + only = just now; a moment ago	411/366
刚刚	just recently; just a moment ago	411/411
刚好	just; exactly; to happen to be	411/039
阳刚	manly; masculine	583/411
刚正	honest; upright	411/339
刚正不阿 (ē)	upright and plainspoken	411/339/007/001

注释 **Note**

* 行 háng=business firm; trade; line; row; MW

Example Sentences

1/411	我刚刚还看见他，怎么一下就不见了？ I saw him just now. Where has he gone now?
2/411	刚才你在和谁讲电话呢？ Who were you on the phone with just now?
3/411	他刚刚成年。 He has only just come of age.
4/411	我正想去找你，刚好你就来了。 You came just when I was going to look for you.
5/411	我们找房子的事才刚刚开始，我知道从找房子到跟银行 * 借钱，最少得半年的时间。 We have just recently started house hunting. I know that from finding a house to borrowing the money from a bank, it needs at least half a year.

G | 412 糕 cake gāo

Chinese	English	Character codes
蛋 + 糕 = 蛋糕	egg + cake = cake	204/412
雪糕	ice cream	314/412
年糕	rice cake	090/412
糕点	cakes and pastries	412/016
糕点店	pastry shop	412/016/018

Example Sentences

1/412	这是我所吃过的最好吃的蛋糕。 This is the best cake I have ever eaten.
2/412	尝尝这些蛋糕吧，都是自己家里做的。 Try these cakes, they are all homemade.
3/412	我天天上班时路过一家糕点店，从里面冒出来的香味儿让我心情大好。 I pass a cake shop on my way to work every day. The lovely smell that comes from it really puts me in a good mood.
4/412	过去的一年，我每星期三晚上都跟蛋糕张 * 学做各种糕点，现在我已经出师了。 I learnt to make various kinds of cakes with Teacher Zhang every Wednesday evening last year, and I have completed my apprenticeship.
5/412	大热的天，你不要一口气吃好几个雪糕，那样对身体很不好。 Don't eat lots of ice cream at once on a hot day. It's not good for your health.

注释 Note

* 蛋糕张，the nick name of Mr. Zhang, a cake making professional

根 root/basis gēn 413 G

Chinese	English	Character codes
根 + 据 = 根据	basis + according to = according to; based on; basis; foundation	413/468
根除	to eradicate	413/378
根本	fundamental; basic; root; simply; absolutely (not); (not) at all	413/006
病根	an incompletely cured illness; an old complaint; the root cause of trouble	192/413
牙根	root of tooth	582/413
草根	grassroots	368/413

Example Sentences

1/413	你这样做有什么根据？ On what basis are you doing this?
2/413	我们的担心是有根据的。 Our fears were well-founded.
3/413	她要说什么就说什么，我根本不在乎。 Whatever she says, I simply don't care.
4/413	我的牙这几天疼得很，今天上午去看了牙医，他说是我的牙根出了问题。 I have had a toothache for a few days so I went to see the dentist this morning, and he said it was the root problems.
5/413	要想根除多年的坏习惯是非常不容易的。 It's not easy to eradicate bad habits that have formed over the years.

G 414 跟 follow/with/heel of feet/towards/same as gēn

Chinese	English	Character codes
跟 + 着 = 跟着	to follow + to follow after = immediately afterwards	414/337
脚跟	heel	450/414
跟班	attendant; footman (servant)	414/182
跟前	in front of; close to; nearby; the time just before	414/099
跟进	to follow; to follow up	414/235
跟不上	not able to keep up with	414/007/108
跟上	to catch up with; to keep pace with	414/108
跟头 (tou)	tumble; fall; somersault	414/554
跟从	to follow; (old) attendant	414/201
跟风	to go with the tide; to blindly follow the crowd; to follow the trend	414/405

注释 Note

* 怎么都……不，whatever the way still cannot...

Example Sentences

1/414	我见过她，但没跟她说过话。 I have seen her but never spoken with her.
2/414	他走得很快，走在他旁边的妻子怎么都 * 跟不 * 上他。 He walked so fast. His wife next to him couldn't keep up at all.
3/414	不用自己头脑想事情的人，当然就只能跟风了。 If you are unable to think for yourself, then you can only follow the crowd.
4/414	我以前还以为他跟谁都能成为朋友呢，实际上，他连和他姐姐弟弟的关系都不怎么好。 I figured he could become friends with anyone. In fact, he even cannot keep good relations with his sisters and brothers.
5/414	弟弟的狗总是跟着他，弟弟走到哪儿，狗就跟到哪儿。 My brother's dog always follows him, wherever he goes the dog goes as well.

更 change gēng; more/even more/further gèng 415 G

Chinese	English	Character codes
更 + 加 = 更加	more + more (than sth else); even more	415/442
更好	better; more	415/039
更多	more; even more	415/023
更大	bigger; even bigger	415/014
更高	higher; even higher	415/030
更 * 新	to replace the old with the new; to renew; to renovate; to upgrade; to update; to regenerate	415/311
更 * 正	to correct; to make a correction	415/339
更 * 衣室	changing room; dressing room; locker room; toilet	415/153/283
自力更 * 生	regeneration through one's own efforts (idiom); self-reliance	616/483/415/112

Example Sentences

1/415	现在雪下得更大了。 The snow is getting heavy now.
2/415	请问男更 * 衣室在哪儿？ Where is the men's changing room, please?
3/415	下雨的时候我开车总是更加小心。 I always drive more carefully when it is raining.
4/415	他的工作做得比过去更多更好了。 He is doing more and better work than he used to.
5/415	我的电脑是五年前买的，上起网来慢极了，该更 * 新了。 My computer was bought five years ago, and its internet connection is very slow, so it's the time to replace it.

注释 Note

* 更 gēng=change (All other examples are pronounced as gèng.)

G | 416 故 reason/old/cause/therefore/deliberately/original/die gù

Chinese	English	Character codes
故 + 事 = 故事	past + matter = narrative; story; tale	416/281
事故	accident	281/416
典故	allusion (to classic story or saying); classical quotation; parable	391/416
故居	former residence	416/466
故而	therefore	416/399
故意	deliberately; on purpose	416/324
故里	hometown	416/070
变故	an unforeseen event; accident; misfortune	364/416
饱经世故	sophisticated; worldly-wise	360/237/536/416
已故	the late; deceased	322/416

Example Sentences

1/416	今年一场意外的事故让他没了工作。 An accident this year made him lose his job.
2/416	我知道，他是因为爱面子才故意说的那些话。 I know that he made those remarks on purpose in order to save face.
3/416	一家报纸发表了他们两人的爱情故事，他们很生气。 One of newspapers published their love story. They are very angry.
4/416	走在伦敦大大小小的街道上，你常可以看到名人故居。 When walking through the streets of London, you often come across celebrities' former residences.
5/416	说起这个典故话就长了，让我先把一些重要的短信发完，然后慢慢地告诉你。 It's a long story of this classical quotation. Let me send some important messages first, then I will tell you the whole story.

顾 to look/to look after/to advice gù 417 G

Chinese	English	Character codes
照 + 顾 = 照顾	according to + attend to = take care of; to show consideration; to attend to; to look after	607/417
不顾	in spite of; regardless of	007/417
只顾	solely; preoccupied (with one thing); engrossed; focusing (on sth); to look after only one aspect	340/417
环顾	to look around; to survey	430/417
顾不上	cannot attend to or manage	417/007/108
顾不得	unable to change sth; unable to deal with	417/007/207
顾客	client; customer	417/063
回顾	to look back; review	048/417

Example Sentences

1/417	感谢你对我们照顾得这么周到。 Thank you for looking after us so well.
2/417	她只顾看书，饭都忘了吃了。 She was engrossed in reading her book and forgot to eat.
3/417	这一早上忙到现在，他午饭都顾不上吃。 He has been busy since this morning and haven't had time for lunch.
4/417	妈妈一晚上都没睡，一直在照顾生病的奶奶。 Mum stayed up all night to look after grandma who was sick.
5/417	顾春容环顾了一下四周，低声对我说，他刚刚发现了一件别人都还不知道的事情。 Gu Chunrong glanced around before whispering to me the matter he had discovered that no one else knew yet.

G | 418 刮 to scrape/to blow guā

Chinese	English	Character codes
刮 + 风 = 刮风	to blow + wind = to be windy	418/405
刮脸	to shave one's face	418/485
耳刮子	(coll.) to slap on one's face	400/418/172
刮目相看	to have a whole new level of respect for sb or sth; to sit up and take notice (of sb's improved performance etc)	418/500/569/062

Example Sentences

1/418	我现在每天早上都得刮脸了。 I have to shave every morning now.
2/418	刮风也好，下雨也好，她从来没迟到过。 Whether it's windy or raining, she has never been late.
3/418	叔叔的成就让很多人对他刮目相看。 Uncle's achievements make many people sit up and take notice.
4/418	今天又是刮风又是下雪的，我实在不想出门了。 It's windy and snowing today and I really don't want to go out.
5/418	这几天因为刮风下雨的关系，我们商场的顾客少了不少，因而，我们的老板很着急。 There are less customers in our shop because it has been windy and raining in the last few days, therefore, our boss feels anxious.

怪 strange/eccentric/blame guài 419 G

Chinese	English	Character codes
奇 + 怪 = 奇怪	strange + odd = strange; odd; to marvel; to baffled	516/419
怪人	strange person; eccentric	419/104
作怪	(of a ghost) to make strange things happen; to act up; to act behind the scenes; to make mischief; odd	176/419
见怪	to mind; to take offense	054/419
难怪	(it's) no wonder (that...); (it's) not surprising (that...)	503/419
怪不得	no wonder; so that's why	419/007/207
千奇百怪	fantastic oddities of every description	268/516/181/419
见怪不怪	to keep one's calm in the face of the unexpected; not to wonder at strange sights	054/419/007/419

Example Sentences

1/419	这件事情有点奇怪。 There is something weird about this matter.
2/419	前后门都大开着，难怪风这么大。 No wonder it's so draughty. The front door and the backdoor are all widely open.
3/419	你不好好吃饭，怪不得老是生病。 You don't eat properly, that's why you are ill all the time.
4/419	你花钱这么大手大脚 *，不能怪你父母生你的气。 You are a reckless spender, no wonder your parents are upset with you.
5/419	说起来 ** 也怪，姐姐的工作是游戏开发，可是她平时几乎是不玩游戏的。 Strange to say, my sister's job is game development but she hardly plays games.

注释 Note

* 大手大脚，the idiom means extravagant spender

** 说起来，in fact

G | 420 惯 accustomed to/to be used to/habit guàn

Chinese	English	Character codes
习 + 惯 = 习惯	habit + accustomed to = habit; custom; usual practice; to be used to	136/420
惯用	to use habitually; habitual; customary	420/594
惯孩子	spoil children	420/227/172
看不惯	cannot bear to see; to hate; to dislike; to disapprove	062/007/420
看惯	to be used to the sight of	062/420
习惯用语	idiom; idiomatic expression; habitual; form of speech	136/420/594/159
习惯成自然	habit becomes nature; get used to something and it seems inevitable; second nature	136/420/375/616/273

Example Sentences

1/420	奶奶平时没有午睡的习惯。 Grandma is not usually in the habit of taking a nap in the afternoon.
2/420	多年来他已习惯早睡早起。 For many years he has been in the habit of going to bed early and getting up early.
3/420	学习外语时，最难的就是做到天天练习；但是如果你这样做一段时间后就会习惯成自然了。 The hardest thing about learning a foreign language is practising every day, but if you persevere, it will become a habit.
4/420	妈妈习惯于天天晚上睡觉前喝一杯热牛奶。 Mum usually drinks a cup of hot milk before going to bed every night.
5/420	我小弟弟做的很多事爸爸都看不惯，特别是他花钱大手大脚的习惯。其实，他是被我爸爸惯坏了的。 My dad disapproves of a lot of things my youngest brother did, especially his bad habit of wasting money. Actually, he has been spoiled by Dad.

害 harm/injurious/disadvantage/destructive/kill hài 421 H

Chinese	English	Character codes
害 + 怕 = 害怕	harm + scare = to be afraid; to be scared	421/507
公害	public hazard; nuisance	221/421
有害	destructive; harmful; damaging	158/421
要害	vital part; (fig) key point; crucial	319/421
害人	to harm sb; to inflict suffering; to victimise; pernicious	421/104
加害	to injure; do harm to	442/421
正中 * 要害	to hit the nail on the head	339/168/319/421

Example Sentences

1/421	这个地 ** 方真安静，晚上一个人走路还真有点害怕。 This place is so quiet, walking alone at night is a bit scary.
2/421	她总是迟到，害得大家总是等她一个人。 She is always late and makes everyone else always wait for her.
3/421	经理听完报告后，一下子就明白了问题的要害。 After listening to the report, the manager grasped at once the crux of the problem.
4/421	妹妹把水箱里的热水都用完了，害得我只能洗冷水澡。 My sister used up all the hot water in the tank so I could only have a cold shower.
5/421	弟弟把家里的花瓶打坏了，他心里七上八下 *** 的，害怕爸爸妈妈会很生气。 My brother broke a vase at home and he is worried and scared that Mum and Dad will be very angry.

注释 Note

* 中 zhòng=hit the target

** 地 dì=earth; land; ground

*** 七上八下 : cannot calm down

H 422 行 business firm/trade/line/row/MW háng; walk/go/travel/behaviour/competent xíng

Chinese	English	Character codes
行 * 业	industry; business; profession	422/585
银行 *	bank	590/422
商行 *	trading company	107/422
同行 *	people of the same trade or occupation	130/422
本行 *	one's line of work	006/422
总行 *	headquarters (of bank)	617/422
分行 *	branch (of bank)	028/422
外行 *	layman; nonprofessional	297/422
行 * 情	market price; quotation of market price; the current market situation	422/270
行 + 李 + 箱 = 行李箱	to walk + plum + box = suitcase; baggage compartment; (car) boot	422/481/571
进行	to advance; to conduct; underway; in progress; to do; to carry out; to carry on; to execute	235/422
行为	action; conduct; behaviour; act	422/303
自行	voluntary; autonomous; by self	616/422
行动	operation; action; to move; mobile	422/212
运行	to be in motion; to move; (of a computer) to run	333/422
实行	to implement; to carry out; to put into practice	534/422
行事	to execute; to handle; behaviour; action; conduct	422/281
可行	feasible	242/422
出行	to set out on a long journey; to travel afar	012/422
送行	to see someone off; to throw a send-off party	287/422
身体力行	to practise what one preaches	279/294/483/422

Example Sentences

1/422	一共才是一个五天的短假 ** 期，可是我姐姐足足带了两个大行李箱。 My sister took two big suitcases for a short five-day holiday.
2/422	今天我的工作面试要进行一个下午，真可怕！ My job interview will carry on for the whole afternoon today. It's very terrifying!
3/422	他的这种行为让同事们不再相信他了。 Such behaviour lost him his colleagues' trust.
4/422	A: 你的行李多吗？ B: 不多，一个行李箱加一个手提包。 A: Do you have much luggage? B: No, one suitcase and one handbag.
5/422	老师常常说我是一个想法多、行动少的人。今天我要给老师看看，我是怎么把想法变为行动的。 The teacher often says that I am the person who has many ideas and fewer actions. Therefore, today I will show her how I translate my idea into action!

注释 Note

* 行 háng=business firm; trade; line; row; MW (All other examples are pronounced as xíng.)

** 假 jià=vacation; holiday

H | 423 河 river hé

Chinese	English	Character codes
黄 + 河 = 黄河	yellow + river = Yellow River	432/423
河水	river water	423/121
河口	estuary; the mouth of a river	423/475
小河	brook	143/423
河道	river course; river channel	423/206
山河	mountains and rivers; whole country	530/423
运河	canal	333/423

Example Sentences

1/423	历史上黄河的河道变更 * 了很多次。 Historically the Yellow River has changed its course many times.
2/423	我妹妹一早就去河边写生了。 My sister went to the river bank to sketch early in the morning.
3/423	冬天的时候，家门口的那条小河常常结冰。 During the winter, the brook outside my house often froze.
4/423	已经六个多月没下雨了，小河里的河水差不多都干了。 It's been over six months since the last rain. The brook is almost dry.
5/423	那条河把城市分成东西两边，东边是商业中心，西边是老百姓居住的地 ** 方。 That river divides the city into two parts, east and west. The east part is the commercial centre, and the west side is the residential area.

注释 Note

* 更 gēng=change

** 地 dì=earth; land; ground

乎 particle hū 424 H

Chinese	English	Character codes
几 (jī) + 乎 = 几乎	almost + a particle = almost; nearly; practically	052/424
关乎	to relate to; concerning; about	034/424
近乎	close to; intimate	236/424
在乎	to care about	236/424
出乎	due to; to stem from; to go beyond; to go against (expectations)	012/424
不外乎	nothing else but	007/297/424
几乎不	hardly; seems not	052/424/007
几乎没有	scarcely; hardly	052/424/078/158
几乎不可能	almost impossible	052/424/007/242/436
热乎乎	nice and warm	103/424/424
于是乎	therefore	597/117/424
满不在乎	not in the least concerned (idiom); reckless; couldn't give a damn about it; unperturbed; couldn't care less	496/007/163/424
忘乎所以	to get carried away; to forget oneself	561/424/290/323

Example Sentences

1/424	她的腿疼得几乎站不住了。 Her legs were so painful that she could hardly stand.
2/424	天气虽然很冷，但是冬泳的人们一点儿都不在乎。 Even though the weather is very cold, the winter swimmers don't mind at all.
3/424	我弟弟的法语说得非常好，几乎不带一点儿口音。 My brother's French is so good that he hardly has any accent.
4/424	他在公司工作有五年了，但是平时和同事们几乎没什么来往。 Although he has been working in the company for five years, he hardly socialises with his colleagues.
5/424	弟弟在今天的数学比赛上得了第一，高兴得他几乎忘乎所以了。 My younger brother came first in today's maths competition. He was overwhelmed with joy.

H | 425 护 protect hù

Chinese	English	Character codes
护 + 照 = 护照	to protect + photo = passport	425/607
爱护	to cherish; to treasure; to take care of; to love and protect	001/425
护理	to nurse; to tend and protect	425/482
看 (kān) 护	to nurse; to look after; to watch over	062/425
医护	doctors and nurses; medics; medical personnel	154/425
护送	to escort; to accompany	425/287

Example Sentences

1/425	我的护照上个月过期了。 My passport expired last month.
2/425	我有两本护照，一本法国的和一本加拿大的。 I have two passports, a French one and a Canadian one.
3/425	那个病人 24 小时有人看护。 That patient has 24-hour care.
4/425	在中国的公园里常可以看到“请爱护花草树木”的字样。 In China you often see the signs saying “Please take care of plants and trees” in the park.
5/425	他花了很多钱，请了两个医护人员，所以白天、晚上他年老的爷爷都有人护理。 He has spent a lot of money on two nurses for looking after his elderly grandpa day and night.

花 flower/spend/consume/blurred huā 426 H

Chinese	English	Character codes
花 + 朵 = 花朵	flower + MW for flower = flower	426/397
花期	florescence; the flowering period	426/096
花束	bouquet	426/541
眼花	dimmed eyesight; blurred; vague and unclear vision	316/426
老花眼	presbyopia	066/426/316
花钱	to spend money	426/100
花瓶	flower vase; (fig) just a pretty face	426/514
种 * 花	to grow flowers; floriculture	611/426
火花	spark; sparkle	050/426
花房	greenhouse	426/213
五花八门	myriad; all kinds of; all sorts of	133/426/002/257

Example Sentences

1/426	绿色的草地 ** 上开满了一朵朵白色的小花。 The green grass is full of little white flowers.
2/426	晚上迎面的车灯让我眼花。 The car headlights shone in my face dazzle me at night.
3/426	我这张票没花钱，是同事送的。 I got this ticket for free. My colleague gave it to me.
4/426	这个花瓶是我从一家二手店里买来的。 I bought this vase from a second-hand shop.
5/426	假 *** 期我一定要飞回家看爷爷奶奶，花多少钱都没关系。因为我是在他们的关心和爱护下长大的。 I will definitely fly back home to see my grandparents this holiday, even if I have to spend a lot of money, because I grew up under their caring and protection.

注释 Note

* 种 zhòng=plant; farm

** 地 dì=earth; land; ground

*** 假 jià=vacation; holiday

H | 427 化 to make into/change/transform/melt/-ize huà

Chinese	English	Character codes
文 + 化 = 文化	culture + to change into = culture; civilisation	563/427
变化	change; variation; to change; to vary	364/427
感化	corrective influence; to reform (a criminal); redemption (of a sinner); to guide sb back to the right path by persuasion and example	410/427
同化	assimilation (cultural, phonemic, etc)	130/427
老化	to age (of person or object); becoming old	066/427
白热化	to turn white-hot; to intensify; to reach a climax	180/103/427
绿化	make a place green by planting trees	494/427
千变万化	countless changes; constant permutation	268/364/559/427

Example Sentences

1/427	中国有着很久远的文化历史。 China has a long cultural history.
2/427	李老师在中山大学教西方文化。 Teacher Li teaches Western Culture in the Sun Yat-sen University.
3/427	太阳下山时，天空的颜色千变万化。 The sky became a kaleidoscope of colours at sunset.
4/427	十年不见，她的样子有了很大的变化，我都几乎认不出来她了。 I hadn't seen her for ten years. Her appearance has changed a lot. I almost couldn't recognise her.
5/427	一个人在外国生活时间长了，会不知不觉地被这个国家的人文所同化。 A person who has lived in a foreign country for a long time will be unknowingly assimilated by its culture.

画 to draw/to paint/picture huà 428 H

Chinese	English	Character codes
画 + 画儿 = 画画儿	to draw + picture = to draw; to paint	428/428/024
画像	portrait; to do a portrait of sb	428/574
画面	scene; picture; image; screen (displayed by a computer); (motion picture) frame; field of view	428/081
动画	animation; cartoon	212/428
刻画	to portray	473/428
画家	painter	428/053
字画	calligraphy and painting	173/428
作画	to paint	176/428
画报	pictorial (magazine)	428/184

Example Sentences

1/428	我表哥喜欢画画儿，看小说和听音乐。 My cousin likes drawing, reading and listening to music.
2/428	他还是孩子时就喜欢画画儿。 He was fond of drawing when he was a child.
3/428	小乐的画像比她本人还漂亮。 Xiao Le's portrait is prettier than she is.
4/428	你知道怎样在电脑上给人物角色做动画吗？ Do you know how to animate characters on the computer?
5/428	我的邻居家的女儿五岁时画画儿就画得很好了，现在她已经是很有成就的画家了。 My neighbour's daughter drew quite well at the age of five, and now she is a successful artist.

H 429 坏 bad/go bad/harm/damaged/ruined huài

Chinese	English	Character codes
坏 + 话 = 坏话	bad + words = unpleasant talk; malicious words	429/046
坏事	bad thing; misdeed; to ruin things	429/281
坏蛋	bad egg; scoundrel; bastard	429/204
好坏	good or bad; good and bad; standard; quality	039/429
变坏	to get worse; to degenerate	364/429
学坏	to follow bad examples; to be corrupted by bad examples	150/429
坏东西	bastard; scoundrel; rogue	429/019/135
坏人	bad person; villain	429/104
时好时坏	sometimes good, sometimes bad	116/039/116/429

Example Sentences

1/429	她人很好，从不说别人的坏话。 She is kind, and never says a bad word about others.
2/429	一本书的好坏不是作家自己怎么感觉，还得听听读者的看法。 Whether a book is good or bad does not depend on the feelings of the writer, but on the readers' opinions.
3/429	妈妈说哥哥小时候很调皮，没少干 * 坏事。 Mum said my brother was very naughty when he was little, and did many naughty things.
4/429	如果你不自己尝一尝，怎么知道这红酒的好坏呢？ If you don't taste it yourself, how will you know if this red wine is good or bad?
5/429	这半年来，奶奶的身体时好时坏，很让我们担心。 Grandma's health has fluctuated for the last six months, and we are all very worried about her.

注释 Note

* 干 gàn=do; strike; main part

环 ring/hoop/circle huán 430 H

Chinese	English	Character codes
环 + 境 = 环境	to surround + condition = environment; circumstances; surroundings	430/462
环节	round segment; connection; link; sector; annular ring	430/454
环顾	to look around; to survey	430/417
环球	around the world; worldwide	430/272
花环	garland; floral hoop	426/430
环路	ring road; closed circuit; loop	430/250

Example Sentences

1/430	这家饭馆儿的环境很不错。 This restaurant has a nice decor.
2/430	她家的房子四周的环境非常安静。 Her house is located in quiet surroundings.
3/430	因为车辆越来越多，很多城市都有了环行路。 Due to the increasing number of vehicles, many cities have built ring roads.
4/430	我又检查了一次才发现是这个环节出了问题。 I checked again and realised this part was the problem.
5/430	离婚的那天，他最后环顾了一下自己那空空的房间，没带一点儿感情地关上房门走了。 At the divorcing day, he looked around his empty room for a second, closed the door and then left without any emotion.

H 431 换 to exchange/change/convert/to replace huàn

Chinese	English	Character codes
变 + 换 = 变换	change + to exchange = to transform; to convert; to vary; to alternate; a transformation	364/431
更 * 换	to replace; to change (one's address etc)	415/431
换算	to convert; conversion	431/546
包换	to guarantee replacement (of faulty goods); warranty	359/431
换气	to take a breath (in swimming); to ventilate	431/098
换句话说	in other words	431/467/046/122

Example Sentences

1/431	我只用了五分钟就换好了衣服。 It took me only five minutes to get changed.
2/431	自从三年前开始工作，他已经更 * 换了好 ** 几个工作了。 Since he started working three years ago, he has changed jobs several times.
3/431	老师经常变换教学方法，调动 *** 同学们的学习兴趣。 Our teacher has often changed teaching methods to motivate the students' interest in their study.
4/431	要是你想学游泳，那么一定要学会换气才能游得好。 In order to learn to swim well, you must learn how to come up for breath.
5/431	他下班回到家，洗了（一）个澡，换了（一）身衣服，就又急急忙忙地出去了。 He came home after work, had a shower, got changed and rushed out again.

注释 Note

* 更 gēng=change

** 好，used before 儿 or 儿十，儿百，etc., means so many. 好儿个，several; 好儿十个，dozens; 好儿百个，hundreds. 好 also can be used like 很 and placed in front of an adjective, for example, 好漂亮，very pretty; 好大，truly big; even some people using double 好，好好啊，really nice.

*** 调动 diàodòng=arouse; mobilize.

黄 yellow huáng 432 H

Chinese	English	Character codes
黄 + 色 = 黄色	yellow + colour = yellow (colour); pornographic	432/277
黄山	Huangshan Mountain	432/530
米黄	cream-coloured	080/432
黄牛	ox; cattle; scalper of tickets	432/261
蛋黄	egg yolk	204/432
黄瓜	cucumber	432/223
黄鱼	yellow croaker (fish)	432/330

Example Sentences

1/432	那只小鸡是黄色的。 That little chick is yellow.
2/432	我觉得蛋黄比蛋白好吃。 I prefer the egg yolk to the white.
3/432	有些坏人常常把一些黄色的东西放在电脑游戏里。 Some evil men often embed pornographic content into computer games.
4/432	黄瓜明明是绿色的，为什么叫它黄瓜呢？ Cucumber is obviously green. Why is it called yellow melon in Chinese?
5/432	这场足球赛的黄牛票已经卖到两千块一张了。 The price of scalped tickets for this football match has already reached 2,000 yuan per ticket.

H 433 婚 marriage/wedding/wed/marry hūn

Chinese	English	Character codes
结 + 婚 = 结婚	to tie + marriage = to marry; to get married	455/433
婚礼	wedding ceremony; wedding	433/480
婚事	wedding; marriage	433/281
再婚	to remarry	164/433
离婚	to divorce; divorce from	248/433
重 * 婚	bigamy	612/433
复婚	(of a divorced couple) remarry each other	407/433
求婚	to propose (marriage)	522/433
已婚	married	322/433
婚外情	extramarital love	433/297/270
新婚	newly wed	311/433

Example Sentences

1/433	我表姐下个月就要结婚了。 My cousin is getting married next month.
2/433	阿姨的婚礼请了二百多个客人。 Over 200 guests were invited at my auntie's wedding.
3/433	他们离了婚没多久就又复婚了。 They remarried each other soon after they divorced.
4/433	冰冰和小春一见钟情 **，相识六个星期后就结婚了。 Bingbing and Xiaochun fell in love at first sight and got married six weeks after they met.
5/433	他们结婚才一年就离婚了。好在 *** 还没有孩子，不然对孩子很不公平。 They divorced after being married for only a year. Luckily they have no child. Otherwise, it's not fair for the child.

注释 Note

* 重 chóng=repeat; again; overlap; layer

** 一见钟情 : fall in love at first sight

*** 好在 : fortunately

或 or/maybe/perhaps huò 434 H

Chinese	English	Character codes
或 + 者 = 或者	maybe + this = or; possibly; maybe; perhaps	434/608
或是	or; either one or the other	434/117
间或	occasionally; now and then	231/434
或多或少	more or less	434/023/434/109
两个或两个以上	two or more	249/031/434/249/031/323/108
两个或更多	two or more	249/031/434/415/023
相当于或大于	greater than or equal to; at least as great as	569/388/579/434/014/579

Example Sentences

1/434	你去或不去都和我没关系。 It doesn't matter to me whether you go or not.
2/434	如果你现在出发，能坐上四点半的那班火车或者五点零四的。 If you set off now, you might make the 4:30 train or four past five.
3/434	如果你还有不明白的地 * 方，可以给我打电话或者发邮件给我。 If you are still not sure about anything, you can ring or email me.
4/434	好好地跟爸爸说、或者跟妈妈说，他们是会同意你的看法的。 Talk to Dad or Mum nicely, and they might agree with your opinion.
5/434	新电影的主角虽然还没有最后定下来，但大家或多或少都已经知道一点儿了。 Although the casting for the new movie hasn't been finalised yet, everyone more or less knows already.

注释 Note

* 地 dì=earth; land; ground

J | 435 级 level/grade/rank/step jí

Chinese	English	Character codes
年 + 级 = 年级	year + grade = grade; year (in school, college, etc)	090/435
高级	high level; advanced; high-ranking	030/435
超级	super-; ultra-; hyper-	373/435
等级	grade; rank; status	208/435
级别	rank; level; grade	435/190
班级	class; grade	182/435
同级	on the same level; ranking equally	130/435
考级	take a grading examination	241/435

Example Sentences

1/436	王老师是我们四年级时新来的数学老师。 Teacher Wang was our new maths teacher when we were in Grade 4.
2/436	张园是东京大学历史系四年级的学生。 Zhang Yuan is a senior student in Tokyo University's History Department.
3/436	李健的工作能力让他的同级和上级都很看重他。 Li Jian's work ability was greatly valued by his peers and his superiors.
4/436	这次考试我们班级的成绩是年级第一，这是同学和老师共同努力的结果。 Our class's results ranked first in this exam among our grade. This is attributed to joint efforts of the students and teachers.
5/436	我妹妹让我和她一起去参加后天的声乐考级。 My younger sister asked me to go with her to the singing exam the day after tomorrow.

极 extremely/pole/to the utmost jí 436 J

Chinese	English	Character codes
极 + 大 = 极大	utmost + big = maximum; enormous	436/014
极少	very little; very few	436/109
极为 (wéi)	extremely; exceedingly	436/303
极其	extremely	436/515
极力	to make a supreme effort; at all costs	436/483
两极	the two poles; both ends of sth	249/436
极点	extreme point; pole; the origin	436/016
北极星	North Star; Polaris	005/436/148
极乐世界	paradise	436/246/536/457

Example Sentences

1/437	这是一个极其重要的会议，我必须得去。 This is a highly important meeting. I have to attend it.
2/437	我的工作给我带来了极大的乐趣。 My job gives me great pleasure.
3/437	在大学里，他的网球打得极为出色。 He played tennis brilliantly when he was at university.
4/437	这个问题在我看来是极其简单的，就像一加一等于二一样。 It seems to me that this problem is very simple, just like one plus one.
5/437	小刚突然离开公司了，关于他为什么离开，极少有人知道。 Xiaogang left the company suddenly, and hardly anyone knows why he left.

J | 437 急 urgent/anxious/impatient/hurried/eager/hurry jí

Chinese	English	Character codes
着 (zháo) + 急 = 着急	to feel + urgent = to worry; to feel anxious	337/437
急着	urgently	437/337
急忙	hastily	437/254
急于	eager; anxious; impatient	437/597
急用	urgent need	437/594
心急	anxious; impatient	576/437
加急	to become more urgent; more rapid; urgent; to handle a matter urgently	442/437
十万火急	most urgent; post-haste; express	114/559/050/437

Example Sentences

1/438	这本书你慢慢看，不用着急还我。 Take your time to read this book. There is no rush to return it to me.
2/438	别着急，小马会解决这些问题的。 Don't worry, Xiao Ma will solve these problems.
3/438	听到门外的脚步声，小张急忙跑去开门。 Xiao Zhang rushed to open the door when he heard the footsteps outside.
4/438	快要迟到了，弟弟急急忙忙地拿起行李向车站跑去。 As it was almost late, my brother hurriedly picked up his luggage and ran to the station.
5/438	飞机迟迟不起飞，机上所有人都很着急，也都急于想了解出了什么事。 The plane delayed taking off. Everybody on board was worried and anxious to find out what happened.

己 self/oneself/one's own/personal jǐ 438 J

Chinese	English	Character codes
自 + 己 = 自己	self + oneself = oneself; one's own	616/438
你自己	yourself	089/616/438
自己人	those on our side; ourselves; one's own people	616/438/104
己见	one's own viewpoint	438/054
表现自己	to express oneself; to give an account of oneself; to project oneself; to show off	189/141/616/438
红颜知己	close female friend; confidante	229/315/341/438
据为己有	to take for one's own; to expropriate	468/303/438/158

Example Sentences

1/439	弟弟已经大了，可以自己照顾自己了。 My brother is old enough to take care of himself.
2/439	这么多瓶啤酒都是你自己一个人喝的？ You drank all the beer by yourself?
3/439	这是我第一次参加面试，没能好好表现自己，下一次我一定能做好。 This is my first interview and I didn't express myself well, but I will do better next time.
4/439	她动作很快，不一会儿就把自己的房间打扫得干干净净了。 She was really quick; it didn't take her long before her room was spotless.
5/439	A: 你平时自己做饭、洗衣服吗？ B: 衣服我能自己洗，但饭一般是买来吃，我自己不太会做饭。 A: Do you usually do your own cooking and laundry? B: I can do my own laundry, but I can't really cook, so usually I have takeout.

J | 439 记 to remember/record/mark/take note jì

Chinese	English	Character codes
忘 + 记 = 忘记	to forget + mark = to forget	561/439
记住	to remember; to bear in mind; to learn by heart	439/170
日记	diary	275/439
笔记本	notebook (stationery); notebook (computing)	187/439/006
后记	epilogue; afterword	044/439
记事	to keep a record of events; record; to start to form memories (after one's infancy)	439/281
记号	notation; seal; mark	439/040

Example Sentences

1/440	请别忘记六点钟叫我。 Please don't forget to call me at six.
2/440	她从不忘记每周给我打电话。 She never forgets to ring me every week.
3/440	记住，你必须在十一点以前到家。 Remember you must get home before 11 o'clock.
4/440	我忘记带手机了，我把它忘在家里了。 I forgot to bring my cellphone with me and left it at home.
5/440	请你告诉我，法语单词和语法这么难，你是怎样把这些法语单词和那些语法都记住的？ Could you tell me how do you remember all these French words and grammar as they are so difficult for me, please?

季 season jì 440 | J

Chinese	English	Character codes
季 + 节 = 季节	season + section = season; time; period	440/454
四季	four seasons	123/440
雨季	rainy season	160/440
花季	youthful time; prime of youth; flowering season	426/440
月季	Chinese rose	162/440
一年四季	all year round	152/090/123/440

Example Sentences

1/441	现在正是爬山的好季节。 Now it is the best season for mountain climbing.
2/441	雨季总算过去了。 The rainy season has ended at last.
3/441	在所有四季当中，我觉得夏天最热也最不舒服。 Of all the four seasons, I think summer is the hottest and the most uncomfortable.
4/441	一年四季中，你最喜欢哪个季节呢？我是最不喜欢冬季的，因为实在太冷了。 Of all four seasons, which season do you like the best? I really hate winter, it's too cold.
5/441	到了每年的三月，季节才真正地 * 起变化，大地 ** 慢慢地 * 变绿了，树上也开始有鸟唱歌了。 There is a real change in the season when it comes to March, as the land's colour changes to green slowly, and birds begin singing in trees.

注释 Note

* 地 de=grammatical code

** 地 dì=earth; land; ground

J | 441 绩 achievement/accomplishment/merit jì

Chinese	English	Character codes
成 + 绩 = 成绩	achieve + grade = achievement; performance records; grades	375/441
业绩	achievement; accomplishment; performance (of a business, employee etc); results	585/441
成绩单	school report	375/441/386
考试成绩	exam results; grades	241/282/375/441

Example Sentences

1/435	小春在班里的学习成绩中等。 Xiao Chun's grades in class are about mid-level.
2/435	他对自己这次考试的成绩十分担心。 He is very worried about his exam result.
3/435	我的历史成绩不错，但数学不太好。 I'm good at history, but not so good at math.
4/435	小刚的工作成绩一直都远比其他同事好。 Xiaogang's work always stands out from the rest of his colleagues.
5/435	安安的努力从她考试成绩单上的五个满分便一目了然。 An'an's hard work was clearly showed in her exam results: full marks for five subjects.

加 to add/plus jiā 442 J

Chinese	English	Character codes
参 + 加 = 参加	to join + to add = to participate; to take part; to join	367/442
加上	plus; to put in; to add; to add on; to add into; in addition; on top of that	442/108
更加	more (than sth else)	415/442
加工	to process; processing; working (machinery)	442/032
加快	to accelerate; to speed up	442/244
加大	to increase (e.g. one's effort)	442/014
外加	in addition; extra	297/442
加法	addition	442/402
加拿大	Canada	442/501/014

Example Sentences

1/442	好，我答应 * 你，一定会去加拿大参加你的婚礼。 OK, I promise you. I will definitely go to Canada to attend your wedding.
2/442	我晚上开车总是比白天更加小心。 I always drive more carefully at night than daytime.
3/442	他太爱她了，一见到她，他就心跳加快。 He loves her so deeply that his heart beats faster as soon as he sees her.
4/442	我们学校报名参加唱歌比赛的不单单是她一个人。 She is not the only one from our school to sign up for the singing competition.
5/442	我觉得，你可以穿那件黑色的晚礼服或者这条绿色的长裙去参加舞会。 I think that you can wear either that black evening dress or this green long skirt at the ball.

注释 Note

* 答应 dāying=promise

J 443 假 false jiǎ; vacation/holiday jià

Chinese	English	Character codes
请 + 假 *= 请假 *	to ask + vacation = to request leave of absence	101/443
真假	genuine or fake; true or false	338/443
假定	to assume; to suppose; supposed; so-called; assumption; hypothesis	443/392
假 * 期	vacation	443/096
假 * 日	holiday; non-working day	443/275
放假 *	to have a holiday or vacation	404/443
作假	to counterfeit; to falsify; to cheat; to defraud; fraudulent; to behave affectedly	176/443
假如	if	443/526
假想	imaginary; virtual; to imagine; hypothesis	443/142
假情假意	hypocrisy; insincerity	443/270/443/324
病假 *	sick leave	192/443

Example Sentences

1/443	老李，我能在星期一上午请假 * 去看病吗？ Old Li, can I have Monday morning off to see my doctor?
2/443	我发烧了，所以今天请了病假 *。 I've got fever so I took sick leave today.
3/443	现在的新闻报道常常是真假难分。 Nowadays, it is often difficult to tell real news from a fake one.
4/443	昨晚我和朋友们喝高 ** 了，今天早上实在起不来了，只能跟老板请假 * 了。 I drank a lot with friends last night and just couldn't get up this morning, so I had to ask my boss for a leave of absence.
5/443	假如你没有和他结婚的意愿的话，那么就跟他分手吧。 If you have no intention of marrying him, then you should break up with him.

注释 Note

* 假 jià=vacation; holiday (All other examples are pronounced as jiǎ.)

** 喝高了，get drunk

检 to check/examine jiǎn 444 J

Chinese	English	Character codes
检 + 查 = 检查	to examine + check = inspection; to examine; to inspect	444/370
安检	safety check	352/444
体检	physical examination; health check-up	294/352
检点	to examine; to check; to keep a lookout; cautious; restrained (in speech or mannerisms)	352/016
检方	the prosecution; prosecutors	352/403

Example Sentences

1/444	空调好久没用了，得让人来检查一下了。 The air conditioner hasn't been used for a while. It needs to be checked out.
2/444	把护照放起来吧。上了飞机以后就没人检查你的护照了。 Put your passport in a safe place, because no one will check your passport once you have boarded the plane.
3/444	你忘带机票了？没有机票怎么能进安检门呢？ You have forgotten to bring your air ticket? How can you get to the security check without an air ticket?
4/444	昨天医生把检查的结果告诉那位年老的病人了。 Yesterday, the doctor told the aged patient the result of the examination.
5/444	下个星期四我要去医院做一个一年一次的身体检查，我希望什么事都没有。 Next Thursday I need to go to the hospital for my annual health check-up. I hope nothing is wrong.

J 445 简 simple/brief/simplified jiǎn

Chinese	English	Character codes
简 + 单 = 简单	simple + single = simple; not complicated	445/386
不简单	not simple; rather complicated; remarkable; marvellous	007/445/386
简单地说	to put it simply; simply put	445/386/390/122
简要	concise; brief	445/319
简写	to write characters in simplified form; to simplify (a book)	445/146
简明	simple and clear	445/052
简化	to simplify	445/427
简短	brief; short duration	445/394
简直	simply; at all; practically	445/609
简报	brief report	445/184
简单明了	clear and simple; in simple terms	445/386/052/067

Example Sentences

1/445	小刚进步这么大，真不简单。 Xiaogang has made such great progress. It's really not easy.
2/445	这事不简单，需要进一步调查。 This matter is not so simple. It requires further investigation.
3/445	这个星期简直没有一个好天气。 There is no good weather at all this week.
4/445	妈妈认为我把这件事情看得太简单了，其实不是。 Mum thinks I take this matter too simply. In fact, I didn't.
5/445	阿姨又要工作又要照顾她的三个孩子，真是不简单。 It's really not easy for auntie to have to go to work while looking after her three children.

健 sound/healthy/strong/strengthen/invigorate jiàn 446 J

Chinese	English	Character codes
健 + 康 = 健康	healthy + health = health; healthy	446/471
健身	to exercise; to keep fit with exercise; to work out; physical exercise	446/279
健身房	gym	446/279/213
健儿	top athlete; heroic warrior	446/024
健忘	forgetful	446/561
健步行走	to hike	446/193/422/345

Example Sentences

1/446	新鲜的空气对健康很重要。 Clean air is important to good health.
2/446	小雨这个孩子身心都很健康。 Xiaoyu, a little child, is physically and mentally healthy.
3/446	每星期二和星期四我都去健身房。 I go to gym every Tuesday and Thursday.
4/446	从大学时起，我就对健身有了极大的兴趣。 I have gained a real interest in fitness since university.
5/446	健步行走是又安全又简便 * 而且适合所有岁数的人的锻炼。 Walking is safe and easy, and it is a suitable exercise for people of all ages.

注释 Note

* 便 biàn=convenient

J 447 讲 to speak/tell/pay attention to/particular about/speech jiǎng

Chinese	English	Character codes
讲 + 话 = 讲话	to speak + word = a speech; to speak; to talk; to address	447/046
讲课	teach; lecture	447/243
讲解	to explain	447/456
听讲	to attend a lecture	129/447
主讲	to give a lecture; to lecture on	614/447
讲理	to argue; to reason with sb	447/482
讲到	to talk about sth	447/205
讲明	to explain	447/082
讲和	to make peace; to reconcile	447/042
讲师	instructor; lecturer	447/113

Example Sentences

1/447	校长的讲话虽然简短，可是非常有意思。 The headmaster's speech was brief but significant.
2/447	听周老师讲课就像听他讲故事，特别有意思。 Teacher Zhou teaches his lessons like he is telling a story. They are very interesting.
3/447	她真行，喝了一大杯咖啡后，又能接着讲课。 She is super, after drinking a big cup of coffee, she can carry on teaching.
4/447	你在没在听我讲话啊？怎么一点儿声音都不出啊？ Are you still listening to me? How come you haven't made a sound?
5/447	你妻子不是不讲理的人，所以你最好心平气和地跟她说。 Your wife is not an unreasonable person, so it would be best to tell her calmly.

蕉 banana jiāo 448 J

Chinese	English	Character codes
香 + 蕉 = 香蕉	fragrance + banana = banana	570/448
香蕉皮	banana skin	570/448/510
香蕉园	banana plantation; banana field	570/448/601
香蕉树	banana tree	570/448/542
香蕉干	dried banana	570/448/409
香蕉船	banana boat; banana split	570/448/380

Example Sentences

1/448	香蕉、李子、苹果，你最喜欢哪一种？ Bananas, plums, apples, which do you like best?
2/448	我很喜欢那些香蕉，因为看起来很不错。 I like those bananas, because they look very nice.
3/448	我叔叔的公司主要是做咖啡还有香蕉的进口生意的。 The main business of my uncle's company is importing coffee and bananas.
4/448	爸爸昨天买的香蕉很生，要放一放才能吃。 The bananas Dad bought yesterday are not ripe yet, need to be put aside for a few days.
5/448	姐姐早饭吃了一根香蕉、一片面包，还喝了一杯奶茶。 For breakfast my sister had a banana, a piece of bread and a cup of milk tea.

J 449 角 angle/corner/horn/cape/MW jiǎo; contend/tussle/quarrel/role/part in drama jué

Chinese	English	Character codes
主 + 角 *= 主角	main + role = leading role; lead	614/449
角 * 色	persona; character in a novel; role	449/277
口角 *	altercation; wrangle; quarrel; angry argument	475/449
口角	corner of the mouth	475/449
视角	view point; angle on sth; perspective	118/449
眼角	outer or inner corner of the eyes; canthus	316/449
号角	bugle horn	040/449
直角	a right angle	609/449
八角	anise; star anise; aniseed; octagonal	002/449

Example Sentences

1/449	这出戏的角 * 色现在还在选择中，可能明天能定下来。 The roles in this play are still being selected now. Maybe they can confirm them by tomorrow.
2/449	不知道为什么，她经常和她的邻居发生口角 *。 I don't know the reason why she has often clashed with her neighbour.
3/449	说到问题时，要是双方都能换个视角去想想，问题就比较容易解决，是不是？ Don't you think it is easier to solve the problem if both sides can consider it from the other's perspective during the discussion?
4/449	我不是今晚舞会的主角 *，我姐姐才是呢。 I'm not the star of tonight's ball, and my sister is.
5/449	数学里的正三角的每个角都相等。 In geometry, an equilateral triangle has three equal angles.

注释 Note

* 角 jué, all other examples are pronounced as jiǎo.

脚 foot/base jiǎo 450 J

Chinese	English	Character codes
腿 + 脚 = 腿脚	leg + foot = legs and feet; ability to walk	557/450
脚本	script	450/006
山脚	foot of a mountain	530/450
手脚	hand and foot; movement of limbs; action	284/450
脚下	under the foot	450/139
脚注	footnote	450/615
脚步	footstep; step	450/193
从头到脚	from head to foot	201/554/205/450
做手脚	to defraud; to rig up (a scan)	178/284/450
动手动脚	to come to blows; to paw; to grope; to get fresh	212/284/212/450
站不住脚	ill-founded; groundless	166/007/170/450

Example Sentences

1/450	我今年就五十岁了，坐久了我就得站起来活动活动腿脚。 I am going to be 50 years old this year, so if I have been sitting a long time, I need to stand up and stretch my legs.
2/450	天色已黑，又在下雪，路上的行人都加快了回家的脚步。 It was dark already and snowing. The pedestrians on the road quickened their pace on their way back home.
3/450	他昨天从头到脚穿了一身黑，像一只黑猫。 He was dressed in black from top to toe yesterday, like a black cat.
4/450	爷爷老了，腿脚不方便，只好从楼房搬到平房去住了。 Grandad is old now and can't walk much, so he has moved from a flat to a bungalow.
5/450	现在不少年轻人看不太懂古典小说，看的时候就得查看下面的脚注。 Nowadays many youngsters won't be able to understand the meanings of some characters in classics without annotations.

J | 451 较 compare/contrast/fairly/quite jiào

Chinese	English	Character codes
比 + 较 = 比较	to contrast + to compare = to compare; to contrast; comparatively; relatively; quite; comparison	186/451
较大	comparatively large	451/014
较好	preferably; rather or relatively good	451/039
较为（wéi）	comparatively; relatively; fairly	451/303
较差	rather poor; relatively poor	451/371
较少	less	451/109
较长	comparatively long	451/194

Example Sentences

1/451	你和你姐姐的看法，我比较同意你的。 Between your point of view and that of your older sister, I am inclined to agree with you.
2/451	她还是个学生，有些想法比较天真。 She is still a student, so some ideas are a bit naïve.
3/451	医生们定期开会以比较病人病情的轻重。 Doctors meet regularly to compare the severity of the patient's condition.
4/451	这两间房子，东边的那间较大，可是见不到太阳；西边的那间不大，可是阳光好，比较亮。 In these two houses, the east house is larger, but you cannot see the sun. The west one is not big, but sunny and bright.
5/451	苹果和香蕉比较起来，虽然后者较甜，可是我更爱吃苹果。 Between apples and bananas, although the later is comparatively sweeter, but I still prefer apples.

接 to receive/to pick up/next jiē 452 J

Chinese	English	Character codes
接 + 着 = 接着	to catch + particle indicating action in progress = to catch and hold on; to continue; to go on to do sth; to follow; to carry on; then; subsequently; to proceed; to ensure; in turn; in one's turn	452/337
直接	direct; immediate; directly; straightforward	609/452
接下来	to accept; to take; next; following	452/139/065
接到	to receive (letter etc)	452/205
接近	to approach; to get close to	452/236
接见	to receive sb; to grant an interview	452/054
间（jiàn）接	indirect	231/452
接手	to take over (duties etc); catcher (baseball etc)	452/284
接生	to deliver (a new born child)	452/112
接班	to take over (from those working the previous shift); to take over (in a leadership role etc); to succeed sb	452/182
接头	to join; to connect; connection; junction; fitting (plumbing); connector	452/554
接送	picking up and dropping off; greeting and sending off; shuttle (transport service)	452/287

Example Sentences

1/452	我决定直接从北京飞到东京，在那里，有人会来接我。 I decided to fly directly from Beijing to Tokyo, and someone will receive me there.
2/452	他跟我说定了，明天我们在超市接头，我把我的手机号给他了。 He and I have agreed that we will meet at the supermarket tomorrow, and I have told him my mobile phone number.
3/452	你们应该知道做出这个决定的间接后果是什么。 We should know what the indirect consequences of this decision are.
4/452	不知为什么，关于我的请调报告，上级迟迟不做直接的答复。 I don't know what is the reason of the leader who held off answering directly to my request for a transfer.
5/452	看完球赛后，我又和李响去喝了一杯，分手时已接近半夜了。 After the match, Li Xiang and I went for a drink, and it was nearly midnight when we parted.

J 453 街 street jiē

Chinese	English	Character codes
街 + 道 = 街道	street + way = street; sub district; residential district	453/206
街头	street	453/554
大街	street; main street	014/453
上街	to go onto the street; to go shopping	108/453
步行街	car-free zone; pedestrian street	193/422/453

Example Sentences

1/453	师阿姨在大街上开了一家书店，生意非常好。 Auntie Shi opens a bookshop in the high street, and her business is going very well.
2/453	小周飞快地跑着，穿过了一条又一条街道去找他的狗。 Young Zhou was running through the streets at lightning speed, looking for his dog.
3/453	天天上下班时每条街道上都有很多车。 All of streets were packed with vehicles during the rush hours each day.
4/453	出租车司机告诉我长安街是北京最长的一条街。 The taxi driver told me that Chang'an Street is the longest street in Beijing.
5/453	我以为今天过节，街上会有很多人，可是很多街道都是安安静静的，真奇怪。 I thought that today there must be a lot of people in the street to celebrate the festival, but many streets were very quiet, it's very strange!

节 node/joint/section/festival/period/MW jié 454 J

Chinese	English	Character codes
节 + 日 = 节日	festival + day = holiday; festival	454/275
节目	program; item (on a program)	454/500
调节	to adjust; to regulate; to harmonise; to reconcile	552/454
小节	a minor matter; trivia; bar (music)	143/454
节能	to save energy; energy-saving	454/088
时节	season; time	116/454
情节	plot; circumstances	270/454
过节	to celebrate a festival; after the celebration (i.e. once the festival is over)	225/454
关节	joint (physiology); key point; critical phase	034/454

Example Sentences

1/454	新年对每个人来说都是一个快乐的节日。 New Year is a cheerful holiday for everyone.
2/454	中秋节是中国一个重要的节日。 Mid-Autumn Festival is an important festival in China.
3/454	这些桌椅的高矮可以跟据孩子的身高调节，对年轻夫妻来说非常实用。 These desks and seats can be adjusted to the heights of children, so it's very practical for young couples.
4/454	游泳对关节不好的人来说是一个特别好的运动。 Swimming is a good sport for people with joint problems.
5/454	妈妈想变换一下，把今年新年的节日饭搬到酒店去吃，但是爷爷奶奶都不同意，所以没去成。 Mum wanted to have a change, therefore, she would like to have the New Year dinner at a restaurant instead of home, but Grandpa and Grandma didn't agree, so we didn't go.

J 455 结 join/tie/weave/congeal/finish/knot jié; to produce/bear jiē

Chinese	English	Character codes
结 + 果 = 结果	to produce + fruit = outcome; result; conclusion; in the end; as a result; to kill; to dispatch; to bear fruit	455/037
结束	termination; to finish; to end; to conclude; to close	455/541
总结	to sum up; to conclude; summary	617/455
结业	to finish school esp. a short course; to complete a course	455/585
小结	summary; short; brief; wrap-up	143/455
结实 (jiēshi)	sturdy; strong; durable; buff (physique)	455/534
结算	to settle a bill; to close an account	455/546
情结	complex (psychology)	270/455

Example Sentences

1/455	今年的苹果树很早就结果了。 The apple trees are fruiting early this year.
2/455	老师对同学们这次考试的结果很满意。 The teacher is pleased with the students' exam results.
3/455	赛跑结束后，他累得都走不动路了。 After the race, he is too tired to walk.
4/455	音乐会要到晚上十点半才会结束。 The concert won't finish until 10:30.
5/455	小明对自己星期一的面试不特别满意，他要总结一下，准备三天以后的第二次面试。 Xiaoming is not satisfied with his interview on Monday, and he wants to sum up a bit for the second one three days later.

解 dissect/decode/resolve/untie/dismiss jiě 456 J

Chinese	English	Character codes
解 + 决 = 解决	to dissolve + to decide = to settle (a dispute); to resolve; to solve; to dispose of; to dispatch	456/469
了 (liǎo) 解	to understand; to realise; to find out	067/456
理解	to understand; to comprehend; comprehension; understanding	482/456
解答	answer; explanation; solution (to a maths equation)	456/384
调解	to mediate	552/456
解放	to liberate; to emancipate; liberation	456/404
见解	opinion; view; understanding	054/456
解体	to break up into components; to disintegrate; to collapse; to crumble	456/294
分解	to resolve; to decompose; to break down	028/456
化解	to dissolve; to resolve (contradictions); to dispel (doubts); to iron out (difficulties); to defuse (conflicts); to neutralise (fears)	427/456
讲解	to explain	447/456

Example Sentences

1/456	大家都知道，这个问题得马上解决，不能再等了。 Everyone has noticed that this problem calls for an immediate solution, it can no longer wait.
2/456	林医师出生于中医世家，对中医理论有他自己的见解。 Doctor Lin was born in a family with generations of experience in traditional Chinese medicine, so he has his own opinions about traditional Chinese medicine theory.
3/456	我对他是越了解就越喜欢了。 The more I know about him, the more I like him.
4/456	小李和老张的关系出现了问题，经过钱老师的调解，没几天就化解了。 A little trouble between Young Li and Old Zhang was soon resolved by Teacher Qian's mediation.
5/456	在北京有住房和上学难的问题已经到了非解决不可的地 * 步。 The difficult problem of housing and schooling in Beijing has reached a point where it must be solved.

注释 Note

* 地 dì=earth; land; ground

J 457 界 boundary/circles/scope jiè

Chinese	English	Character codes
世 + 界 = 世界	world + boundary = world	536/457
世界杯	World Cup	536/457/004
界定	definition; to delimit	457/392
自然界	nature; the natural world	616/273/457
眼界	field of view; outlook	316/457
边界	boundary; border	188/457
外界	the outside world; external	297/457
开眼界	broaden, expand one's horizons	061/316/457
国界	national boundary; border between countries	036/457
租界	concession	174/457
教育界	education circle	233/598/457

Example Sentences

1/457	爸爸和妈妈打算明年坐船去周游世界。 My parents are planning to travel around the world by ship next year.
2/457	这条小河是这个城市南北的界河。 This river forms the boundary between the northern and southern parts of the city.
3/457	我最喜欢看的电视节目叫“自然界”。 The TV programme I like to watch most is called “The Natural World”.
4/457	昨天晚上九点我和朋友们一起在看世界杯的决赛，你们呢？ I was watching the World Cup final with my friends at 9 o'clock last night, what about you?
5/457	出国留学的五年，不但让我眼界大开，还让我认识了很多知识界的朋友。 The five years of studying abroad allowed me to broaden my horizons and make many intellectual friends.

借 lend/borrow/loan jiè 458 J

Chinese	English	Character codes
借 + 用 = 借用	to borrow + use = to borrow sth for another use; to borrow an idea for one's own use	458/594
借助	to draw support from; with the help of	458/343
借读	to attend school on a temporary basis	458/021
借口	to use as an excuse; on the pretext; excuse; pretext	458/475
租借	to rent; to lease	174/458
假借	to make use of; to use sth as pretext; under false pretences; under the guise of	443/458
借机	to seize the opportunity	458/051
借故	to find an excuse	458/416

Example Sentences

1/458	我可以借用一下你的雨伞吗？ May I borrow your umbrella for a while?
2/458	能不能把你的打字机借给我用用？ Can you lend your typewriter to me?
3/458	市长提议的"自行车以小时数或天数租借"计划，会在今年下半年实行。 The plan the mayor proposed that bicycles can be hired by the hour or by the day will be carried out in the second half of this year.
4/458	姐姐不喜欢聊天，所以在飞机上一直看电影，她的借口是这些电影她都没看过。 My sister doesn't like chatting, so she had watched films throughout the flight. Her excuse was that she never watched those movies before.
5/458	公共图书馆里的书的借用期不得超过三个星期。 All the books in the public library have to be returned within three weeks.

J | 459 斤 a Chinese traditional unit of weight (equal to 0.5 kg) jīn

Chinese	English	Character codes
公 + 斤 = 公斤	international + weight = kilogram	221/459
斤两	weight; (fig) importance	459/249
市斤	Chinese unit of weight (equal to 0.5 kg)	537/459
半斤八两	not much to choose between the two; tweedledum and tweedledee	358/459/002/249

Example Sentences

1/459	这个高个子的运动员有一百公斤重。 This tall sportsman weighs one hundred kilos.
2/459	这箱苹果里里外外一共重二十三公斤。 This box of apples' gross weight is 23 kg.
3/459	男子 56 公斤级的比赛现在开始！ The men's 56 kg category competition is starting now.
4/459	别看弟弟人小，他一下子能提起一包十公斤的大米呢。 Although my brother is little, he can easily lift a 10 kg bag of rice.
5/459	我上次飞南京的时候行李才超重了五公斤，就要了我六百块钱。 The last time I flew to Nanjing I was charged 600 yuan even though my luggage was only 5 kg overweight.

净 clean/make clean/pure/net/mere/empty jìng 460 J

Chinese	English	Character codes
干 + 净 = 干净	dry + clean = clean; neat	409/460
净重	net weight	460/612
白净	(of skin) fair and clean	180/460
净化	to purify	460/427
清净	peaceful and quiet	520/460
净水	clean water; purified water	460/121
明净	bright and clean; luminous	082/460
一干二净	thoroughly (idiom); completely; one and all; very clean	152/409/025/460
不干不净	unclean; filthy; foul-mouthed	007/409/007/460
眼不见为 (wéi) 净	what remains unseen is deemed to be clean; what the eye doesn't see, the heart doesn't grieve over (idiom)	316/007/054/303/460

Example Sentences

1/460	小小，你能不能把手洗得干净一点儿再吃饭？ Can you wash your hands clean before eating meals, Xiaoxiao?
2/460	一到冬天，商店里的空气净化机就特别好卖。 Air purifiers are very popular in the shops during winter.
3/460	姐姐特别爱干净，她的衣服和鞋子总是干干净净的。 My elder sister likes to be clean, her clothes and shoes are always clean and tidy.
4/460	你觉得"不干不净，吃了没病"这句话有没有道理？ Do you agree with the statement that a couple of germs won't do you any harm?
5/460	昨晚下了一场大雨，今天早上的空气都被雨水净化了，所以很新鲜！ There was a heavy downpour last night which cleared the air this morning, so the air is fresh!

J | 461 静 still; calm; quiet jìng

Chinese	English	Character codes
安 + 静 = 安静	still + calm = quiet; peaceful; calm	352/461
冷静	calm; cool-headed	068/461
文静	(of a person's manner or character) gentle and quiet	563/461
静坐	to sit quietly; to meditate; to stage a sit-in	461/177
静心	meditation	461/576
心静	tranquil; calm	576/461
动静	sound of activity or people talking; movement	212/461
平静	calm; without turbulence; serene	513/461
清静	tranquil; peaceful; quiet	520/461
静音	silent; mute; quiet;	461/589

Example Sentences

1/462	这里真安静啊！ It seems so peaceful here!
2/462	我打算到山上去过个周末，静静心。 I plan to go to the mountains for a weekend in order to meditate.
3/462	要想身体好，心静很重要。 Being calm is important for good health.
4/462	那个小女孩哭了一会儿，不久就静下来睡着了。 That little girl cried for a while, but soon quieted down and fell asleep.
5/462	弟弟坐在河边等来等去，把手机也静了音，但是鱼还是一点儿动静都没有。 My younger brother sat by the river waiting and waiting, even silenced his mobile phone, but there was no sign of fish whatsoever.

境 border; boundary; place; area jìng 462 J

Chinese	English	Character codes
环 + 境 = 环境	surround + condition = environment; circumstances; surroundings; ambient	430/462
国境	national border; frontier	036/462
境遇	circumstance	462/599
境地 *	circumstance	462/390
境界	realm; state	462/457
家境	family financial situation; family circumstances	053/462
边境	frontier; border	188/462
过境	to pass through a country's territory; transit	225/462
心境	mood; mental state; frame of mind	576/462

注释 Note

* 地 dì=earth; land; ground

Example Sentences

1/461	我喜欢家里有一个舒服的环境。 I like the comfy environment at home.
2/461	我奶奶的病已经到了没有一点儿希望的境地 *。 My grandma's illness has already come to a hopeless condition.
3/461	这家酒店远离市中心，环境非常好。 This hotel is far away from the city centre in very nice surroundings.
4/461	我表弟在家住惯了，所以他花了一段时间才习惯大学的居住环境。 My cousin is used to living at home, so it took him a little time to settle in university.
5/461	虽然他的家境不好，但是他十分努力，最后成了一名出色的新闻记者。 As he comes from a poor family, he has worked very hard eventually to become an excellent journalist.

J 463 久 long time jiǔ

Chinese	English	Character codes
不 + 久 = 不久	not + long = not long (after); before too long; soon; soon after	007/463
多久	how long	023/463
久远	old; ancient; far away	463/332
好久	quite a while	039/463
长久	(for a) long time	194/463
久久	for a very long time	463/463
已久	already a long time	322/463
久留	to stay for a long time	463/492
不久前	not long ago	007/463/099
前不久	not long ago; not long before	099/007/463
天长地 * 久 ; 地 * 久天长	enduring while the world lasts (idiom)	128/194/390/463; 390/463/128/194

注释 Note

* 地 dì=earth; land; ground

Example Sentences

1/463	你刚走不久，老万就回来了。 Lao Wan came back not long after you left.
2/463	你学中文多久了？ How long have you studied Chinese?
3/463	环球戏院新年过后不久就会有新戏了。 A new play is coming soon after the New Year at the Globe Theatre.
4/463	我哥哥去了法国，没多久就在一家大公司找到了一份理想的工作。 Not long after my old brother went to France, he found an ideal job in a big company.
5/463	你多久以前见过他？我刚来学校不久见过他一次，后来就再也没来往了，已经快一年了。 How long ago did you see him? I saw him once soon after I came to the school, then we didn't meet again. It has been about a year now.

酒 wine/alcohol jiǔ 464 J

Chinese	English	Character codes
喝 + 酒 = 喝酒	to drink + wine = to drink (alcohol)	041/464
啤酒	beer	511/464
酒店	wine shop; pub (public house); hotel; restaurant	464/018
下酒菜	food to accompany wine	464/008
红酒	red wine	229/464
白酒	alcohol	180/464
酒馆儿	tavern; pub	464/035/024
酒杯	wine cup; wine glass	464/004
酒会	drinking party; wine reception	464/049
酒吧	bar; pub; saloon	464/179
酒水	beverage; a drink	464/121

Example Sentences

1/464	你喜欢喝酒吗？你喜欢喝什么酒？ Do you like to drink wine? What kind of wine do you like to drink?
2/464	他一口气喝下了一大瓶啤酒。 He knocked back a big bottle of beer.
3/464	啤酒有的是 *，可是白酒不多，大家多喝啤酒吧！ There is plenty of beer, but Chinese liquor is not much, so drink more beer as much as you like!
4/464	除了我们家的小五，大家都去公司年末的酒会了。 Everyone went to the company's year end wine reception except our Xiaowu.
5/464	我喝酒没法跟你比，我只能喝一小杯，喝第二杯就站不住了。 My capacity for alcohol cannot compare with you. I can only drink a small glass, one more glass will make me fall down.

注释 Note

* 有的是 have a lot of

J 465 旧 old/past/by gone/used/former jiù

Chinese	English	Character codes
旧 + 时 = 旧时	old + time = in former times; olden days	465/116
旧友	old friends	465/157
旧事	old affair; former matter	465/281
旧闻	old anecdote; stories passed on from former times	465/564
照旧	as before; as in the past	607/465
旧居	old residence; former home	465/466
又老又旧	outmoded; old-fashioned	596/066/596/465

Example Sentences

1/465	我的电话号没换，还是旧的。 My telephone number is the same as before.
2/465	他把旧汽车卖了，换了一辆自行车。 He sold his old car and bought a bicycle.
3/465	她病了，可是照旧去上班，一天假 * 都没请，真行！ She was ill, but carried on going to work as before and never took a day off. She is super!
4/465	我哥哥把他的旧电视机送给他的同学了。 My older brother gave his old TV to his classmate.
5/465	放假 * 的时候，我想看看书，听听音乐，或者像以往一样和旧时的朋友们聊聊天。 On my holidays, I like to read, listen to music or chat with my old friends as always.

注释 Note

* 假 jià=vacation; holiday

居 to reside/to live jū 466 J

Chinese	English	Character codes
居＋住 ＝居住	to reside + to live = to reside; to dwell; to live in a place; resident in	466/170
居然	unexpectedly; to one's surprise; do so far as to	466/273
起居	everyday life; regular pattern of life	097/466
居所	residence	466/290
居多	to be in the majority	466/023
分居	to separate (married couple); to live apart (of husband and wife, family members)	028/466
同居	to live together	130/466
居心	to harbour (evil) intentions; to be bent on; a tranquil heart or mind	466/576
安居乐业	to live in peace and work happily (idiom)	352/466/246/617

Example Sentences

1/466	搬进这个新楼里的，年轻人居多。 The people who moved in this new building are mostly young people.
2/466	在我居住的大楼旁边有一家小小的面包房。 There is a small bakery next to the building I live in.
3/466	在过去的二十五年里，他们一直同居，昨天男方突然告诉我，他们居然分居了。 During the last twenty-five years, they lived together. Surprisingly the man suddenly told me yesterday they are separated.
4/466	如果你有机会去北京的话，你打算居住多长时间？ If you had an opportunity to go to Beijing, how long would you plan to live there?
5/466	居住在这条小街上离铁路最近的一家人是老张和他的妻子，虽然他们的钱不多，工作也一般，可是两个人的感情很好，是安居乐业的一对儿。 Old Zhang and his wife live in this small street nearest to the railway. Although they don't have much money and are doing ordinary jobs, they have a good relationship and are a couple who live in peace and work happily.

J | 467 句 sentence/MW jù

Chinese	English	Character codes
字 + 句 = 字句	word + sentence = words; expressions; writing	173/467
句子	sentence	467/172
说两句	(say) a few words	122/249/467
一句	a sentence	154/467
一句话	a sentence; in a word; in short	154/467/046
句号	period (punctuation); full stop	467/040

Example Sentences

1/467	对这件事，他打定主意一句话也不说。 He made up his mind not to say a word about this matter.
2/467	这本书写得真好，字字句句都很感人。 This book is very well-written, and the words are very touching.
3/467	这几个句子又长又难，换几句简单的吧。 These sentences are long and difficult, please replace them with some simple ones.
4/467	这个句子被分成了两个分句和三个短语。 This sentence was divided into two clauses and three phrases.
5/467	我知道他现在很难，所以我试图给他写几句话，发个短信；可是我想了好半天还是没写出一个让他能安下心来的句子。 I know that he is in a very difficult situation now, so I tried to write a few words and send him a text message, but I thought about it for a long time, but still couldn't frame a sentence that can comfort him.

据 according to/depend on/occupy/evidence jù 468 J

Chinese	English	Character codes
根 + 据 = 根据	root + according to = according to; based on; on the basis of; basis; foundation	413/468
数据	data; numbers; digital	543/468
据说	it is said that; reportedly	468/122
据点	stronghold; defended military base; base for operations; strategic point; foothold; (market) presence	468/016
单据	receipts; invoices; transaction records	386/468
据报道	according to a report; it is reported that...	468/184/206

Example Sentences

1/468	有力的话语一定是有根有据的。 A powerful statement should be based on facts.
2/468	他总是根据自己的意愿来办事。 He is always doing things according to his own wishes.
3/468	据说谢小平自学了三门外语，真了不起！ It is said that Xie Xiaoping has taught himself three foreign languages. It's amazing!
4/468	据新闻报道说，今明两天北京会有一场大雪。 It is reported that Beijing will have heavy snow today and tomorrow.
5/468	电脑参照数据办事，人根据思考办事，所以常常电脑和人得出的结果很不一样。不过，最后应该还是人来做决定。 Computers do things according to data, and people do things based on their thinking, so computers and people often get very different results. However, in the end, things should be decided by mankind.

J | 469 决 burst/break out/to decide/determine jué

Chinese	English	Character codes
解 + 决 = 解决	to untie + to decide = to settle (a dispute); to resolve; to solve; to dispose of; to dispatch	456/469
决定	to decide (to do sth); to resolve; decision	469/392
决口	burst (of a river bank)	469/475
先决条件	prerequisite; precondition	140/469/295/232
决心	determination; resolution; determined; firm and resolute; to make up one's mind	469/576
表决	to decide by vote; to vote	189/469
决不	not at all; simply (can) not; definitely not	469/007

Example Sentences

1/469	我大姐很早就决心当一名牙医，现在终于实现了她的愿望。 Long since my eldest sister has decided to become a dentist, finally she realized her wish now.
2/469	她的主意已定，决不更 * 换。 Her mind is made up, and she simply won't change her mind.
3/469	别着急，他正在努力解决这个问题呢。 Don't worry, he is trying hard to solve this problem.
4/469	她从不把问题留到第二天解决，所以当天就进行了表决。 She never leaves a problem until the next day, so on the same day we have carried on a vote.
5/469	爸爸思前想后，最后决定自己一个人去南京。 Dad has thought about it carefully and finally decided to go to Nanjing by himself.

注释 Note

* 更 gēng=change

卡 card/to stop/be blocked kǎ; grip/clip/wedge qiǎ 470 K

Chinese	English	Character codes
信 + 用 + 卡 = 信用卡	to trust + use + card = credit card	577/594/470
电话卡	telephone card	017/046/470
关卡 *	customs post; road safety inspection station; outpost	034/470
发 ** 卡 *	hair grip; hair clip	401/470
发 *** 卡	to issue a card	401/470
卡片	card	470/512
卡车	truck	470/101
卡 * 住	to jam; to choke; to clutch; wedge	470/170
卡路里	calorie	470/250/070
房卡	room card	213/470
绿卡	United States permanent resident card; green card	494/470

Example Sentences

1/470	我虽然拿着姐姐的银行 **** 卡呢，可是我不会用。 I have my sister's bank card, but I don't know how to use it.
2/470	生日时，朋友们给我发了电子生日卡。 On my birthday, friends sent me e-cards.
3/470	没想到，我又在第三个问题上卡 * 住了！ Unexpectedly, I'm stuck on the third question again!
4/470	你可以帮我把这张电话卡带给我妈吗？ Can you do me a favour to bring this phone card to my mum?
5/470	今晚吃饭我请客，爱吃什么就点什么，我带着信用卡呢！ Tonight's dinner is on me. Order whatever you like, I have my credit card!

注释 Note

* 卡 qiǎ=grip; clip; wedge (All other examples are pronounced as kǎ.)

** 发 fà=hair

*** 发 fā=distribute; to send out; rise

**** 行 háng=business; trade; line; row; MW

K | 471 康 healthy/well-being/sumptuous/broad/peaceful kāng

Chinese	English	Character codes
健 + 康 = 健康	healthy + healthy = health; healthy	446/471
康复	to recuperate; to recover (health); to convalesce	471/407
安康	peaceful and healthy	352/471
康乐	peace and happiness	471/246
小康	moderately affluent; well-off; period of peace and prosperity	143/471

Example Sentences

1/471	我爷爷身体健康，很少生病。 My grandad is very healthy, and he hardly ever gets ill.
2/471	这家书店里卖很多关于健康方面的书。 This bookshop sells lots of books about health.
3/471	虽然我有些瘦，但是我很健康。 Although I'm thin, I'm very healthy.
4/471	一个人不能什么都有，其实，能有一个健康的身体才是最重要的。 A person cannot own everything. In fact, having a healthy body is the most important thing.
5/471	前一段时间奶奶病得不轻，现在有一位很好的中医大夫在小心地为她调理，奶奶正在慢慢地康复。 Grandma was very unwell a while ago, now a good traditional Chinese medicine doctor is carefully nursing her. As the result, she is slowly recovering.

渴 thirsty kě 472 K

Chinese	English	Character codes
口 + 渴 = 口渴	mouth + thirsty = thirsty	475/472
渴求	to long for; to crave; to greatly desire	472/522
解渴	to quench	456/472
干渴	parched; dry mouth	409/472
渴望	to thirst for; to long for	472/302
远水不解近渴	lit. distant water does not cure present thirst; fig. urgent need; a slow remedy does not address immediate needs	332/121/007/456/236/472

Example Sentences

1/472	你渴吗？我有点儿渴。 Are you thirsty? I'm a bit thirsty.
2/472	天热，为了解渴，他喝了一大杯啤酒。 As the weather is hot, to quench his thirst, he has drunk a large glass of beer.
3/472	孩子们都渴望听到这个故事。 The children were all eager to hear the story.
4/472	多年来笑笑一直渴望着一个能环游世界的假 * 期，现在他终于有机会了。 For years Xiaoxiao has been longing for a trip around the world, and finally he got the opportunity now.
5/472	回到家，我又累又渴，喝了一瓶汽水还不解渴，又喝了一杯绿茶。 When I got home, I was tired and thirsty. A whole bottle of soda still didn't quench my thirst, so I also had a cup of green tea.

注释 Note

* 假 jià=vacation; holiday

K | 473 刻 moment/to cut/engrave kè

Chinese	English	Character codes
时 + 刻 = 时刻	time + moment = moment; constantly; always	116/473
片刻	short period of time; a moment	512/473
刻板	stiff; inflexible; mechanical; stubborn; to cut blocks for painting	473/356
刻意	meticulous; painstaking; deliberate	473/324
每时每刻	at all times; at every moment	255/116/255/473
时时刻刻	at all times	116/116/473/473

Example Sentences

1/473	真奇怪，只片刻，我就对她有了好感。 I liked her at that moment I met her. It's unusual!
2/473	我真不明白你们公司的头头为什么刻意要见我。 I really don't understand why your company's boss deliberately wants to see me.
3/473	虽然儿子年年都从国外回来看我，可是每当看到他的那一刻，我都会心跳加快。 Although my son comes back to see me from abroad each year, every time I see him, my heart is always pounding fast.
4/473	虽然我不在妈妈身边，但我心里每时每刻都想着她。 Although I don't live with my mum, I miss her all the time.
5/473	他一拿到作文题就写了起来，片刻间已经写了满满的一张纸。 As soon as he got the essay title, he promptly started to write and in no time he had filled a whole page.

空 empty/air kōng; vacant/blank kòng 474 K

Chinese	English	Character codes
空 + 调 = 空调	air + adjust = air conditioning	474/552
空间	space	474/231
天空	sky	128/474
空气	air; atmosphere	474/098
空想	daydream; fantasy; fantasise	474/142
上空	overhead; in the sky	108/474
空中	in the sky; in the air	474/168
空话	empty talk; bunk	474/046
空手	empty-handed; unarmed	474/284
空手道	karate	474/284/206
空 * 地 **	vacant land; open space	474/388
高空	high altitude	030/474
空 * 位	empty space; room (for sb)	474/562
空 * 白	blank space	474/180
空前	unprecedented	474/099
真空	vacuum	338/474
空心	hollow	474/576
司空见惯	a common occurrence	285/474/054/420

Example Sentences

1/474	太热了，你能开一下空调吗？ It's too hot! Could you turn on the air conditioner?
2/474	天气太热了，妈妈不得不开开空调。 It's so hot, Mum has to put the air conditioning on.
3/474	这班的班机已经客满了，没有空位子了。 This flight is full. There are no spare seats.
4/474	事故发生的那一刻，我的脑子一片空白，什么也想不起来了。 When the accident happened, my mind went blank, and I couldn't remember anything.
5/474	晚上天空中的星星就像灯火，把天空照得亮亮的。 In the evening, the stars in the sky are like lights that illuminate the sky brightly.

注释 Note

* 空 kòng=vacant (All other examples are pronounced as kōng.)

** 地 dì=earth; land; ground

K 475 口 mouth/hole kǒu

Chinese	English	Character codes
出口	exit; to speak; to export; (of a ship) to leave a port	012/475
人口	population; people	104/475
对口	(of two performers) to speak or sing alternately; to be fit for the purpose of a job or task; (of food) to suit sb's taste	022/475
进口	to import; imported; entrance; inlet (for the intake of air, water etc)	235/475
大口	big mouthful (of food, drink, smoke etc); open mouth; gulping; gobbling; gaping	014/475
口头	oral; verbal	475/554
口号	slogan; catchphrase	475/040
口试	oral examination; oral test	475/282
满口	a mouthful; (of speech) pure; perfect accent; substance of speech all of a kind (e.g. all lies); unreservedly (accept, agree, promise etc)	496/475
可口	tasty; to taste good	242/475
口吃	to stammer; to stutter	475/011
门口	doorway; gate	257/475

Example Sentences

1/475	她喜欢坐在路口看着太阳下山。 She likes to sit at the intersection of the road, watching the sunset.
2/475	这件事他觉得很不好意思，所以没说出口。 He feels very embarrassed about this matter, so he never puts it into words
3/475	你的足球票是进 3 号口的，这是 1 号口。 Your football ticket is in No 3 Gate，this is No 1 Gate.
4/475	你上星期还满口答应 *，怎么这么快就忘了？ You made a definite promise last week, how come you have already forgotten?
5/475	他把她送到家门口，然后一直看着她进了家门才离开。 He walked her to her front door, saw her get in and then left.

注释 Note

* 答应 dāying=promise

哭 to cry kū 476 K

Chinese	English	Character codes
哭 + 声 = 哭声	to cry + sound = sound of weeping	476/533
大哭	to cry loudly	014/476
哭鼻子	to snivel (usually humorous)	476/362/172
哭笑不得	lit. not to know whether to laugh or cry (idiom)	476/310/007/207
放声大哭	to burst into tears; to sob loudly; to bawl	404/533/014/476

Example Sentences

1/476	那个孩子突然大哭起来，可能是找不到妈妈了。 That child suddenly burst into tears. Maybe she cannot find her mum.
2/476	没有人知道她哭着穿过马路向家的方向跑去是为了什么。 She crossed the road crying and ran home, but no one knows why.
3/476	她什么也不说，就在那儿一直哭。 She didn't say a word, just kept crying.
4/476	亮亮边说边哭，说了老半天我都没听明白他要说什么。 Liangliang burst into tears as he spoke, he went on and on and I couldn't understand anything he was saying.
5/476	他爱跟他的姐姐们开一些不太高明 * 的玩笑，常常让她们哭笑不得。 He likes to tease his sisters in an insensible way, therefore, often made them feel unsure whether they should laugh or cry.

注释 Note

* 不太高明 not smart; insensible

K 477 裤 trousers kù

Chinese	English	Character codes
裤 + 子 = 裤子	trousers + suffix = trousers; pants	477/172
短裤	shorts; short pants	394/477
长裤	trousers	194/477
裤长	the length of trousers	477/194
三角裤	briefs; panties	106/449/477
裤腿	trouser leg	477/557
裤脚	the bottom of trousers	477/450
单裤	unlined trousers; summer trousers	386/477
秋裤	long underwear pants	521/477
穿一条裤子	(of male friends) to have been through thick and thin together; to be like family; to share the same view of things	198/152/295/477/172

Example Sentences

1/477	这条裤子真漂亮！ What a smart pair of trousers!
2/477	夏天又来了，穿短裤的时候到了。 Summer is here again. It's time for wearing shorts.
3/477	弟弟又长高了，他的裤子又短了。 My brother has grown again. His trousers are now too short again.
4/477	他穿着黄色的运动衫和新的黑色的裤子，看起来很舒服！ He wore a yellow sports shirt and a new pair of black trousers which make him look nice.
5/477	每个星期六我都会把裤子和衬衫拿到洗衣店去干洗。 Every Saturday, I'll take my trousers and shirts to the dry cleaners to have them cleaned.

筷 chopstick kuài 478 K

Chinese	English	Character codes
筷 + 子 = 筷子	chopstick + suffix = chopsticks	478/172
公筷	serving chopsticks	221/478
一双筷子	a pair of chopsticks	152/545/478/172
银筷子	silver chopsticks	590/478/172
一根筷子	one chopstick	152/412/478/172
一把筷子	a few chopsticks	152/353/478/172

Example Sentences

1/478	饭桌上还少一双筷子和一只碗。 There are still a pair of chopsticks and a bowl lacking on the dinner table.
2/478	真好玩，这是我第一次用筷子吃饭。 It's fun, this is the first time I use chopsticks to eat.
3/478	请你教我怎么用筷子好吗？ Can you please teach me how to use chopsticks?
4/478	你筷子用得真好，是在哪儿学的？ You are very good at using chopsticks. Where did you learn that?
5/478	这把筷子七长八短，颜色也不一样，我们怎么用啊？ These chopsticks are not the same length and even the colours are not the same. How can we use them?

L 479 蓝 blue lán

Chinese	English	Character codes
蓝 + 色 = 蓝色	blue + colour = blue	479/277
蓝天	blue sky	479/128
蓝本	blueprint; source material on which later works are based	479/006
蓝图	blueprint	479/556
蓝皮书	an official report	479/510/119
蓝牙	Bluetooth	479/582

Example Sentences

1/479	弟弟的梦想是长大后能飞上蓝天。 My younger brother has a dream of flying a plane when he grows up.
2/479	我喜欢蓝色，每当看到蓝色的天空，心情就特别好。 I like blue. Whenever I see the blue sky, it makes me happy.
3/479	我们家除了我妹妹以外都喜欢蓝色。 My family all like blue apart from my younger sister.
4/479	小鸟在蓝天里越飞越高，很快就成了一个小黑点了。 The little bird is flying higher and higher in the blue sky. It quickly becomes a black dot.
5/479	今天姐姐穿着她新买的那条蓝色裙子去参加公司的新年舞会了。 My sister wore her newly purchased blue skirt to the company's New Year party.

礼 gift/courtesy/ceremony lǐ 480 L

Chinese	English	Character codes
礼 + 物 = 礼物	gift + things = gift; present	480/565
洗礼	baptism	309/480
礼遇	courtesy; deferential treatment; polite reception	480/599
典礼	celebration; ceremony	391/480
非礼	insolence; harassment; indecent assault	214/480
礼节	etiquette	480/454
行礼	to salute; to make one's salutation	422/480
礼服	ceremonial robe; formal attire (dinner suit, evening gown etc)	480/029

Example Sentences

1/480	这个礼物是送给你小姨的。 This present is for your younger auntie.
2/480	老板决定典礼一结束就分发礼物。 The boss has decided to distribute the gifts as soon as the ceremony is over.
3/480	我叔叔假 * 期回来了，他给家里所有人都带了礼物。 My uncle has brought presents back from his holiday for everyone at home.
4/480	这是我的一点儿小意思，送给你做生日礼物吧。 This is just a small token from me for your birthday.
5/480	今天，我们班的同学准备了很多礼物去医院看望住院的万老师。 Today, our classmates have taken many gifts to go and visit Teacher Wan in the hospital.

注释 Note

* 假 jià=vacation; holiday

L | 481 李 plum/a popular surname lǐ

Chinese	English	Character codes
行＋李＝行李	to walk + a surname = luggage	422/481
行李箱	suitcase; baggage compartment; overhead bin; (car) trunk; boot	422/481/571
一件行李	a piece of luggage	152/232/422/481
李子	plum	481/172

Example Sentences

1/481	把你的行李放下来，坐一会儿吧！ Put down your luggage and have a seat!
2/481	把你的行李条给我，我去给你拿行李。 Give me your baggage tag, and I'll get it for you.
3/481	你的行李会在明天下午五点送到你家。 Your luggage will be delivered to your house tomorrow afternoon at five.
4/481	每次出门，我妈妈总是带很多没用的行李。 My Mum always takes lots of useless luggage every time she goes away.
5/481	今年我家院子里的李子树开满了花，希望几个月以后，会结满树的李子。 This year, the plum tree in my yard is full of flowers. I hope that after a few months, the tree will be full of plums.

理 reason/logic/sense lǐ 482 L

Chinese	English	Character codes
道 + 理 = 道理	way + reason = reason; argument; sense; principle; basis; justification	206/482
理想	an ideal; a dream; ideal; perfect	482/142
心理	mental; psychological	576/482
情理	reason; sense	270/482
常理	common sense; conventional reasoning and morals	195/482
办理	to handle; to transact; to conduct	357/482
条理	arrangement; order; tidiness	295/482
地 * 理	geography	390/482
物理	physics; physical	565/482
料理	to arrange; to handle; to cook; cuisine; art of cooking	490/482
经理	manager; director	237/482
有条有理	properly and logically arranged	158/295/158/482

Example Sentences

1/482	这事是他一手办理的，没有别人帮忙。 He dealt with this matter all on his own without others' help.
2/482	她写的报告用词简洁，有条有理。 The report she wrote is concise and well-organised.
3/482	弟弟出国前的成绩不是很理想，现在他进步很大。 My brother's school grades were poor before he went abroad, and now he has progressed a lot.
4/482	这本书对刚开始学法语的人来说是最理想的了。 This book is ideal for French beginners.
5/482	新房子的地 * 点虽不算理想，但新居本身我相当满意。 The location of the new house is not ideal, but I'm quite happy with its building.

注释 Note

* 地 dì=earth; land; ground

L 483 力 power/strength lì

Chinese	English	Character codes
努 + 力 = 努力	to strive + strength = great effort; to strive; to try hard	505/483
能力	capability; ability	088/483
影响力	influence; impact	156/572/483
实力	strength	534/483
动力	power; motion; propulsion; force	212/483
有力	powerful; forceful; vigorous	158/483
大力	energetically; vigorously	014/483
物力	physical resources (as oppose to labour resources)	565/483
人力	manpower; labour power	104/483
想象力	conception; imagination	142/574/483
力求	to make every effort to; striving to do one's best	483/522
力图	to try hard to; to strive to	483/556
得 (dé) 力	able; capable; competent; efficient	207/483
身体力行	to practise what one preaches	279/294/483/421
力不从心	less capable than desirable; not as strong as one would wish; the spirit is willing but the fresh is weak	483/007/201/576

Example Sentences

1/483	因为快过节了，街边卖花的男孩在努力地叫卖。 As the festival is approaching, the flower boy is trying hard to sell his flowers at the roadside.
2/483	他看上去是那么有能力，那么有信心。 He looked so competent and confident.
3/483	他哥哥得到经理的重视以后，工作更加努力了。 Since his brother gained recognition from his manager, he has worked even harder.
4/483	有些学校常常根据学生们的能力把他们分成不同的班。 Some schools often divides students into classes according to their ability.
5/483	小李学习画画儿不是不努力，而是力不从心，更重要的是没有什么想象力，所以他画的画儿很刻板，一点儿都不动人。 It is not that Xiao Li doesn't work hard to learn drawing, but that he couldn't reach the level as he would wish. What is more important is that he has no imagination. Therefore, his paintings are very rigid and not touching at all.

历 to experience/to go through lì 484 L

Chinese	English	Character codes
历 + 史 = 历史	experience + history = history	484/535
经历	experience; to experience; to go through	237/484
历来	always; throughout (a period of time); (of) all-time	484/065
学历	educational background; academic qualification	150/484
历时	to last; to take (time); period; diachronic	484/116
历经	to experience; to go through	484/237
来历	history; antecedents; origin	065/484
日历	calendar	275/484
月历	monthly calendar	162/484
年历	yearly calendar	090/484
简历	curriculum vitae; résumé; biographical notes	445/484
历年来	over the years; bygone years	484/090/065
游历	to tour; to travel	328/484

Example Sentences

1/484	今天历史课的作业是什么？ What's today's history homework?
2/484	我叔叔这个人经历多，见识也多。 My uncle is a man of wide knowledge and experience.
3/484	一定不要打开来历不明的电子邮件和附件。 Do not open unknown emails and attachments.
4/484	昨天来了几个新同事，可是他们的来历，除了经理谁都不清楚。 A few new colleagues came yesterday, but nobody knew them except the manager.
5/484	我哥哥游历回来后，给我们讲了很多他的有趣的经历。 After coming back from his travels, my brother recounted many interesting experiences.

L | 485 脸 face/reputation liǎn

Chinese	English	Character codes
脸 + 蛋 + 儿 = 脸蛋儿	face + egg + word suffix = cheek; face	485/204/024
脸色	complexion; facial expression	485/277
脸红	to blush	485/229
笑脸	smiling face	310/485
满脸	across one's whole face; from ear to ear	496/485
洗脸	wash the face	309/485
一张 * 脸	one face	152/606/485
没脸	ashamed	078/485
不要脸	to have no sense of shame; shameless	007/319/485
变脸 **	face changing; suddenly turn hostile	364/485

Example Sentences

1/485	她一大声说话就脸红。 She blushes every time she speaks loudly.
2/485	妈妈的脸上写满了关心。 Mum's face shows great care.
3/485	妹妹的小脸蛋儿红得像苹果。 My younger sister's little cheeks are as red as apples.
4/485	你的脸色很不好，是不是生病了？ You don't look well. Are you ill?
5/485	人家 *** 几句话就把他说得脸上下不来了。 He was visibly embarrassed by a few words said by others.

注释 Note

* 张，MW

** 变脸 "Face Changing" is an ancient Chinese dramatic art that is part of the more general Sichuan opera. Performers wear brightly coloured costumes and move to quick, dramatic music. They also wear vividly coloured masks, typically depicting well-known characters from the opera, which they change from one face to another almost instantaneously with the swipe of a fan, a movement of the head, or wave of the hand.

*** 人家，other people

练 practise/train/exercise/drill liàn 486 L

Chinese	English	Character codes
练 + 习 = 练习	exercise+ review = to practise	486/136
练声	vocalize; train one's voice	486/533
老练	experienced; seasoned; sophisticated	066/486
练笔	to practise writing	486/187
教练	coach; instructor; trainer	233/486

Example Sentences

1/486	学校的手球教练是个东北人。 The school's handball coach is from northeast China.
2/486	对不起，我得出去，在家里我没法儿练声。 Sorry, I have to go out. I can't practise singing at home.
3/486	下个月就要书法比赛了，这一段时间你得回家好好练一练。 The calligraphic competition will be held next month. You need to go home and practise for the period.
4/486	书法需要经常练习才能写好。 Calligraphy needs constant practice in order to write well.
5/486	你们还练吗？不练的话，我就回家了。 Are you still going to practise? If not, I'm going home.

L | 487 炼 refine/smelt liàn

Chinese	English	Character codes
锻 + 炼 = 锻炼	forge + refine = exercise; training	396/487
提炼	to extract; to refine; to purify	550/487
喜欢锻炼	to like to exercise	137/047/396/487
常锻炼	to exercise regularly	195/396/487
炼铁	smelt iron	396/553

Example Sentences

1/487	我天天都锻炼身体。 I exercise every day.
2/487	他不喜欢锻炼。 He doesn't like exercise.
3/487	爸爸经常锻炼，所以身体很好。 Dad exercises regularly, so his health is very good.
4/487	每天早上走路上班也是一种很好的锻炼方法。 Walking to work every morning is a good way to exercise.
5/487	今天下午你想不想和我一起去锻炼? Would you like to go and exercise with me this afternoon?

辆 MW for vehicles liàng 488 L

Chinese	English	Character codes
车 + 辆 = 车辆	vehicle + quantity measuring = vehicle	010/488
机动车辆	motor vehicle	051/212/010/488
两辆	two vehicles	152/488
几辆	several vehicles; How many vehicles?	052/488
数十辆	dozens of vehicles	543/114/488

Example Sentences

1/488	弟弟刚买了一辆新车。 My brother just bought a new car.
2/488	那辆车的颜色很漂亮。 That car's colour is very nice.
3/488	我家还有几辆旧的自行车，虽然旧，还能骑。 There are a few old bicycles in my house. Although they are old, they are still rideable.
4/488	你的那辆车呢？坏了吗？好久没见你开了。 Where is your car? Is it broken? I haven't seen you driving it for a long time.
5/488	我妹妹每天上学要换三辆公共汽车才能到学校。 My sister has to change buses three times to get to school every day.

L | 489 聊 chat/merely/just/slightly liáo

Chinese	English	Character codes
聊 + 天 + 儿 = 聊天儿	chat + sky+ word suffix = to chat; to gossip	489/128/024
聊天室	chat room	489/128/283
聊一聊	have a chat	489/152/489
聊不下去了	can't continue the chat any further	489/007/139/102/067
聊表心意	just a token of gratitude; just to show my appreciation	489/189/576/324

Example Sentences

1/489	我们几个人常在一块儿聊天儿。 A few of us often have a chat together.
2/489	晚饭后我们聊一聊吧。 Let's have a chat after the dinner.
3/489	不要再聊了，已经很晚了。 Stop chatting, it's very late.
4/489	你们在聊什么呢？这么开心！ What are you talking about? You look so happy.
5/489	我几年没见他了，我们聊起过去的事聊个没完 *，聊了一下午都不觉得累。 I had not seen him for years, we were chatting away about the old times for the whole afternoon and we didn't feel tired.

注释 **Note**

* 聊个没完，to chat endlessly

料 stuff/material/anticipate liào 490 L

Chinese	English	Character codes
衣 + 料 = 衣料	cloth + material = clothing material	153/490
笑料	laughable thing	310/490
饮料	drinks; beverage	591/490
料酒	cooking wine	490/464
料理	to manage, to arrange; art of cooking	490/482
料想	to suppose, to presume	490/142
意料	expected	324/490
料到	to anticipate, to expect	490/205
料不到	didn't anticipate; unexpected	490/007/205

Example Sentences

1/490	你想喝什么饮料？ What do you want to drink?
2/490	这块衣料的颜色真鲜亮。 The colour of this clothing material is very bright.
3/490	她这次的考试成绩是出乎意料的好。 Her results are well over expectation for this exam.
4/490	爸爸的料理小有名气，常常有朋友来家里吃饭。 Dad's cooking is well-known. Friends often come round for dinner.
5/490	她把家里的事儿料理得有条有理。 She is very organised in her home life.

L | 491 邻 neighbour/beside lín

Chinese	English	Character codes
邻 + 居 = 邻居	adjacent + live = neighbour	491/466
邻近	nearby	491/236
邻里	neighbourhood	491/070
邻国	neighbouring countries	491/036

Example Sentences

1/491	小王的邻居有一只大黑猫。 Xiao Wang's neighbour has a big black cat.
2/491	中国的东邻除了日本还有别的国家。 China has other countries to the east besides Japan.
3/491	我们和方家做了二十年的邻居了，我们的关系很好。 Fang's family has been our neighbour for twenty years, and we have a good relationship.
4/491	小红一直帮助邻居王奶奶做家务。 Xiaohong is always helping her neighbour Grandma Wang with her housework.
5/491	邻家的小女孩跟我妹妹是同班同学。 Next door's little girl and my sister are in the same class.

留 stay/keep/remain/reserve liú 492 L

Chinese	English	Character codes
留 + 学 = 留学	stay + study = to study abroad	492/150
留学生	oversea student	492/150/112
留意	be careful; keep one's eyes open; be cautious about; pay attention to; to be mindful	492/324
留后路	keep a way open for retreat; leave a way out	492/576
留下	to leave behind; stay (for); detain; keep; not to let (sb) go	492/139
居留	residence; reside	466/492

Example Sentences

1/492	小谢明年秋天去外国留学。 Xiao Xie is going to study abroad in the autumn of next year.
2/492	是去还是留？请你自己决定。 Go or stay? You decide by yourself.
3/492	学校的信息交换板上都是有关找工作的信息。 The school message board is full of job information.
4/492	这是新鲜的蛋糕，我给你留了一块。 This is freshly baked cake. I've saved a piece for you.
5/492	下课后你能留下来帮我把今天的笔记看一下吗？ After the lesson, can you stay behind and help me have a look at today's notes?

L | 493 楼 storied building/tower/story/floor lóu

Chinese	English	Character codes
城 + 楼 = 城楼	city + building = city gate tower	376/493
茶楼	teahouse	009/493
钟楼	bell tower	169/493
高楼	high building	030/493
楼道	corridor; passageway	493/206
楼市	real estate market	493/537
楼梯	stairs	493/549
办公大楼	office building	357/221/014/493
五角大楼	the Pentagon	133/449/014/493
楼上；楼下	upstairs; downstairs	493/108; 493/139
上楼；下楼	to go upstairs; to go downstairs	108/493; 139/493

Example Sentences

1/493	这个中等城市里有很多高楼。 There are many high-rise buildings in this medium-sized city.
2/493	昨天楼上的老张搬走了。 Lao Zhang who lived upstairs has moved out yesterday.
3/493	爷爷每天下午去茶楼，一边儿喝茶一边儿听说书的人说故事。 Grandad goes to the teahouse every afternoon to drink tea and listen to story-telling.
4/493	那家酒店的二楼有一家很不错的咖啡馆儿。 There is a very nice coffee shop on the second floor of that hotel.
5/493	我叔叔家在七楼，可是没有电梯，天天得上下楼梯，真累人。 My uncle's flat is on the seventh floor. There are no lifts, so he has to go up and down the stairs every day. It is very tiring.

绿 green lǜ 494 L

Chinese	English	Character codes
绿 + 色 = 绿色	green + colour = green	494/277
绿茶	green tea	494/009
绿灯	green light	494/389
红绿灯	traffic lights	229/494/389
绿地 *	green area or land	494/390
绿树	green tree	494/542
绿化	make a place green by planting trees	494/427

注释 Note

* 地 dì=earth; land; ground

Example Sentences

1/494	请注意：红灯不可以走，绿灯才能走！ Please pay attention: Red light means stop, green light means go!
2/494	我最喜欢的颜色是绿色。 My favourite colour is green.
3/494	街口新开张的小超市里只卖绿色健康的东西。 The newly opened shop at the street corner only sells green and healthy products.
4/494	今天天气特别好，所以午休的时间办公楼前面的那块绿地 * 上坐满了人。 The weather is very sunny, therefore, there are lots of people sitting on the green in front of the office building during the lunch break.
5/494	学校门口那条路上的那个红绿灯坏了，所以行人过马路很不方便。 The traffic light outside the school gate is broken, so it is very inconvenient for pedestrians.

M | 495 马 horse mǎ

Chinese	English	Character codes
马 + 上 = 马上	horse + on = at once; immediately; on horseback	495/108
上马	to get on a horse; to mount; start a project	108/495
下马	to dismount from a horse; (fig) to abandon (a project)	139/495
马车	carriage; cart	495/010
骑马	to ride a horse	517/495
人马	troops; group of people	104/495
马夫	groom	495/216
赛马	horse race; horse racing	527/495
一马当先	be in the forefront; take the lead	152/495/388/140

Example Sentences

1/495	电影马上就要结束了，我们再等等吧。 Shall we wait for a while? The movie is nearly finished.
2/495	小李马上就到了，我们再等她一会儿吧。 Xiao Li is almost here. Let's wait a bit longer.
3/495	她很不简单，从五岁开始就学习骑马了。 She is amazing and started learning to ride when she was five years old.
4/495	他真是一个工作认真的人，每天都把马场打扫得干干净净。 He really takes his work seriously, and makes sure the stable is well cleaned every day.
5/495	马姓是中国较为常见的姓，在《百家姓》* 中是第五十二位。 The surname Ma is a very common surname in China. It ranks the 52nd in *Hundred Family Surnames*.

注释 **Note**

* The *Hundred Family Surnames* is a classic Chinese book containing common Chinese surnames. The book was composed in the early Song Dynasty (960-1279). It originally contained 411 surnames, and was later expanded to 504.

满 satisfied/full/fill/filled/completely mǎn 496 M

Chinese	English	Character codes
满 + 意 = 满意	full + desire = satisfied; pleased	496/324
满足	to satisfy; to meet (the needs of)	496/346
不满意	dissatisfied	007/496/324
不满	resentful; discontented	007/496
满口	a mouthful; unreservedly	496/475
满目	full of	496/500
满天飞	to rush around everywhere	496/128/027
自满	complacent; self-satisfied	616/496
满月	full moon; baby's one-month old birthday	496/162
满分	full marks	496/028
心满意足	perfectly contented	576/496/324/346

Example Sentences

1/496	我对你做的这件事很不满意。 I'm not happy with what you have done.
2/496	这次数学考试小朵得了满分。 Xiao Duo got full marks for this maths test.
3/496	我选的这间茶馆儿你还满意吗？ Are you happy with the teahouse I picked?
4/496	今晚的天空真漂亮，满天都是星星。 The sky is so pretty tonight, full of stars.
5/496	最近太忙了，能放两天假 * 我已经心满意足了。 I've been very busy recently. I'm perfectly happy to have two days off.

注释 Note

* 假 jià=vacation; holiday

M | 497 冒 emit/give off/send up/crop up/risk/brave mào

Chinese	English	Character codes
感 + 冒 = 感冒	sense + emit = cold; flu	410/497
冒雨	brave the rain	497/160
冒火	get angry; flare up	497/050
冒名	pose under a false name	497/083
假冒	pretend to be; palm off a fake as genuine	443/497
火冒三丈	to get really angry	050/497/106/335

Example Sentences

1/497	看，从草地 * 上冒出了一朵朵的小黄花。 Look, there are lots of little yellow flowers cropping up from the grass.
2/497	我感冒了，今天不能去上班了。 I have a cold so I won't be able to go to work today.
3/497	这个人假冒他人的名字，轻易地 ** 就走进了会议中心场地 *。 Posing under someone else's name, this person managed to get into the conference centre easily.
4/497	他的意见把她气得火冒三丈。 She was seething with rage at his remarks.
5/497	工人们冒着雨把舞台的音响调好了。 The builders braved the rain to fix the sound on the stage.

注释 Note

* 地 dì=earth; land; ground

** 地 de=grammatical code

帽 hat/cap mào 498 M

Chinese	English	Character codes
帽 + 子 = 帽子	hat + (noun) suffix = hat	498/172
草帽	straw hat	368/498
礼帽	bowler hat	480/498
笔帽	the cap of a pen, pencil or writing brush	187/498
衣帽间	cloakroom	153/498/231
方帽	square academic cap	403/498

Example Sentences

1/498	你找的人在酒店的衣帽间工作。 The person you are looking for works in the hotel's cloakroom.
2/498	弟弟最爱听小红帽的故事了。 Little Red Riding Hood is my younger brother's favourite story.
3/498	你的帽子找着了吗? Did you find your hat?
4/498	在工地 * 上，用安全帽是必需的。 A safety helmet is a must on a construction site.
5/498	下车时我把帽子忘在火车上了，等我想起来的时候火车已经开走了。 I left my hat on the train when I got off, and the train drove off just as I realised.

注释 Note

* 地 dì=earth; land; ground

M 499 末 final/end/last/tip mò

Chinese	English	Character codes
周 + 末 = 周末	week + end = weekend	613/499
末日	doomsday	499/275
岁末	end of the year	124/499
末了	finally	499/067
末班车	last bus/train	499/182/010
始末	from the beginning to the end; the whole story	280/499

Example Sentences

1/499	这种果树在每年夏末结果。 This kind of fruit tree produces fruit at the end of summer.
2/499	他末了还是同意了大家的意见。 He agreed with everybody in the end.
3/499	我们每个周末都去健身房打网球。 We go to the gym to play tennis every weekend.
4/499	爸爸三月末才回山东。 Dad will only come back to Shandong at the end of March.
5/499	总算没白 * 跑，我刚好坐上了去市中心的末班公共汽车。 I didn't run for nothing. I just got on the last bus to the city centre.

注释 Note

* 白 for nothing; 白忙了半天 go through a lot of trouble for nothing; 白 free of charge 白看戏 go to a theatre free of charge.

目 eye/item mù 500 M

Chinese	English	Character codes
面 + 目 = 面目	face + eye = appearance	081/500
节目	programme	454/500
过目	look over	225/500
目前	present	500/099
数目	number; amount	543/500
名目	items	083/500
目的	destination; purpose	500/015
耳目	eyes and ears; one who spies for sb else	400/500
耳聪目明	have good eyesight and hearing; (fig) have one's wits about one	400/382/500/082
历历在目	come clearly into view; to flood back	484/484/163/500

Example Sentences

1/500	没有别的办法，所以这是目前最好的选择。 This is the best choice at the moment and there is no other way.
2/500	学习的目的是为了长知识。 The purpose of studying is to gain knowledge.
3/500	我一到东京就感到耳目一新。 I found myself in an entirely new world the moment I arrived in Tokyo.
4/500	他耳聪目明，极 * 少上当。 He has his wits about him and is rarely fooled.
5/500	你给我的数目是错的，要重 ** 新算一次。 The amount you gave me is wrong. You need to calculate it again.

注释 Note

* 极 jí=extreme

** 重 chóng=repeat; again; overlap; layer

N | 501 拿 pick up/take/hold/seize/capture ná

Chinese	English	Character codes
拿 + 笔 = 拿笔	take + pen = take pen; hold pen	501/187
拿主意	make a decision; make up one's mind	501/614/324
拿手	expert; be good at	501/284
拿不出手	not be presentable	501/007/012/284
拿不准	be in doubt; not sure of; feel uncertain	501/007/344

Example Sentences

1/501	他从家里拿来了一箱啤酒。 He brought a case of beer from home.
2/501	我一个人拿不了这么多东西。 I can't carry all these things on my own.
3/501	别的饭菜我不会做，只有做面条还拿手。 I can't cook anything, but I'm good at making noodles.
4/501	这道题我还真拿不准，要不我去问问老师？ I'm not sure about this question. Shall I ask the teacher?
5/501	A: 你能拿多少行李？ B: 我能拿多少就拿多少。 A: How much luggage can you carry? B: As much as I can.

南 south nán 502 N

Chinese	English	Character codes
南 + 方 = 南方	south + square = the south	502/403
南半球	the Southern Hemisphere	502/358/272
南极	South Pole	502/437
南瓜	pumpkin	502/223
南下	to go south	502/139
南站	the south station	502/166

Example Sentences

1/502	中国南方的雨季很长。 The monsoon in south China is quite long.
2/502	他的弟弟考上了南开大学。 His younger brother got into Nankai University.
3/502	北方不比南方，三四月老 * 刮风。 Unlike the south, the north is very windy in March and April.
4/502	天南地 ** 北，我哪儿都想去。 I want to go to whatever the places, far and wide.
5/502	那只船在慢慢地 *** 向东南方向前行。 That boat is moving slowly southeastward.

注释 Note

* 老 lǎo=always

** 地 dì=earth; land; ground

*** 地 de=grammatical code

N | 503 难 difficult/hard/troublesome nán; disaster/adversity/misfortune/scold nàn

Chinese	English	Character codes
难 + 过 = 难过	difficult + pass = to feel bad; to feel unwell; to be difficult (of life)	503/225
难听	unpleasant to hear; vulgar; offensive	503/129
难题	difficult problem	503/293
难看	ugly; unsightly	503/062
难得	seldom; rare; hard to come by	503/207
遇难 *	to be killed; die in an accident	599/503
难忘	unforgettable; memorable	503/561
万事开头难	the first step is the hardest (idiom)	559/281/097/554/503

Example Sentences

1/503	我觉得这件事很难说哪种是最好的方法。 I think it's very hard to say what the best solution to this matter is.
2/503	看见她一天都不开心的样子，我心里很难过。 I feel bad seeing her upset all day.
3/503	你的脸色很难看，一定是有哪儿不舒服吧？ You don't look well. Are you feeling unwell?
4/503	这音乐真难听，把它关了吧。 This music is unpleasant. Please turn it off.
5/503	大家都被这个问题难住了。 Everyone is stuck on this question.

注释 Note

* 难 nàn=disaster; adversity; misfortune; scold (All other examples are pronounced as nán.)

鸟 bird niǎo 504 N

Chinese	English	Character codes
小 + 鸟 = 小鸟	small + bird = little bird	143/504
鸟儿	bird	504/024
鸟市	bird market	504/537
鸟语花香	lit. singing birds and fragrant flowers; fig. the intoxication of a beautiful spring day	504/159/426/570

Example Sentences

1/504	公园里鸟语花香，一片生机。 The park is alive with singing birds and blossoming flowers.
2/504	一大早小鸟儿们就在树上唱起歌来了。 The birds are starting to sing in the trees in the early morning.
3/504	看，有数十只鸟正在飞往南方去过冬。 Look! A lot of birds are flying to south China for the winter.
4/504	小猫一来，树上的鸟儿就都飞走了。 As soon as the little cat came, all the birds in the tree flew away.
5/504	在这个远离城市的大山里，从早到晚都是鸟、鸡和狗叫声。 In this mountain far from the city, birds, roosters, and dogs are making sounds from morning till night.

N | 505 努 make an effort/exert effort/strive/to pout/bulge nǔ

Chinese	English	Character codes
努 + 力 = 努力	make an effort + strength = make an effort	505/483
努嘴	to pout; to stick out one's lips	505/618
共同努力	to work together; to collaborate	222/130/505/483
好好努力	to try harder; to redouble one's effort	039/505/483

Example Sentences

1/505	他不很聪明，但是一直很努力。 He is not very smart but always makes an effort.
2/505	真好，我们的努力开始有了成绩。 Our efforts are beginning to show results. It's really good.
3/505	她正在努力想办法，我相信这个难题会得到解决。 She is trying hard to solve this problem and I believe the problem will be solved.
4/505	你只要现在好好努力，明年就能考上好的大学。 As long as you work hard now, you will get into a good university next year.
5/505	让我们共同努力把学校办好。 Let's work together to run the school well.

爬 climb/crawl/creep pá 506 P

Chinese	English	Character codes
爬 + 山 = 爬山	climb + mountain = climb	506/530
爬行	creep	506/422
爬泳	the crawl	506/327
吃里爬外	live off one person while secretly helping another	011/070/506/297

Example Sentences

1/506	山不高，他们一口气就爬上去了。 The hill is not high, so they climbed up in one go.
2/506	这双鞋是便鞋，爬山时不能穿。 These shoes are casual shoes, and they are not suitable for climbing.
3/506	一口气爬上八楼的她已经上气不接下气了，没有力气再接着做这事了。 She is out of breath after climbing up to the eighth floor, so she has no energy to do the work.
4/506	对不起，今天没有电梯，我们得爬六层楼梯。 Sorry, there is no lift, so we have to climb six stories of stairs.
5/506	这个小孩儿居然爬上了那张高桌子，真行！ This little boy climbed up onto that tall table. He is amazing!

P | 507 怕 afraid/fear/dread/unable to endure pà

Chinese	English	Character codes
害 + 怕 = 害怕	harm + afraid = to be afraid	421/507
可怕	awful; dreadful; formidable; frightful; horrible	242/507
哪怕	even; even if; even though; no matter how	085/507
怕生	fear of strangers; to be shy	507/112
生怕	afraid; extremely nervous; to avoid; so as not to	112/507
怕事	timid; to be afraid of getting into trouble	507/281

Example Sentences

1/507	我怕这么做会不给他面子。 I'm afraid doing in this way will make him feel ashamed.
2/507	他很担心，但不害怕。 He is worried but not afraid.
3/507	我害怕得感冒，所以多穿了一件衣服。 I wore extra clothing as I was afraid of catching a cold.
4/507	她小心地把花瓶包了起来，生怕把它打坏了。 She wrapped up the vase carefully for fear that it could get damaged.
5/507	哪怕有再多的难处，我也要坚持到最后。 I will stick to the end no matter how difficult it is.

盘 plate/tray/dish/coil/check/transfer/MW pán 508 P

Chinese	English	Character codes
盘 + 子 = 盘子	plate + suffix = plate	508/172
茶盘	tea tray	009/172
水果盘	fruit plate	121/037/172
算盘	abacus	546/508
盘算	to plot; to scheme; to calculate	508/546
盘问	to interrogate; to cross-examine; to inquire	508/304
开盘	to commence trading (stock market)	061/508

Example Sentences

1/508	这个茶盘子里有四个小茶杯。 There are four little tea cups on this tray.
2/508	妈妈说盘子里都是好吃的。 Mum said the plate is full of delicious food.
3/508	这个算盘是爷爷留给我的。 This abacus was given to me by my grandad.
4/508	他不得不自已先盘算一下再做决定。 He has to calculate first before making the decision.
5/508	吃完饭请你把盘子洗了。 You wash the dishes after the meal.

P | 509 胖 fat/stout pàng

Chinese	English	Character codes
胖 + 子 = 胖子	fat + suffix = fatty	509/172
发胖	to put on weight	401/509
胖乎乎	chubby; plump; pudgy	509/424/424

Example Sentences

1/509	你最近发胖了吧？ Have you put on weight recently?
2/509	他越来越胖了。 He is getting fatter and fatter.
3/509	他比过去胖多了。 He is much fatter than before.
4/509	那个小孩儿胖乎乎的，十分可爱。 That kid is chubby and very cute.
5/509	她在电话里告诉我，她比以前更胖了。 She told me on the telephone that she is even fatter than before.

皮 skin/cover/leather/naughty pí 510 P

Chinese	English	Character codes
皮 + 鞋 = 皮鞋	leather + shoes = leather shoes	510/575
调皮	naughty; mischievous	552/510
皮球	(leather) ball	510/272
皮包	handbag; briefcase	510/359
眼皮	eyelid	316/510

Example Sentences

1/510	这双皮鞋真好看。 This pair of leather shoes looks nice.
2/510	孩子们在草地 * 上踢皮球呢。 Children are kicking the ball on the grass.
3/510	我哥哥的儿子很调皮。 My brother's son is naughty.
4/510	已经很晚了，我的眼皮越来越重了。 It's getting late. I'm feeling sleepy.
5/510	我跑了三家店才买到这双皮鞋。 I went round three shops before buying this pair of leather shoes.

注释 Note

* 地 dì=earth; land; ground

P 511 啤 beer pí

Chinese	English	Character codes
啤 + 酒 = 啤酒	beer + alcohol = beer	511/464
啤酒节	Beer Festival	511/464/454
啤酒花	hops	041/511/464
黑啤	stout	511/464/004
生啤	draft beer	112/511

Example Sentences

1/511	我不爱喝啤酒。 I don't like to drink beer.
2/511	他一口气喝了两大杯啤酒。 He drank two big glasses of beer in one go.
3/511	她只要一喝啤酒就会脸红。 Her face gets red when she drinks beer.
4/511	啤酒有的是，大家放开喝吧。 There is plenty of beer, drink as much as you want.
5/511	爸爸喜欢一边喝啤酒一边和朋友聊天。 Dad likes to drink beer while chatting with his friends.

片 piece/slice/flake/part of place/a vast sheet piàn; Orally Rhotic piān 512 P

Chinese	English	Character codes
照 + 片 = 照片	photo + piece = photograph	607/512
图片	image; photograph	556/512
影片	film; movie	156/512
短片	short film; video clip	394/512
一片	a piece; one slice; a vast sheet	152/512
名片	(business) card	083/512
片面	one-sided	512/081
片 * 子	film; disc	512/172
照片 * 儿	photo (colloquial usage)	607/512/024

Example Sentences

1/512	大多数旧影片都是黑白的。 Most old movies are black and white.
2/512	这张照片 * 儿是去年在法国照的。 This photo was taken in France last year.
3/512	下雪了，一片片雪花在天空中飞舞。 It's snowing, snowflakes are floating all over the sky.
4/512	你从哪儿拿到这么多图片？ Where did you get all these photographs?
5/512	这一大片树木和房子都被大火给烧了。 All these trees and houses were burnt down by the fire.

注释 **Note**

* 片 piān=(colloquial)film; disc (All other examples are pronounced as piàn.)

P | 513 平 flat/level/smooth/even píng

Chinese	English	Character codes
水 + 平 = 水平	water + flat = level (of achievement etc); standard	121/513
平安	safe and sound; well	513/352
平常	usually	513/195
和平	peace; peaceful	042/513
公平	fair; impartial	221/513
平时	ordinarily; in normal times	513/116
心平气和	good-humoured and even-tempered; calmly and without stress	576/513/098/042
平易近人	amiable and easy of approach	513/588/236/104
平心静气	dispassionately in attitude; calmly	513/576/461/098

Example Sentences

1/513	这件事做得一点儿都不公平。 This way of dealing with this matter is not at all fair.
2/513	平时你们都去哪儿吃饭？ Where do you usually go out to eat?
3/513	你平安到家后给我发个短信好吗？ Text me once you have got home safely, OK?
4/513	经理平心静气地听她说完了这件事情的经过。 The manager listened calmly to her whole story.
5/513	在这次比赛中，中国选手的水平还真让人耳目一新。 The Chinese athletes' performance during this match is a breath of fresh air.

瓶 bottle/vase/MW píng 514 P

Chinese	English	Character codes
瓶 + 子 = 瓶子	bottle + suffix = bottle	514/172
花瓶	flower vase	426/514
奶瓶	feeding bottle	258/514
药瓶	medicine bottle	318/514
热水瓶	thermos	103/121/514

Example Sentences

1/514	我每天早上都喝一瓶牛奶。 I drink a bottle of milk every morning.
2/514	这瓶汽水多少钱？ How much does this bottle of fizzy drink cost?
3/514	桌上的花瓶是昨天新买的。 The vase on the table was bought yesterday.
4/514	他们怎么把我的五瓶酒都喝完了。 How come they drank all my five bottles of wine.
5/514	我家里有的是 * 空瓶，你要几个？ There are lots of empty bottles at my home. How many do you want?

注释 Note

* 有的是，there are lot of; so many of

Q | 515 其 it/such/that/pronoun qí

Chinese	English	Character codes
其 + 实 = 其实	such + fact = actually; in fact	515/534
其他	other; (sth or sb) else; the rest	515/125
其次	next; secondly	515/200
其中	among; in	515/168
其间	in between; in the meantime	515/231
突如其来	to arise abruptly; to arrive suddenly; happening suddenly	555/526/515/065
出其不意	to do sth when least expected; to catch sb off guard	012/515/007/324
乐在其中	to take pleasure in sth	246/163/515/168
只知其一，不知其二	know a part of the whole matter only	340/341/515/152, 007/341/515/025

Example Sentences

1/515	我不行，其实我也是第一次玩儿这种游戏。 I am not really good, actually it's my first time playing this game.
2/515	你还有什么其他的事吗？要是没有，我就走了。 Do you have anything else? If not, I will leave.
3/515	在外国留学期间，她去了法国、西班牙和一些其他的国家。 She has also been to France, Spain and other countries during her study abroad.
4/515	姐姐非常喜欢老师这个工作，她简直是乐在其中。 My sister likes being a teacher and takes real pleasure in it.
5/515	动物园里有很多可爱的动物，其中老百姓 * 最喜欢的是大熊猫。 There are lots of cute animals in the zoo, of which the big panda is the most popular.

注释 Note

* 老百姓，common people, general public

奇 strange/rare/odd/unusual/wonder/astonish qí 516 Q

Chinese	English	Character codes
奇 + 怪 = 奇怪	odd + strange = strange; odd	516/419
好奇	inquisitive; curious	039/516
出奇	exceptional; unusual	012/516
奇特	peculiar; queer	516/547
新奇	novelty; novel	311/516
奇才	genius	516/366
奇遇	happy encounter; fortuitous meeting	516/599
千奇百怪	fantastic oddities of every description	268/516/181/419

Example Sentences

1/516	他人不一般，穿着 * 也很奇特。 His is an unusual person, and his dress is also very peculiar.
2/516	她的声音很奇怪，很不好听。 Her voice is very strange and unpleasant to listen to.
3/516	姐姐又聪明又努力，总是考第一一点儿也不奇怪。 My sister is clever and hardworking, so it's not surprising she always comes top.
4/516	我实在太好奇了，这件事这么难，他是怎么做到的？ I'm really curious about how he did such a difficult matter so well.
5/516	在这大千世界 ** 里，什么新奇的事情都有可能发生。 Anything can happen in this big wide world.

注释 Note

* 穿着 (zhuó)，dressing; clothing

** 大千世界，the boundless universe; world wide

Q | 517 骑 to ride/sit on the back of qí

Chinese	English	Character codes
骑 + 马 = 骑马	to ride + horse = horse-riding	517/495
骑车	to cycle	517/010
骑手	jockey; horse rider	517/284
坐骑	saddle horse; mount	177/517
骑着马找马	sit on one horse and look for another	517/337/494/336/494

Example Sentences

1/517	小张每天骑车上下班。 Xiao Zhang cycles to work every day.
2/517	下雪天骑车要十分小心。 Be careful cycling in the snow.
3/517	这个周末我教你骑自行车怎么样？ How about I teach you to ride a bicycle this weekend?
4/517	他一边骑着车一边听着音乐，自得其乐。 He enjoys riding his bicycle whilst listening to music.
5/517	张先生骑马骑得跟骑手一样好。 Mr. Zhang rides a horse like a jockey.

且 also/and/even more/still/yet/just/while/last qiě 518 Q

Chinese	English	Character codes
而 + 且 = 而且	and + even more = (not only...) but also...; moreover; in addition; furthermore	399/518
且不说	not to mention	518/007/122
且……且……	whole; as	518/518
且慢	to wait a moment; do not go too soon	518/253
得过且过	satisfied just to get through; to muddle through without high ambitions	207/225/518/225

Example Sentences

1/518	她不但歌唱得好，而且舞跳得也很好看。 She sings well and dances beautifully.
2/518	这本书很有趣，而且非常容易理解。 This book is interesting and easy to understand.
3/518	弟弟那种得过且过的样子，让妈妈很生气。 Mum is angry with my younger brother's way of muddling along.
4/518	小奇今天很不听话，不但不写作业而且还不吃饭。 Xiaoqi is very naughty today. Not only did he not do the homework, but he also didn't eat his food.
5/518	小明不但自己学习成绩好，而且还愿意帮助别人，同学们都很喜欢他。 Xiaoming is not only good in his studies but is also willing to help others, and he is well liked by his classmates.

Q | 519 轻 light/gentle/belittle/not serious/hasty qīng

Chinese	English	Character codes
轻 + 轻 +(地)= 轻轻(地)	light + light = lightly; softly	519/519 (390)
年轻	young	090/519
轻快	light and quick; brisk; effortless	519/244
轻重	weight; severity (of the case); degree of seriousness	519/612
轻视	contempt; to despise	519/118
轻信	to easily trust; gullible; naïve	519/577
重男轻女	prefer sons to daughters	612/259/519/091

Example Sentences

1/519	她看上去很年轻。 She looks very young.
2/519	这个包儿很轻，我自己能拿。 This bag is very light. I can take it myself.
3/519	爷爷八十多岁了，走起路来脚步还是很轻快。 Granddad is over eighties, and he still walks with springy steps.
4/519	他很有主张，但不轻视别人的意见，说话做事也知道轻重，所以是个学生头儿。 He is his own man but he doesn't ignore others' advice and knows the proper way to talk and act, therefore, he is a leader among the students.
5/519	在一些国家，出于习惯上重男轻女的原因，很多家长不愿送女孩子去学校读书。 In some countries, families are unwilling to send their daughters to school, because the custom is patriarchal.

清 pure and clear/unmixed/uncorrupted qīng 520 Q

Chinese	English	Character codes
清 + 楚 = 清楚	clear + distinct = clear; distinct	520/379
不清楚	unclear; not understand	007/520/379
不清	unclear	007/520
看不清	not able to see clearly	062/007/520
分清	to distinguish (between different things)	028/520
高清	high definition (television etc)	030/520
清高	noble and virtuous; aloof from petty politics and material	520/030
清水	fresh water; clear water	520/121
清明 (节)*	5th of the 24 solar terms; Tomb-Sweeping Day (in early April)	520/082 (454)

Example Sentences

1/520	这字太小了，看不清楚。 The word is too small to see.
2/520	雨实在太大了，路都看不清了。 The rain is too heavy to see the road clearly.
3/520	啊？我听不清楚你在说什么，能说大声点吗？ What? I can't hear what you're saying. Can you speak a bit louder?
4/520	她把那个数据算得清清楚楚。 She has computed the data clearly.
5/520	这条河的水真清，一眼就能望到水里的鱼。 The river is very clear. You can see the fish in it.

注释 Note

* 清明 (节): The Qingming Festival also known as Tomb-Sweeping Day in English (sometime also called Chinese Memorial Day or Ancestors' Day) is a traditional Chinese festival.

Q | 521 秋 autumn qiū

Chinese	English	Character codes
秋 + 天 = 秋天	autumn + sky = autumn	521/128
秋色	colour of autumn	521/277
秋雨	autumn rain	521/160
秋季	autumn season	521/440
秋千	swing	521/268
千秋	a thousand years	268/521

Example Sentences

1/521	秋天了，树上都结满了果实。 The tree is full of fruits in the autumn.
2/521	秋天来到了，白天慢慢地变短了。 It's autumn now, and the day slowly gets shorter.
3/521	秋雨又冷又长，很不舒服。 Autumn rain is cold and constant. It's very uncomfortable.
4/521	中秋的满月又大又亮，真好看。 The full moon in Mid-Autumn Festival is big and bright, and it is very beautiful.
5/521	我朋友那里七月的天气，像秋天一样舒服。 The weather of my friend's place in July is as comfortable as in autumn.

求 beg/to seek/to ask/solicit qiú 522 Q

Chinese	English	Character codes
要 + 求 = 要求	want + to seek = to request; to require; to stake a claim	319/522
求助	to request help; to appeal (for help)	522/343
需求	requirement; to require; (economic) demand	580/522
请求	to ask; to request; petition; appeal	101/522
求知	anxious to learn; seek knowledge	522/341
求人	to ask for help; to ask a favour	522/104
力求	to make every effort to; striving to; do one's best	483/522
渴求	long for; eagerly yearn for; greatly desire	472/522
实事求是	seek truth from facts; be practical and realistic	534/281/522/117
有求必应 *	to grant whatever is asked for; to accede to every plan	158/522/363/592

Example Sentences

1/522	我想请求同学们帮我一个忙。 I'd like to ask my classmates to help me.
2/522	请告诉我你有什么需求。 Tell me your requirements, please.
3/522	他想都没想就一口答应 ** 了我的要求。 He agreed my request without thinking.
4/522	学校要求每个学生在校时必须穿校服。 The school requires every student to wear school uniform while in school.
5/522	他不但热心而且又很能干 ***，对别人的求助总是有求必应 *。 He is kind and capable, and he never refuses anyone's request.

注释 Note

* 应 yìng=answer; echo; meet the demand; cope with

** 答应 dāying=promise

*** 干 gàn=do; strike; main part

Q 523 趣 fun/interest qù

Chinese	English	Character codes
兴 + 趣 = 兴趣	excitement + interest = interest; hobby	149/523
感兴趣	to be interested	410/149/523
有兴趣	interested; interesting	158/149/523
有趣	interesting; fascinating; amusing	158/523
乐趣	delight; pleasure; joy	246/523
情趣	inclinations and interests	270/523
没趣	embarrassing; dull; unsatisfactory	078/523
知趣	tactful; sensible; discreet	341/523

Example Sentences

1/523	这个故事十分有趣。 This story is very funny.
2/523	他这个人很没趣，不爱开玩笑，也听不懂笑话。 He is dull and doesn't like joking. He doesn't understand jokes either.
3/523	你最感兴趣的是什么？ What are you most interested in?
4/523	妹妹的兴趣爱好 * 非常多，天天从早忙到晚。 My sister has many interests, so she is busy all day long.
5/523	你没看见他正不高兴呢吗？知趣点儿，别现在去问他。 Can't you see that he is in a bad mood? Don't ask him now, if you know what's good for you.

注释 Note

* 爱好 àihào=hobby

裙 skirt qún 524 Q

Chinese	English	Character codes
裙 + 子 = 裙子	skirt + suffix = skirt	524/172
短裙	short skirt	394/524
长裙	long skirt	194/524
睡裙	nightgown	120/524
裙带关系	through petticoat influence; with the help of one's female relatives	524/385/034/138

Example Sentences

1/524	这条裙子的颜色真好看。 The colour of this skirt is really pretty.
2/524	这条短裙实在 * 太短了。 This short skirt is truly too short.
3/524	我一年四季都穿裙子。 I wear a skirt all year round.
4/524	她穿上这条裙子就更 ** 漂亮了。 She is even prettier when she wears this skirt.
5/524	把你这条黑长裙借给我去参加舞会时穿好吗？ Could you lend me your black long skirt for the ball?

注释 Note

* 实在 shízài=truly; really

** 更 gèng=more; even more

R | 525 容 accommodate/hold/capacity/contain/tolerant/appearance róng

Chinese	English	Character codes
容 + 易 = 容易	to tolerate + easy = easy; likely; apt to	525/588
从容	to go easy; unhurried; calm	201/525
包容	to pardon; to forgive; to show tolerance	359/525
市容	appearance of a city	537/525
动容	to be emotionally moved	212/525
笑容	smiling expression	310/525
容人	tolerant	525/104
好不容易	with great difficulty; very difficult	039/007/525/588

Example Sentences

1/525	新老师面带笑容地走进了教室。 The new teacher walks into the classroom with a smile.
2/525	这道题很容易，我一下子就算出来了。 This question is quite easy. I get the answer straight away.
3/525	张阿姨那甜甜的笑容时时出现在我的眼前。 Auntie Zhang's sweet smile keeps coming up in my mind.
4/525	他从容地看了一下四周，然后就走了。 He calmly looked around and then left.
5/525	他们好不容易 * 才找到这儿。 With great difficulty, they finally found this place.

注释 Note

* 好不容易 = 好容易 . The two phrases are the same, meaning very difficult. The similar phrases are 差一点儿 = 差一点儿没，for example，我昨天上课差一点儿晚了 I was almost late for the class yesterday. You also can say 我昨天上课差一点儿没晚 .

如 similar/as if/like/such as/supposing rú 526 R

Chinese	English	Character codes
如 + 果 = 如果	as + fruit = if; in case; in the event that	526/037
比如	for example; such as	186/526
如下	as follows	526/139
如同	like; same as; as	526/130
自如	smoothly; with facility; calm and at ease; unobstructed; with ease; freely	616/526
不如	not equal to; not as good as; inferior to; it would be better to	007/526
还不如	might as well	226/007/526
如今	nowadays	526/058
正如	just as; precisely as	339/526
如愿	have one's wish or dream come true; fulfilled	526/602
假如	if	443/526
如鱼得水	like a fish back in water; glad to be back in one's proper surroundings	526/330/207/121
突如其来	to arise abruptly; to arrive suddenly	555/526/515/065

Example Sentences

1/526	太阳就如同一个大大的火球。 The sun is like a big fireball.
2/526	过去打电话很不方便，如今人们大都有手机了。 In the past making telephone calls was not convenient; nowadays, most people have mobile phones.
3/526	如果明天下雨，就不去公园了。 If it's raining tomorrow, we won't go to the park.
4/526	如果明天天气好，我们就去爬山吧？ If tomorrow's weather is good, shall we go hiking?
5/526	节日里大街上都是人，还不如在家里看书呢。 There are lots of people in the street during the holiday. One had better stay at home and read a book.

S | 527 赛 match/competition/race/game/better than sài

Chinese	English	Character codes
比 + 赛 = 比赛	to compare + match = competition; match	186/527
复赛	semi-final; intermediary heat of a competition	407/527
半决赛	semi-final	358/469/527
决赛	finals (of a competition)	469/527
赛场	race track; field (for athletics competition)	527/196
开赛	to start a match; the kick-off	061/527
赛跑	race (running); to race	527/263

Example Sentences

1/527	今年的比赛我参加，明年的比赛我也想参加。 I will participate in this year's competition and also next year's.
2/527	昨天晚上大家都在电视机前看这场比赛，没有人出去。 Everyone was in front of the TV watching the game last night. No one went out.
3/527	让我们来比一比赛跑，看谁先跑到终点。 Let's have a race to see who reaches the finishing line first.
4/527	因为要参加网球决赛，所以他今天没来上课。 He didn't come to the lesson today because he has a tennis finals match.
5/527	每次的足球世界杯决赛我场场必看。 I watch every single football match of World Cup finals.

伞 umbrella/sth shaped like an umbrella sǎn 528 S

Chinese	English	Character codes
雨 + 伞 = 雨伞	rain + umbrella = umbrella	160/528
阳伞	parasol	583/528
打伞	to hold up an umbrella	013/528
跳伞	to parachute; parachute jumping	296/528

Example Sentences

1/528	我去年夏天旅游的时候，在南京买了把太阳伞。 I bought a parasol in Nanjing during last summer's trip.
2/528	放在门口的那把伞是谁的？ Whose umbrella is it by the door?
3/528	下雨了，可是我没带雨伞。 It's raining, but I haven't got an umbrella.
4/528	跳伞是爸爸一生的爱好，直到现在七十多岁了他还在跳伞。 Parachuting is my dad's lifelong hobby; he is still doing it in his seventies.
5/528	他一手拿着行李一手打着伞急急忙忙地向火车站跑去。 He rushed to the train station with an opened umbrella in one hand and his luggage in the other.

S | 529 扫 sweep/eliminate sǎo; clear away/broom sào

Chinese	English	Character codes
清 + 扫 = 清扫	clear + to sweep = to tidy up; to mop up	520/529
打扫	to clean; to sweep	013/529
扫地 *	to sweep the floor	529/390
扫 (sào) 把 **	broom	529/353
扫兴	to have one's spirits dampened; to feel disappointment	529/149
一扫而空	to sweep clean; to clean out	152/529/399/474

Example Sentences

1/529	清扫工正在打扫房间。 The cleaner is cleaning the room.
2/529	他的行为让他名声扫地 *。 His action destroyed his reputation.
3/529	一听到妈妈在电话上的声音，她不安的心情就一扫而空了。 When she heard her mum' s voice on the telephone, all her nervousness disappeared.
4/529	这把扫把 ** 把儿 *** 太短了，给我换一把吧。 The handle of this broom is too short. Please change it for me.
5/529	明天晚会的节目一定不会让你扫兴。 You won't be disappointed with tomorrow's party programme.

注释 Note

* 地 dì=earth; land; ground

** 扫把 sàobǎ=broom

*** 把儿 bàr=handle or grip

山 hill/mountain shān 530 S

Chinese	English	Character codes
高 + 山 = 高山	high + hill = high mountain	030/530
大山	big mountain	014/530
上山	to go uphill	108/530
山上	on the mountain	530/108
火山	volcano	050/530
假山	rock garden; rockery	443/530
冰山	glacier; iceberg	365/530
山水画儿	landscape painting	530/121/428/024

Example Sentences

1/530	我们大家体力都很好。很快就爬上了那个山头儿。 All of us had great physical energy and climbed very quickly up to the mountain.
2/530	这个周末我们去爬山好吗？ Shall we go to a mountain for hiking this weekend?
3/530	山上的空气清新，是休假 * 的好地 ** 方。 The mountains are a good place for a holiday because of the fresh air.
4/530	有火山的国家自然环境都很漂亮，是不是？ The countries that have volcanoes have a pretty landscape, isn't that right?
5/530	她在上山的路上遇到了其他的同事，感到非常意外。 She met her other colleagues on the way up to the mountain. It's completely unexpected.

注释 Note

* 假 jià=vacation; holiday

** 地 dì=earth; land; ground

S | 531 衫 shirt/robe/unlined upper garment shān

Chinese	English	Character codes
衬 + 衫 = 衬衫	lining + garment = shirt	374/531
衣衫	clothing	153/531
运动衫	sport shirt	333/212/531
长衫	traditional Asian dress for men; long gown	194/531

Example Sentences

1/531	那几件衬衫都是旧的。 Those shirts are old.
2/531	天气冷了，多加一件长衫吧。 It's cold, add one more layer of long gown.
3/531	这件衬衫是我新买的，好看吗？ This is the shirt that I just bought, isn't it nice?
4/531	弟弟平时最爱穿的就是运动衫。 Sport shirt is my brother's favourite clothes.
5/531	那件白衬衫被洗衣机洗坏了。 That white shirt was ruined by the washing machine.

烧 burn/cook/set fire to/fever shāo 532 S

Chinese	English	Character codes
发 + 烧 = 发烧	give out + burn = have a fever	401/532
烧香	to burn incense	532/570
火烧	to burn down; burning hot	050/532
烧开	to boil	532/061
烧水	to boil water; to heat water	532/121
红烧鸡	braised chicken	229/532/230
烧包	to forget oneself in extravagance; be drunken with success	532/359
烧心	heartburn	532/576

Example Sentences

1/532	水烧开了，要喝绿茶吗？ The water has boiled. Do you want some green tea?
2/532	昨晚我感冒发烧了。 I got a cold and a fever last night.
3/532	哥哥最爱吃他太太做的红烧鸡了。 My brother loves his wife's braised chicken most.
4/532	上周末和朋友一起吃饭吃得太多了，到现在我还觉得有点烧心呢。 I ate too much with my friends last weekend, and I still feel a little heartburn.
5/532	上个月，一个坏人放了一把火，把很多房子都烧着了。 A bad man has set a fire and burned down a lot of buildings last month.

注释 Note

* 着 zháo=burn; be ignited; be lit

S 533 声 sound/voice/MW shēng

Chinese	English	Character codes
声 + 音 = 声音	sound + tone = voice; sound	533/589
大声	loud voice; in a loud voice; loudly	014/533
轻声	quietly; softly; neutral tone	519/533
心声	thoughts; feelings; heartfelt wishes; inner voice	576/533
声明	to state; to declare; statement; declaration	533/082
名声	reputation	083/533
回声	echo	048/533
声调	tone; note	533/552
歌声	singing voice	219/533
有声有色	having sound and colour; vivid and dramatic	158/533/158/277
口口声声	to keep on saying; to repeat over and over again	475/475/533/533

Example Sentences

1/533	学校新开的中文课办得有声有色。 The school's new Chinese lessons are going well.
2/533	小声点儿，别让妈妈听见。 Lower your voice. Don't let mum hear.
3/533	办公室里静静的，一点儿声音都没有。 It's quiet in the office. There is not a single sound.
4/533	虽然教室很大，不过钟老师讲课声音响亮，所以我们都能听得清清楚楚。 Even the size of classroom is large, Teacher Zhong's voice is loud and clear, so we can hear it very well.
5/533	会场里所有的人都被她甜美的歌声打动了。 Her sweet singing moved everyone in the conference room.

实 real/solid/true/full/sincere/reality/fruit shí 534 S

Chinese	English	Character codes
其 + 实 = 其实	such + fact = actually; in fact	515/534
真实	true; real	338/534
实现	to achieve; to implement	534/141
实用	practical; functional; applied (science)	534/594
事实	fact	281/534
事实上	in fact; in reality; actually; as a matter of fact	281/534/108
实事求是	be practical and realistic	534/281/522/117
实在	really; indeed; true; real	534/163
实行	to implement, to carry out; to put into practice	534/422
实力	strength	534/483

Example Sentences

1/534	其实，明天我也要去那里，你不必等我了。 In fact, I also need to go there tomorrow, so you don't need to wait for me.
2/534	我刚才找了半天都没发现，其实我要找的书就在我面前。 I have been looking for the book for ages, eventually, it is right in front of me.
3/534	她的画儿画得实在太好了。 Her drawing is really brilliant.
4/534	事实上，这是一本根据真实的故事写的小说，非常感人。 In fact, this book is based on a real story. It's really impressive.
5/534	虽然这个主意不错，然而，实事求是地说，它可行吗？ Although this idea is good, to be realistic, can it work?

S | 535 史 history shǐ

Chinese	English	Character codes
历 + 史 = 历史	experience + history = history	484/535
历史上	historical; in history	484/535/108
文学史	history of literature	563/150/535
史书	history book	535/119
史前	prehistory	535/099
有史以来	since the beginning of history	158/535/323/065
历史新高	record high	484/535/311/030
史学家	historian	535/150/053
史料	historical material	535/490
史实	historical facts	535/534

Example Sentences

1/535	王先生在北京大学教历史。 Mr Wang teaches history at Peking University.
2/535	我哥哥边看新闻边跟我说，这是有史以来最快的火车。 This is the fastest train ever. While watching the news, my older brother told me that.
3/535	他是北大历史上最年轻的校长。 He is the youngest president in the history of Peking University.
4/535	中国的春节历史很久远。 Chinese Spring Festival has a long history.
5/535	这学期教我们班历史的安老师刚刚完成大学的学业，是我们大学最年轻的助教。 Teacher An, who is teaching us history this term, has just finished his college education and is the youngest teaching assistant of the university.

世 lifetime/life/generation/era/world/society shì 536 S

Chinese	English	Character codes
世 + 界 = 世界	life + boundary = world	536/454
世界杯	world cup	536/454/004
问世	to be published; to come out	304/536
世事	affairs of life; things of the world	536/281
一世	generation; one's lifetime; lifelong	152/536
一生一世	all one's life; throughout one's life time	152/112/152/536
在世	to be alive	163/536
去世	to die; to pass away	102/536
身世	one's life experience; one's past history	279/536

Example Sentences

1/537	他今天要请假 * 在家看世界杯。 He will take time off to watch the World Cup at home today.
2/537	我哥哥的房间里有一张世界地 ** 图。 There's a world map in my older brother's room.
3/537	经过两年的调查，他终于知道了自己的身世。 After two years investigation, at last he knew his origins.
4/537	她花了五年时间写的小说终于问世了。 The book that she spent five years writing is finally published.
5/537	老万和他的妻子是生活在两个完全不同世界里的人。 Old Wan and his wife are living in totally different worlds.

注释 Note

* 假 jià=vacation; holiday

** 地 dì=earth; land; ground

S | 537 市 city/market shì

Chinese	English	Character codes
城 + 市 = 城市	town + city = city	376/537
超市	supermarket	373/537
市场	marketplace	537/196
市长	mayor	537/194
上市	to hit the market (of a new product); to list (on the stock market)	108/537
黑市	black market	228/537
市容	the appearance of a city	537/525

Example Sentences

1/536	那家超市又大又干净。 That supermarket is big and clean.
2/536	我爱我生活的这个城市。 I love the city I'm living in.
3/536	这个“大熊猫”的电脑游戏上市第一天就被卖完了。 The Panda computer game sold out on the first day on the market.
4/536	爱护环境是每一个市民都应该做的。 Caring for the environment is every city resident's duty.
5/536	每个星期三这个街头市场的人都很多，有卖衣服的、卖日用品的，还有卖来自不同地 * 方的小吃的。 Every Wednesday the street market is full of people; it sells clothing, daily necessities and food from different places.

注释 Note

* 地 dì=earth; land; ground

瘦 thin/slim shòu 538 S

Chinese	English	Character codes
瘦 + 子 = 瘦子	thin + person = thin person	538/172
瘦身	to lose weight (intentionally); to slim down	538/279
瘦长	long and thin;	538/194
瘦肉	lean meat	538/276
清瘦	meagre; slander	520/538
高矮胖瘦	one's physique (tall or short, thin or fat)	030/351/509/538

Example Sentences

1/538	妈妈年轻的时候又高又瘦。 When Mum was young, she was tall and thin.
2/538	那个身高瘦长的女孩儿是我姐姐。 That tall slim girl is my sister.
3/538	好久没见了，你瘦了。 I haven't seen you for a while. You've lost weight.
4/538	他虽然瘦小，但是力气大得很。 Even though he is thin and small, he has great strength.
5/538	她虽然看上去很瘦但是很健康，很少生病。 Although she is slender, she is very healthy and rarely gets ill.

S | 539 叔 uncle/father's younger brother shū

Chinese	English	Character codes
叔 + 叔 = 叔叔	uncle + uncle = uncle; father's younger brother	539/539
大叔	uncle (term used to address a man about the age of one's father)	014/539
小叔叔	father's youngest brother	143/539/539
表叔	father's younger male cousin	189/539
叔公	great uncle; grandfather's younger brother	539/221

Example Sentences

1/539	马大叔是个做事干 * 练的人。 Uncle Ma is capable and experienced in handling affairs.
2/539	我叔叔的女儿今年上中学了。 My uncle's daughter started secondary school this year.
3/539	我小叔叔自小就去西班牙读书了。 My youngest uncle went to study in Spain when he was little.
4/539	我有两个叔叔，我爸爸是老大。 I have two younger uncles, my dad is the eldest.
5/539	邻居大叔家的小黑猫每天下午都跑到我家的花园里睡觉，她很可爱。 My neighbour uncle's small black cat comes to my garden to sleep every afternoon. She is so cute.

注释 Note

* 干 gàn=do; strike; main part

舒 stretch/spread/leisurely/soothe shū 540 S

Chinese	English	Character codes
舒 + 服 = 舒服	to stretch + serve = comfortable; feeling well	540/029
不舒服	unwell; feeling ill; uneasy	007/540/029
舒张	diastole	540/606
舒心	comfortable; at ease; no worry	540/576
舒一口气	heave a sigh of relief	540/152/475/098
舒舒服服	comfortable; with ease	540/540/029/029

Example Sentences

1/540	新买的那张床很舒服。 That new bed is very comfortable.
2/540	黄非今天不舒服，没来上班。 Huang Fei is not well today therefore he didn't come to work.
3/540	下半场球赛已经到了最后五分钟，双方球员你来我往，都想最后再进一个球，当终场的钟声响起时，大家都舒了一口气。 It was the last five minutes of the second half of the match. Both sides' players were neck and neck in possession of the ball, trying to score the last goal. When the final buzzer sounded, everyone sighed with relief.
4/540	因为天气坏，我们的假 * 期过得很不舒心。 We didn't have a good holiday because of the bad weather.
5/540	听我的话：回家后舒舒服服地洗个澡，好好睡一觉，明天你就会觉得好多了。 Listen to me: when you get home, have a nice shower and a good sleep and you will feel better tomorrow.

注释 Note

* 假 jià=vacation; holiday

S | 541 束 bind/tie/beam/restrain/overcautious/MW shù

Chinese	English	Character codes
结 + 束 = 结束	knot + to control = termination; to finish; to end; to conclude; to close	455/541
花束	bouquet	426/541
束手束脚	be over-cautious	541/284/541/450
束身	to bind oneself; submission	541/279
一束	a bunch	152/541

Example Sentences

1/541	这么好的电影，还没结束她们就离开了。我真不明白为什么。 They had left before such an interesting film ended. I really don't know why.
2/541	比赛上半场结束时，意外的事发生了…… An accident happened at the end of the first half of the game.
3/541	我的经理对我说，不要担心别人的看法而做事束手束脚。 My manager told me that there is no need to worry about other people's opinions and do things over-cautiously.
4/541	去年生日的时候，同事们送了我很大的一束鲜花。 My colleagues gave me a big bunch of flowers on my birthday last year.
5/541	别再跟我提他了，我们已经结束了。 Don't talk about him to me anymore. We broke up.

树 tree/cultivate/set up shù 542 S

Chinese	English	Character codes
果 + 树 = 果树	fruit + tree = fruit tree	037/542
树种 *	tree species	542/611
种 ** 树	to plant tree	611/542
树皮	tree bark	542/510
树干 ***	tree trunk	542/409
茶树	tea tree	009/542
小树	small tree; shrub	143/542

注释 Note

* 种 zhǒng=MW; type; sort; guts

** 种 zhòng=plant; farm

*** 干 gàn=do; strike; main part

**** 参天 cāntiān=reach to the sky

Example Sentences

1/542	这些和公路平行的树都是新种 ** 的。 These trees which stand in parallel with the road are newly planted.
2/542	花园里的苹果树上结满了小苹果。 The apple tree in the garden is full of little apples.
3/542	这些都是百年以上的老树。 These trees are over a hundred years old.
4/542	道路两旁参天 **** 的大树已经有几十年的历史了。 The towering trees along the roadside have more than several decades' history.
5/542	在这些大树下的长椅上，三三两两地坐着休息的人们。 People are sitting on the long benches to have a rest under these big trees in groups of two or three.

S 543 数 number shù; count/be reckoned as shǔ

Chinese	English	Character codes
数 + 学 = 数学	number + to learn = mathematics	543/150
次数	number of times	200/543
数字	numeral; digit; figure	543/173
多数	majority; most	023/543
大多数	(great) majority	014/023/543
少数	small number; few; minority	109/543
半数	half the number; half	358/543
人数	number of people	104/543
数据	data; numbers	543/468
数 * 数	counting numbers	543/543
数 * 一数 * 二	reckoned to be first or second; one of the very best	543/152/543/025

Example Sentences

1/543	大多数老年人都喜欢看老电影。 The old movies are enjoyed by most of elderly people.
2/543	李先生是国内数 * 一数 * 二的心理医生。 Mr. Li is one of the best psychologists in the country.
3/543	小明这学期数学成绩进步很大。 Xiaoming's maths grade has greatly improved this term.
4/543	你近来晚睡的次数越来越多了，这可不好。 You are sleeping late more often. It's not good.
5/543	除了少数几个人，大多数人都准时完成了作业。 Most people have finished their homework.

注释 Note

* 数 shǔ=count; be reckoned as (All other examples are pronounced as shù.)

刷 scrub/brush/eliminate shuā 544 S

Chinese	English	Character codes
刷 + 牙 = 刷牙	brush + teeth = to brush teeth	544/582
牙刷	toothbrush	582/544
刷新	to renovate; to refresh (computer window); to write a new page (in history); to break (a record)	544/311
洗刷	wash; scrub	309/544
刷了	brush	544/172
雨刷	windshield wiper	160/544
刷卡	to swipe a card	544/470

Example Sentences

1/544	妈妈对我说，饭后记得要刷牙。 Mum told me to remember to brush my teeth after a meal.
2/544	这是新上市的电子牙刷，很好用。 This is the latest electric toothbrush. It's quite easy to use.
3/544	小李又一次刷新了自己的最好成绩。 Young Li broke his own best record again.
4/544	这把刷子太小了，我能换一把大（一）点儿的吗？ This brush is too small. Can I exchange it for a bigger one?
5/544	这个黑点儿怎么刷都刷不干净。 No matter how hard I brush, I still can't get rid of this black dot.

S 545 双 two/double/dual/even/MW shuāng

Chinese	English	Character codes
双 + 方 = 双方	two + square = both sides; both parties involved	545/403
双边	bilateral	545/188
双重 *	double	545/612
双向	bidirectional; two way; interactive	545/573
双手	both hands	545/284
双语	bilingual	545/159
双眼	the two eyes	545/316
双人舞	pas de deux; dance for two performers	545/104
成双成对	to form pairs; to be in couples	375/545/022

注释 Note

* 重 chóng=repeat; again; overlap; layer

Example Sentences

1/545	你知道吗，这么做对我们双方都有影响。 Do you know that it will affect both sides if you do it like that.
2/545	在双休日我去商场买了一双鞋。 I went to the shopping centre and bought a pair of shoes during my two days off.
3/545	她双眼都是红红的，好像是刚刚哭过了。 Both her eyes are red, it seems that she has been crying.
4/545	你脚上穿的那两只鞋子不是一双的。 The two shoes you are wearing on your feet are not a pair.
5/545	看着朋友们都成双成对的，他也想给自己找个女朋友了。 Seeing that his friends where all in pairs, he also wanted to find himself a girlfriend.

算 calculate/reckon/count/consider/regard as suàn 546 S

Chinese	English	Character codes
打 + 算 = 打算	make + to calculate = to plan; to intend; to calculate; plan; intention; calculation	013/546
就算	granted that; even if	239/546
算是	considered to be; at last	546/117
算出	to figure out	546/012
盘算	to plot; to scheme; to calculate	508/546
算盘	abacus	546/508
总算	at long last; finally; on the whole	617/546
算了	let it be; let it pass; forget about it	546/067
说了算	to have the final say; to be the one in charge	122/067/546

Example Sentences

1/546	阿姨说，她打算在山上长久地住下去了。 Auntie said that she plans to live in the mountains for a long time.
2/546	今年的假 * 期你打算去哪儿？ Where are you planning to go for this year's holiday?
3/546	他也不算小了，一点儿人情世故 ** 都不懂。 He is not so young, but he doesn't know the world at all.
4/546	这点儿工作对她来说不算什么，一会儿就做完了。 This work is nothing to her. It didn't take her long to finish it.
5/546	这家饭店门口这么多人在等着，我们还是算了，换一家吧。 There are so many people waiting outside this restaurant, forget about it. Let's go to another one.

注释 Note

* 假 jià=vacation; holiday

** 人情世故，worldly wisdom

T | 547 特 special/extraordinary/out of ordinary tè

Chinese	English	Character codes
特 + 别 = 特别	special + do not = especially; particular; unusual	547/190
特定	specific; designated	547/392
特点	characteristic; trait	547/016
特有	specific (to); characteristic (of); distinctive	547/158
特色	characteristic; distinguishing feature or quality	547/277
特长	personal strength; one's special ability or strong points	547/194
特地 *	specially; for a special purpose	547/390
特意	specially; intentionally	547/324
特务	special agent; spy	547/306

Example Sentences

1/547	我觉得这个孩子很特别。 I think this kid is very special.
2/547	画画儿是她的特长，音乐不是。 Painting is her special skill, and music is not.
3/547	啤酒鸡是这儿特有的名菜，我们去吃吧。 Beer chicken is the distinctive dish here, shall we go to eat?
4/547	我哥哥特地 * 从法国飞回来参加他朋友的婚礼。 My brother flew back from France especially for his friend's wedding.
5/547	这些都是当地 * 的特色小吃，每一样都有自己的特点。 These are local speciality dishes, each with their own characteristics.

注释 Note

* 地 dì=earth; land; ground

疼 pain/ache/love dearly/dote on téng 548 T

Chinese	English	Character codes
疼 + 爱 = 疼爱	pain + love = to love dearly	548/001
头疼	headache	554/548
心疼	to love dearly; to feel sorry for sb; to regret; to grudge; to be distressed	576/548
疼不疼	does it hurt	548/007/548

Example Sentences

1/548	不知道为什么，我今天头疼了一天。 I had a headache all day today. I don't know the reason.
2/548	我有三个女儿，她们的爷爷最疼爱老二。 Of the three daughters I have, their grandad loves the middle one best.
3/548	我真心疼花了这么多钱买了这么个包儿。 I regret spending so much money on this bag.
4/548	你还疼吗？如果疼得实在不行的话就去医院吧。 Are you still in pain? If it hurts too much you should go to the hospital.
5/548	这双高跟鞋穿得我脚疼得都走不了路了。 These high heels are too painful to walk on.

T | 549 梯 ladder/steps/stairs tī

Chinese	English	Character codes
电 + 梯 = 电梯	electricity + stairs = elevator; escalator; lift	017/549
楼梯	stair; staircase	493/549
梯子	ladder; stepladder	549/172
楼梯口	head of a flight of stairs; landing	493/549/475
楼梯间	staircase; flight of stairs	493/549/231
盘梯	spiral staircase	508/549

Example Sentences

1/549	楼梯口的灯不亮了，怎么办？ The lights are out at the top of the stairs. What can we do?
2/549	这个梯子看着一点儿都不结实，换一个吧。 This ladder doesn't look strong enough. Let's change it.
3/549	等了这么久电梯还没来，我们不如走楼梯上去。好吗？ It's been a long wait for the elevator. Let's use the stairs, is that OK?
4/549	A: 请问楼梯间在哪儿？ B: 一直走，右手第三道门。 A: Where is the staircase please? B: Straight down, third door on the right.
5/549	我正需要用梯子的时候，妈妈把梯子借给邻居了。 When I need to use the ladder, my mum lends it to the neighbour.

提 lift/raise/carry in one's hand with the arm down tí 550 T

Chinese	English	Character codes
提 + 高 = 提高	to lift + high = to raise; to increase; to improve	550/030
提出	to raise (an issue); to purpose; to put forward; to suggest	550/012
提问	to question; to quiz; to grill	550/304
提到	to mention; to refer to	550/205
提起	to mention; to speak of; to lift; to pick up	550/097
提要	summary; abstract	550/319
提前	to shift to an earlier date; to do sth ahead of time; in advance	550/099
前提	presupposition; premise	099/550
提早	ahead of schedule; sooner than planned; to bring forward (to an earlier time)	550/334
提名	to nominate	550/083
提成	to take percentage	550/375
手提	portable	284/550

Example Sentences

1/550	我换工作了，所以我们得提前搬家。 I have changed my job, so we have to move out ahead of time.
2/550	他提出的方法可以试一试，你觉得呢？ We can give his suggestion a try. What do you think?
3/550	只要人一提到老张的儿子，他就特别开心。 As soon as Lao Zhang's son is mentioned, he is very happy.
4/550	对于刚才提出的问题，你们要好好想一想。 You need to have a think about the issue that has been raised.
5/550	如果没有人提问的话，今天的会议就结束了。 If no one has any questions, then today's meeting is finished.

T | 551 甜 sweet/pleasant tián

Chinese	English	Character codes
香 + 甜 = 香甜	fragrant + sweet = fragrant and sweet; sound (sleep)	570/551
甜点	dessert	551/016
甜心	sweetheart	551/576
甜头	sweet taste (of power, success etc); benefit	551/554
甜菜	beetroot	551/008

Example Sentences

1/551	这是什么水果？又香又甜真好吃。 What kind of fruit is this? It's fragrant and sweet, really delicious.
2/551	苹果和甜瓜是妈妈喜欢吃的水果。 Apple and honey melon are Mum's favourite fruits.
3/551	上学期考了高分以后，弟弟尝到了努力学习的甜头。 My brother benefits from his hard studying after he got high marks last term.
4/551	两岁的妹妹那甜甜的笑容好像一朵开放的鲜花。 My two-years-old sister's sweet smile is like a blossoming flower.
5/551	来试试我新调的水果酒，味道香甜，很适合没有酒力的你。 Come and try my new fruit cocktail mix. It's fragrant and sweet and is suitable for you as you can't hold your drink.

调 adjust/fit in/regulate tiáo; tone/allocate/shift/deploy diào 552 T

Chinese	English	Character codes
空 + 调 = 空调	air + adjust = air conditioning	474/552
调皮	naughty; mischievous; unruly	552/510
调和	harmonious; to mediate; to reconcile; to compromise; to mix; to blend	552/042
调试	to debug; to adjust components during testing	552/282
调节	regulate; adjust	552/454
调理	to nurse one's health; to recuperate; to discipline; to train	552/482
调料	condiment; seasoning; flavouring	552/490
上调	to raise (price); to adjust upwards	108/552
调情	to flirt	552/270
情调 *	sentiment	270/552
声调 *	tones	533/552
调 * 动	shift; transfer; mobilize	552/212
调 * 换	exchange; swap	552/431

注释 Note

* 调 diào=pronunciation; tones (All other examples are pronounced as tiáo.)

Example Sentences

1/552	这个商场里开足了空调，很舒服。 This shopping centre's air conditioning is strong, so it is quite comfortable.
2/552	两个第三声的汉字在一起时，第一个字的声调 * 变为第二声，第二个字的声调 * 不变。 When two Chinese characters are together and in third tone, the tone of the first character becomes the second tone, and the second character doesn't change its tone.
3/552	你的病只要休息和调理一下就会好。 Your illness will be alright as long as you take rest to recuperate.
4/552	他们两个人谁都不喜欢谁，很难调和。 As they don't like each other, it's hard to reconcile them.
5/552	她眼中那调皮的表情让我想起了自己儿时的好朋友。 The naughty expression in her eyes reminds me of my childhood best friend.

T 553 铁 iron/strong/indisputable/solemn tiě

Chinese	English	Character codes
地 * + 铁 = 地 * 铁	ground + iron = underground; subway; metro	390/553
高铁	high speed rail	030/553
地 * 铁站	underground station; metro station	390/553/166
铁路	railway	553/250
铁道	railway line; railway track	553/206
铁人	ironman	553/104
打铁	to forge ironware	013/553

Example Sentences

1/553	我叔叔每天都坐地 * 铁上下班。 My uncle uses the underground to get to and from work.
2/553	东京的地 * 铁又快又准时。 Tokyo's metro is fast and on time.
3/553	新年期间高铁的车票很难买到。 It's difficult to buy a high speed rail ticket during the New Year.
4/553	我家里离地 * 铁站才五分钟的路，很方便。 It's only a five-minute journey from my house to the underground station. It's convenient.
5/553	钟小路是我们学校的名人，学校到如今还留着他参加“铁人”比赛时的照片呢。 Zhong Xiaolu is very famous in our school, which still keeps the photos of his Ironman Competition.

注释 Note

* 地 dì=earth; land; ground

头 head/as a root of a noun or a verb/suffix of a locality tóu 554 T

Chinese	English	Character codes
街 + 头 = 街头	street + head = street	453/554
头发 *	hair (on the head)	554/401
头条新闻	lead story on the news	554/295/311/564
头像	portrait; bust	554/574
带头	to take the lead; to be the first; to set an example	384/554
口头	oral; verbal	475/554
分头	separately	028/554
头等	first-class; first-rate	554/208
头头是道	clear and systematic in speech or action	554/554/117/206

Example Sentences

1/554	"总理大选"上了今天的头条新闻。 The Prime Minister's General Election has made today's headline news.
2/554	有事找张楚楚 **，他是我们的头儿。 If you need anything you should talk to Zhang Chuchu, he is our leader.
3/554	我已经口头上答应 *** 了同事的请求。 I already agreed to my colleague's request verbally.
4/554	他知道，问题越难，他头脑越要冷静。 He knows that the harder the question the calmer he has to be.
5/554	他口才极好，说起话来头头是道，很让人信服。 He is extremely articulate and can be very persuasive and convincing when he talks.

注释 Note

* 发 fà=hair

** 楚楚 a name

*** 答应 dāying=promise

T | 555 突 protrude/prominent/sudden tū

Chinese	English	Character codes
突 + 然 = 突然	sudden + suffix = sudden; abrupt; unexpected	555/273
突然间	suddenly	555/273/231
突出	prominent; outstanding; to protrude	555/012
突变	sudden change; mutation	555/364
突发	sudden outburst	555/401
突如其来	to arise abruptly; to arrive suddenly; happening suddenly	555/526/515/065
突发奇想	suddenly have a thought (idiom); suddenly be inspired to do something	555/401/516/142

Example Sentences

1/555	电灯突然不亮了，房间里黑乎乎的，我什么都看不见了。 The lights suddenly went out. The room is dark, and I can see nothing.
2/555	我朋友说，她妹妹结婚的信息来得很突然。 My friend said that the news of her young sister's marriage was really sudden.
3/555	因为他有突出的成绩，才一年的时间他就成为了我们的经理。 Because of his outstanding achievements, he was promoted to be our manager after only one year.
4/555	因为这场突如其来的大雪，学校决定放假 * 一天。 Because of the sudden heavy snow, the school decides to close for one day.
5/555	听到爸爸和妈妈的对话以后，她突然间明白自己错怪他们了。 Overhearing her mum and dad's conversation, she suddenly realised that she had wrongly blamed them.

注释 Note

* 假 jià=vacation; holiday

图 picture/intent/attempt/plan to tú 556 T

Chinese	English	Character codes
图 + 书 + 馆 = 图书馆	picture + book + building = library	556/119/035
地 * 图	map	390/556
图片	image; picture	556/512
力图	to try hard to; to strive to	483/522
图像	image; graphic	522/574
试图	to attempt; to try	282/522
平面图	a plan	513/081/556
图画	drawing; picture	556/428
画图	to draw design, map etc	428/556
草图	a sketch; rough drawing	368/556
意图	intent; intention; to intend	324/556
图表	chart; diagram	556/189

Example Sentences

1/556	每天晚上自习的时间，图书馆里都坐满了学生。 Every day the library is full of students during the evening self-study period.
2/556	谢谢，我已经很习惯用电脑画图了，好像已经不会用笔画图纸了。 Thank you. I'm so used to using a computer to draw. It seems I can't draw sketches with a pen anymore.
3/556	你如果需要的话 **，可以用图书馆的电脑上网。 You can use the library's computer to go online if you need to.
4/556	他这么做的意图让人难以理解 **。 His intention of doing this way is hard to understand.
5/556	姐姐试图说服我和她一起去参加周末的舞会。 My sister tried to persuade me to go to the party with her this weekend.

注释 Note

* 地 dì=earth; land; ground

** 的话 dehuà= if, used to express a condition

*** 难以理解 , difficult to understand

T | 557 腿 leg tuǐ

Chinese	English	Character codes
腿 + 脚 = 腿脚	leg + feet = legs and feet; ability to walk; strides	557/450
小腿	calf (of the leg)	143/557
大腿	thigh	014/557
跑腿（儿）	to run errands	263/557（024）
火腿	ham	050/557
双腿	legs; both legs; two legs	545/557
盘腿	to sit cross-legged; to sit in lotus position	508/557
狗腿子	lapdog; fig. one who follows a villain; henchman; hired thug	033/557/172

Example Sentences

1/557	我早上经常吃火腿、鸡蛋和面包。 I often have ham, eggs and bread in the morning.
2/557	聪聪个子很高，长 * 得长 ** 手长腿的。 Congcong has grown very tall, with long arms and legs.
3/557	我不会烧菜，但是跑跑腿儿、打个下手还行。 I can't cook, but I can help and run errands.
4/557	每当感觉累的时候，她就会盘腿打会儿坐。 Whenever she feels tired and stressed, she would cross her legs to meditate.
5/557	因为他有两条长腿，所以每次坐飞机他都选走道边的位子。 Because of his long legs, he always chooses an aisle seat when he travels by plane.

注释 Note

* 长 zhǎng=grow

** 长 cháng=long

碗 bowl/MW wǎn 558 W

Chinese	English	Character codes
饭 + 碗 = 饭碗	rice + bowl = rice bowl; fig. livelihood; job; way of making a living	026/558
茶碗	teacup	009/558
洗碗	to wash the dishes	309/558
洗碗机	dishwasher	309/558/051
找饭碗	to look for a job	336/026/558
铁饭碗	secured job	554/026/558

Example Sentences

1/558	我做饭你洗碗怎么样? I'll cook, and you wash the dishes, is it alright?
2/558	请放心用吧，洗碗机里的碗都是干净的。 Don't worry, the bowls in the dishwasher are clean.
3/558	现在想找个铁饭碗的工作越来越不容易了。 It's getting more and more difficult to find a stable and lifelong job.
4/558	你真能吃，中午才吃了一大碗面，这么快又饿了! You really have an appetite! You've just had a big bowl of noodles for lunch and you're hungry again so soon.
5/558	这两个老茶碗儿是我好不容易才买到的，花了不少钱呢。 These two old teacups are not easy to get. I spent a lot of money on them.

W | 559 万 ten thousand/large number/under all circumstances wàn

Chinese	English	Character codes
万 + 人 = 万人	ten thousand + people = ten thousand people; all the people; everyman	559/104
十万	hundred thousand	114/559
千万	ten million; countless; many; must; make sure to	268/559
万一	just in case; if by any chance; contingency	559/152
万丈	lit. ten thousand fathoms; fig. extremely high or deep; lofty; bottomless	559/335
万般	every kind; manifold	559/354
万分	very much; extremely; one ten thousandth part	559/028
万物	all living things	559/565
千变万化	countless changes; constant permutation	268/364/559/427

Example Sentences

1/559	我们的飞机正在一万米的高空上飞行。 Our aircraft is flying at 10,000-metre altitude.
2/559	他最新写的小说有十万多字。 His new book has more than one hundred thousand words.
3/559	你过马路时千万要小心车辆。 Please do watch out for the cars when you cross the road.
4/559	万一这些都是错的，我们该怎么办呢？ If by any chance these are all wrong, what should we do?
5/559	山上的天气，一会儿晴空万里，一会儿又是风又是雨，真是千变万化。 Weather in the mountains can change very quickly; it can be sunny one minute, then rainy and windy the next.

网 net/net like/network/enmesh/MW wǎng 560 | W

Chinese	English	Character codes
上 + 网 = 上网	up + net = to go online; to connect to the internet	108/560
网上	online	560/108
网站	website	560/166
网吧	internet café	560/179
网友	online friend; internet user	560/157
球网	net (for ball games)	272/560
网球	tennis; tennis ball	560/272

Example Sentences

1/560	我姐姐是个网球运动员。 My elder sister is a tennis player.
2/560	你看，这是我们新成立的公司网站。 Look, this is our new company website.
3/560	现在用手机上网的人数越来越多了。 Nowadays the number of people using mobile phones to go online is getting bigger all the time.
4/560	学校旁边的网吧一到放学后总是坐满了学生。 The internet café next to the school is full of students after school.
5/560	面对这些五花八门的网站，我都不知道应该相信哪一家了。 There are so multifarious different websites. I really don't know which one can be trusted.

W 561 忘 forget wàng

Chinese	English	Character codes
忘 + 记 = 忘记	forget + note = to forget	561/439
健忘	forgetful	446/561
难忘	unforgettable	503/561
忘我	selflessness	561/132
忘不了	cannot forget	561/007/067
忘乎所以	to get carried away; to forget oneself	561/424/290/323

Example Sentences

1/561	对不起，我把你的名字忘了。 Sorry, I forgot your name.
2/561	这是一个难忘的假 * 期。 This is an unforgettable holiday.
3/561	是不是人老了就容易健忘了？ The older we get the more forgetful we becom, don't we?
4/561	我今天早上急急忙忙地出门，忘记带钱包了，还好没忘带手机。 I rushed to go out this morning and forgot my wallet. Luckily I didn't forget my mobile phone.
5/261	真对不起，我把那件事忘得一干二净。 I am terribly sorry. I completely forgot about that.

注释 Note

* 假 jià=vacation; holiday

位 location/position/place/MW wèi 562 W

Chinese	English	Character codes
单 + 位 = 单位	single + position = unit (of measure); work unit; place of employment	387/562
这位	this (person)	167/562
地 * 位	position; status	390/562
位于	to be located at; to be situated at	562/597
定位	to orientate; to position; to categorise; positioning	392/562
学位	academic degree; title granted by an institution of higher learning; place in school	150/562
方位	direction; position of the compass; bearing	403/562
位子	place; seat	562/172

Example Sentences

1/562	对不起，这个位子已经有人了。 Sorry, this seat is taken.
2/562	在我们家，妈妈的地 * 位是 ** 最高的 **。 Mum has the highest status in our family.
3/562	我哥哥特别会学习，居然读了三个学位。 My elder brother is good at learning. He actually has got three degrees.
4/562	单位离我家很远，开车要一个多小时。 My work place is far from my house, over an hour's drive.
5/562	一读完大学我就去这家单位上班了，一直到如今。 I started working in this company right after I finished university, and I'm still there.

注释 Note

* 地 dì=earth; land; ground

** 是……的 pattern

W | 563 文 character/language/literature/civilian/refined/MW/certain natural phenomena wén

Chinese	English	Character codes
文 + 化 = 文化	language + change = culture	563/427
文字	character; script; writing	563/173
文明	civilised; civilisation	563/082
文件	document; file	563/232
文法	grammar	563/402
条文	clause	295/563
明文	to state in writing	082/563
天文	astronomy	128/563
一文钱	a copper coin (in old time)	152/563/100

Example Sentences

1/563	我们可以从中国的文字中看到几千年的文明。 Through Chinese characters, we can see their evolution over thousands of years of civilisation.
2/563	她一拿到作文试题就开始写起来了。 She started to write as soon as she got the essay topic.
3/563	Smith 先生对中国文化很感兴趣。 Mr. Smith is very interested in Chinese culture.
4/563	他把自己所有有关历史的文件都送给了图书馆。 He gave all his historical papers to the library.
5/563	她从小被西方文化所 * 影响，所以思考和做事方法都很西化。 She has been influenced by Western culture ever since she was little, so her thinking and the way she does things are very Westernised.

注释 Note

* 所 is used before a verb to emphasize or highlight the noun it modifies.

闻 to hear/to smell wén 564 W

Chinese	English	Character codes
新 + 闻 = 新闻	new + to hear = news	311/564
要闻	important news story; headline	319/564
闻名	well-known; famous; renowned	564/083
耳闻	to hear of; to hear about	400/564
见闻	what one has seen and heard; knowledge; one's experience	054/564
奇闻	sth inconceivable; anecdote; unbelievable story	516/564
闻到	to smell; to sniff out; to perceive by smelling	564/205
所见所闻	what one hears and sees	290/054/290/564

Example Sentences

1/564	房先生是世界闻名的歌唱家。 Mr. Fang is a well-known singer in the world.
2/564	我爸爸总是早上一边喝咖啡一边看报纸上的要闻。 In the morning my dad always drinks coffee while reading the important news in the paper.
3/564	你知道这条新闻在网上有不小的影响吗？ Do you know this news is having a big impact online?
4/564	我回国后会把在加拿大 * 的所见所闻都告诉你。 When I get back, I'll tell you about my experiences in Canada.
5/564	我一进家门就闻到饭菜香，突然觉得饿了。 As soon as I enter my home, I smell the delicious food and suddenly I feel hungry.

注释 Note

* 加拿大 =Canada

W | 565 物 thing/object wù

Chinese	English	Character codes
动 + 物 = 动物	move + thing = animal	212/565
人物	person; character (in play, novel etc); protagonist	104/565
生物	organism; living creature; biological	112/565
礼物	present	480/565
物理	physics	565/482
物色	to look for; to seek; to choose	565/277

Example Sentences

1/565	我妹妹最喜欢的小动物是狗。 My sister's favourite small animals are dogs.
2/565	我已经物色好给你的生日礼物了。 I have already chosen your birthday present.
3/565	如果明天不下雨，我们就去动物园。 If it isn't raining tomorrow, we'll go to the zoo.
4/565	BBC 花了四年时间才做完《动物世界》节目。 The BBC spent whole four years making the Animal World programme.
5/565	动物园有很多动物，最被人喜爱的要数 * 大熊猫了。 There are many animals in the zoo. Big pandas are the most popular.

注释 Note

* 数 shǔ=count; be reckoned as

戏 play/drama/frolic/show xì 566 X

Chinese	English	Character codes
游 + 戏 = 游戏	to swim + drama = game; to play	328/566
戏院	theatre	566/161
把戏	acrobatics; jugglery; cheap trick; game; frolic; show	353/566
马戏	circus	495/566
没戏	not a chance; beyond hope; no way; hopeless	078/566
地 * 方戏	local opera	390/403/566
京戏	Beijing Opera	059/566
拿手好戏	one's speciality	501/284/039/566

注释 Note

* 地 dì=earth; land; ground

Example Sentences

1/566	讲笑话是她的拿手好戏。 Telling jokes is her speciality.
2/566	我已经看穿了你的小把戏。 I've seen through your little tricks.
3/566	你和小月没戏，她已经有喜欢的人了。 You and Xiaoyue don't stand a chance. She already has someone she likes.
4/566	他天天打游戏机，作业也不做，学习都没心思了。 He plays games every day, doesn't do his homework and has lost interest in his study.
5/566	我有两张今天晚上的戏票，跟我一起去看戏好吗？ I have two theatre tickets for tonight. Will you come with me?

X | 567 夏 summer xià

Chinese	English	Character codes
夏 + 季 = 夏季	summer + season = summer	567/440
夏天	summer	567/128
夏日	summertime	567/275
西夏	Western Xia Dynasty of China (1038-1227)	135/567

Example Sentences

1/567	一年四季里我最喜欢夏季。 Summer is my favourite season in a year.
2/567	明年夏天我们打算去北京。 We are planning to go to Beijing next summer.
3/567	今年夏天的世界杯真让人难忘。 This summer's World Cup was unforgettable.
4/567	西瓜是夏日里最解渴的水果，也是爸爸最喜欢吃的。 Watermelon is the most thirst-quenching fruit in summer, and it is also my dad's favourite.
5/567	我怕冷更怕热，所以夏天一定要有空调。 I fear the cold and even more the heat, so I definitely need air conditioner in summer.

鲜 fresh/bright/delicious/delicate xiān 568 X

Chinese	English	Character codes
新 + 鲜 = 新鲜	new + fresh = fresh; freshness; novel; uncommon	311/568
鲜明	clear-cut; distinct; in bright colours	568/082
鲜亮	shining bright colour; shiny	568/069
鲜花	fresh flower	568/426
鲜红	scarlet; bright red	568/229
鲜 * 为人知	rarely known to anyone; almost unknown; secret to all but a few	568/303/104/341

注释 Note

* 鲜 xiǎn=rare

Example Sentences

1/568	今天有贵宾来，宾馆门口放满了鲜花。 Today some VIPs will come. The front door of the hotel is full of fresh flowers.
2/568	一场大雨后空气变得新鲜多了。 The air becomes much fresher after a heavy rain.
3/568	那辆鲜红的汽车是你的吗？ Is that bright red car yours?
4/568	早上空气很新鲜，所以公园里都是来锻炼的人们。 The air is very fresh in the morning and the park is full of people who come to exercise.
5/568	衣着和心情很有关系，当我们心情好的时候，常常会选择一些鲜亮的衣服。 Clothing has something to do with mood. When we are happy, we often choose to wear something bright.

X 569 相 mutually/each other xiāng; appearance of a person or object /looks/posture xiàng

Chinese	English	Character codes
照 + 相 *+ 机 = 照相 * 机	photo + appearance + machine = camera	607/569/051
相关	related; relevant; pertinent	569/034
相比	to compare	569/186
相对	opposite to each other; relative; comparatively	569/022
相信	to believe; to be convinced (that sth is true); to accept sth as true	569/577
相应 **	to correspond; answering (one another); to agree (among the part)	569/592
相同	identical; same	569/130
相当于	equivalent to	569/388/579
亮相 *	to strike a pose (Chinese opera); (fig) to make a public appearance; to come out in public (revealing one's true personality, opinion etc); (of a product) to appear on the market or at trade show etc	069/569
真相 *	the truth about sth; the actual facts	338/569
相 * 片	image; picture	569/512

注释 Note

* 相 xiàng=appearance of a person or object; looks; posture (All other examples are pronounced as xiāng.)

** 应 yìng=answer; echo; meet the demand; cope with

Example Sentences

1/569	这张相 * 片已经很旧了，人都看不清楚了。 This picture is very old. The images can't be seen clearly.
2/569	我相信你一定能考上医学院。 I am sure you will get into medical school.
3/569	你放心吧，我会努力查出这件事的真相 *。 No need to worry, I will try to find out the truth of this matter.
4/569	我的照相 * 机是今年才买的，相当不错。 I just bought my camera this year. It's quite good.
5/569	在下次开会的时候，请你把所有相关的文件都准备好。 Please prepare all the relevant documents for the next meeting

香 fragrant/aromatic/savoury/incense xiāng 570 X

Chinese	English	Character codes
香 + 蕉 = 香蕉	fragrant + banana = banana	570/448
香料	spice; flavouring; condiment; perfume	570/490
香火	incense burning in front of a temple; burning joss sticks	570/050
香水	perfume; cologne	570/121
香甜	fragrant and sweet; sound (sleep)	570/551
书香门第	a family of scholars	119/570/257/210
鸟语花香	lit. birds singing and fragrant flowers; fig. the intoxication of a beautiful spring day	504/159/426 /570

Example Sentences

1/570	知道吗，这道菜用了九种不同的香料呢。 You know, this dish has five different spices.
2/570	我不爱吃香蕉，也不爱吃苹果。 I don't like bananas, nor do I like apples.
3/570	姐姐昨晚没睡好，所以吃饭也不香。 My sister didn't sleep well last night and has lost her appetite.
4/570	从很远就能闻到她身上的香水，这让我想起了鲜花。 I can smell her perfume from far away. It reminds me of fresh flowers.
5/570	我已经饿了一天了，现在吃什么饭菜都觉得特别香。 I have been hungry for a whole day. Whatever the food I have taken is delicious now!

X | 571 箱 box/trunk/case/chest/MW xiāng

Chinese	English	Character codes
冰 + 箱 = 冰箱	ice + box = icebox; refrigerator	365/571
行李箱	luggage case; suitcase	422/481/571
信箱	mailbox; post office box	577/571
邮箱	mailbox; post office box	595/571
电子邮箱	email address or box	017/172/595/571
箱子	trunk; box; suitcase	571/172
水箱	water tank; radiator (automobile); cistern	121/571
纸箱	carton; cardboard box	342/571

Example Sentences

1/571	这个皮箱子是我出门时常用的。 This leather suitcase is the one I often use when I travel.
2/571	这么多行李箱你一个人怎么拿啊？ There are so many suitcases. How can you manage all by yourself?
3/571	冰箱里有妈妈今天刚买的蛋糕，你吃吧。 In the fridge are some cakes that mum bought today. You can eat some.
4/571	家里卫生间的水箱坏了，得请工人换新的了。 My toilet flush tank is broken. I need to call a plumber.
5/571	为了给周末的晚会做准备，请把你们的电子邮箱都写给我。 In order to prepare for the weekend's party, please send me all your email addresses.

响 sound/noise/loud/make a sound/echo xiǎng 572 X

Chinese	English	Character codes
影 + 响 = 影响	shadow + sound = influence; effect; to influence; to disturb	156/572
影响力	influence; impact	156/572/483
响当当	resounding; loud; well known; famous	572/388
响亮	loud and clear; resounding	572/069
响应 *	to respond to; answer	572/592
响声	noise	572/533
声响	sound; noise	533/572
音响	sound; acoustics	589/572
不声不响	wordless and silent; without speaking; taciturn	007/533/007/572

Example Sentences

1/572	她不但样子好，而且她的歌声也很响亮。 She not only is nice-looking, but also has a loud and clear singing voice.
2/572	这件事的影响越来越大，慢慢地被大家注意到了。 This matter is having a bigger and bigger effect, and it has slowly caught everyone's attention.
3/572	在他的影响下 **，弟弟也爱上了网球。 My brother has also started to like tennis under his influence.
4/572	他在音乐方面有很高的成就，是个响当当的音乐家。 His achievement in music is very high. He is a well-known musician.
5/572	为了不影响别人，同学们在图书馆里都轻轻地走路。 Students are walking quietly in the library in order not to disturb other people.

注释 Note

* 应 yìng=answer; echo; meet the demand; cope with

** 在 …… 下 : under a certain condition or circumstances, such as a person, the media, a matter, even a war

X | 573 向 towards/face to/direction/from xiàng

Chinese	English	Character codes
方 + 向 = 方向	square + towards = direction; orientation	403/573
向前	forward; onward	573/099
面向	to face; to turn towards	081/573
向上	upward; up; to advance; to try improve oneself; to make progress	573/108
走向	direction; inclination; trend	345/573
去向	the position of sth; whereabouts	102/573
向往	to yearn for; to look forward to; desire to	573/301
一向	always; a period of time in the recent past; all along	152/573

Example Sentences

1/573	他做事一向小心，很少出错。 He is always careful and rarely makes mistakes.
2/573	我哥哥考上了他心中一直向往的那所大学。 My older brother got into the university that he always wanted.
3/573	小高的男朋友答应 * 等她回来。可是两年后她回来时，他早已不知去向。 Young Gao's boyfriend said that he would wait until she came back. After two years, when she got back, he had been long gone.
4/573	李飞的方向感很差，出门总要带本地 ** 图。 Li Fei's sense of direction is poor, so he always carries a map when he goes out.
5/573	A: 请问图书馆怎么走？ B: 过了红绿灯，再向前走 50 米就到了。 A: Which way goes to the library, please? B: After the traffic lights, walk straight on another 50 metres and you're there.

注释 Note

* 答应 dāying=agree; promise

** 地 dì=earth; land; ground

像 resemble/be like/image/seem/such as xiàng 574 X

Chinese	English	Character codes
好 + 像 = 好像	good + resemble = as if; to seem like	039/574
画像	portrait; to do a portrait of sb	428/574
影像	image; portrait; figure	156/574
头像	portrait; bust	554/574
成像	to form an image; imaging	375/574
像样	presentable; decent; up to par	574/151
相 * 像	to resemble one another; to be alike; similar	569/574

注释 Note

* 相 xiāng=mutually

Example Sentences

1/574	太阳就像一个大大的火球。 The sun is really looks like a big fireball.
2/574	我好像听到了一声猫叫，你听见了吗？ I seem to hear a cat's meow. Have you heard it?
3/574	他不像大家想象的那么聪明。 He is not as clever as everyone imagines.
4/574	她的电影天马行空，影像总是非常有想象力。 Her films are powerful and unconstrained, full of creative images.
5/574	月亮在一个月当中一直在变化，有时像条小船，有时又像个雪亮的大盘子。 The moon is always changing in the month, sometimes it looks like a small boat, and other times it looks like a big round shinny plate.

X 575 鞋 shoe xié

Chinese	English	Character codes
皮 + 鞋 = 皮鞋	leather + shoe = leather shoes	510/575
鞋子	shoes	575/172
鞋带	shoelace	575/384
球鞋	athletic shoes	272/575
草鞋	straw sandals	368/575
雨鞋	rain shoes	160/575

Example Sentences

1/575	（买 *）这双皮鞋花了我不少钱。 This pair of leather shoes costs me much money.
2/575	这双球鞋的鞋带太长了，没必要。 The shoelaces of this pair of trainers are too long. It is unnecessary.
3/575	你的鞋太多了，你还留了好几双鞋在我家呢！ You have too many shoes, and even a few pairs of shoes are left in my house!
4/575	这双鞋子已经很旧了，可他还是不愿意换新的。 These shoes are very old, but he still doesn't want to change them.
5/575	不到一个月，儿子就把这双新鞋穿坏了，又得买新的。 My son wore out his shoes in less than a month. I have to buy a new one again.

注释 Note

* 买 =to buy (Here it can be omitted.)

心 heart/mind/feeling/centre/core xīn 576 X

Chinese	English	Character codes
小 + 心 = 小心	small + heart = to be careful; to take care	143/576
放心	to feel relieved; to feel reassured; to be at ease	404/576
担心	anxious; worried; uneasy; to worry	387/576
开心	to feel happy; to have a great time; to make fun of sb	061/576
心理	mental; psychological	576/482
心情	mood; frame of mind	576/270
信心	confidence; faith (in sb or sth)	577/576
心病	sore point; secret trouble; worry	576/192
心地 *	moral nature; person's character	576/390
心得	what one has learned (through experiences, reading etc); knowledge; insight; understandings; tips	576/207
变心	to cease to be faithful	364/576
用心	motive; intention; to be diligent or attentive	594/576
得心应 ** 手	lit. what the heart wishes, the hand accomplishes; skilled at the job; entirely in one's element; going smoothly and easily	207/576/592/284
心安理得	feel ease and justified; feel no qualm	576/352/482/207

注释 Note

* 地 dì=earth; land; ground

** 应 yìng=answer; echo; meet the demand; cope with

Example Sentences

1/576	可能是快要结婚了吧，最近我们经理的心情不错。 The manager is in a good mood recently. Maybe because he is about to get married.
2/576	爸爸太忙，没有工夫关心这些事情。 Father is to busy to have time to care about these things.
3/576	我非常担心，因为很久都没收到她的音信了。 I'm so worried that I haven't received any news from her for quite a long time.
4/576	对不起，我一不小心把门关上了。 I am sorry to have accidentally closed the door.
5/576	跟我们讲讲你这几年学中文的心得好不好？ Can you share with us your experience of learning Chinese in the last few years?

X | 577 信 trust/mail/post/believe/at will/message xìn

Chinese	English	Character codes
相 + 信 = 相信	each other + to believe = to be convinced (that sth is true); to believe; to accept sth as true	569/577
自信	to have confidence in oneself; self-confidence	616/577
信用	to trust; credit (commerce); trust worthiness; reputation	577/594
信号	signal	577/040
来信	incoming letter	065/577
信息	information; news; message	577/308
信服	to believe; to be convinced; to convince sb	577/029
轻信	to easily trust; gullible; naïve	519/577
信口开河	talk irresponsibly; wag one's tongue too freely	577/475/061/423
信心十足	full of confidence	577/576/114/346

Example Sentences

1/577	她做起事来总是信心十足。 She is always full of confidence in her work.
2/577	上个星期我刚收到妈妈发来的短信，短信上说她很好。 Just last week I received a text message from my mum saying she was very well.
3/577	我相信她一定能做好这个月的报表。 I am convinced she will definitely create a good monthly report.
4/577	一定要知道自己有没有能力做到，千万不要信口开河地轻易答应 * 别人的请求。 You must think whether you have the ability to fulfil others' requests before you go running your mouth.
5/577	因为做了很多的准备工作，所以他有信心能把这次的活动完成得很出色。 Because he did plenty of preparation work, he is confident this event will go well.

注释 Note

* 答应 dāying=agree; promise

熊 bear/scold/coward xióng 578 X

Chinese	English	Character codes
熊 + 猫 = 熊猫	bear + cat = panda	578/076
大熊猫	giant panda	014/578/076
熊猫眼	to have dark circle under one's eyes; to have eyes like panda	578/076/316
北极熊	polar bear	005/436/578
狗熊	black bear; coward	033/578
熊包蛋	good for nothing; coward	578/359/204
熊市	bear market (i.e. period of falling share price)	578/537
熊熊大火	raging fire; flaming	578/578/014/050

Example Sentences

1/578	东京动物园里有一对大熊猫。 Tokyo Zoo has a pair of giant pandas.
2/578	大山里常有狗熊出没 *。 There are often black bears roaming in the mountains.
3/578	地 ** 球的温度一年比一年高，这让北极熊的生活环境越来越差 ***。 The temperature on earth has increased over the years, which has caused the polar bears' living environment to get worse.
4/578	熊熊大火把天空照得红红的。 The raging fire turned the sky red.
5/578	小马看了一晚的足球赛，所以今天一早带着一对“熊猫眼”来上班。 Xiao Ma watched football matches all night, so he came to work with “panda eyes”.

注释 Note

* 没 mò=disappear; vanish.

** 地 dì=earth; land; ground

*** 差 chà=poor; not up to standard

X 579 须 beard/must xū

Chinese	English	Character codes
必 + 须 = 必须	must + must = to have to; must; compulsory; necessarily	363/579
须要	must; have to	579/319
须知	key information; instructions	579/341
须发 *	beard and hair	579/401
留须	grow a beard	492/579
刮须	shave beard	418/579

注释 Note

* 发 fà=hair

Example Sentences

1/579	考生必须知道“考试须知”。 Exam candidates must know the exam instructions.
2/579	这是必须的，没的商量。 This is a must.
3/579	他病得很重，必须马上送往医院。 He is very ill, and should be sent to hospital immediately.
4/579	学习中文光会说还不行，还必须得会写。 Learning Chinese is not just about speaking, and you must also learn to write.
5/579	时间已经晚了，我们必须出发了，要不就坐不上末班车了。 It's getting late, and we must get going now, otherwise we won't make the last bus.

需 need/require/needs/demand xū 580 X

Chinese	English	Character codes
需 + 要 = 需要	to require + need = to need; to want; to demand; to require; requirement; need	580/319
不需要	unnecessary; not required	007/580/319
需求	requirement; demand (economic); to require	580/522
所需	necessary (for); required	290/580
特需	special need; particular requirement	547/580
必需	to need; to require; essential; indispensable	363/580
急需	to urgently need; urgent need	437/580

Example Sentences

1/580	她的"老爷车"突然坏了，为了换新车她急需一笔钱。 Her beat-up car has broken down, so she is badly in need of some money to get a new car.
2/580	他这个人很特别，没人能满足得了 * 他的需求。 He is special, and nobody can satisfy his needs.
3/580	下星期四晚上的音乐会票你需要吗？ Do you need tickets for next Thursday evening's concert?
4/580	奶奶的腿脚不便，上下楼梯需要帮助，我常常去帮助她。 Grandma's legs are weak, so she needs help going up and down the stairs. I often help her.
5/580	她需要时间好好想一想下一步该怎么做。 She needs time to have a good think about her near future.

注释 Note

* 了 liǎo=end; for example 没完没了 means endless.

X | 581 选 choose/select/pick/elect xuǎn

Chinese	English	Character codes
选 + 择 = 选择	choose + select = to select; to pick; choice; option; alternative	581/605
选中	pick on; choose; settle upon; decide upon a candidate; to be selected for some role	581/168
大选	general election	014/581
选用	to choose for some purpose; to select and use	581/594
人选	choice of person; candidate	104/581
当选	to be elected	388/581
选票	vote; ballot	581/265
选手	athlete; contestant; candidate	581/284
选出	to pick out; to select; to elect	581/012
选定	to select; to choose; to settle on	581/392

Example Sentences

1/581	因为钱不多了，他只好选择了一家最便宜的酒店。 Because he hasn't got much money left, he has to choose the cheapest hotel.
2/581	太好了，环保会议的地 * 点终于选定了。 It is great that the location for the meeting of protecting the environment has finally been decided.
3/581	学校选出三位选手去参加市数学比赛。 The school picked three contestants to go to the city's maths competition.
4/581	当他知道自己被选中去参加明年的世界杯时，他高兴坏了。 He is deadly happy when he got the notice that he has been chosen to play in next year's world cup.
5/581	周老师今天选了些短句让学生们听写。 Teacher Zhou picked some short sentences for dictation to the students today.

注释 Note

* 地 dì=earth; land; ground

牙 tooth/tooth-like yá 582 Y

Chinese	English	Character codes
牙 + 医 = 牙医	tooth + doctor = dentist	582/154
假牙	false teeth; dentures	443/582
月牙	crescent moon; new moon	162/582
牙刷	toothbrush	582/544
刷牙	brush teeth	544/582
门牙	incisor	257/582
牙根	root of tooth	582/413
牙关	jaw	582/034
牙牙学语	(baby) learning to speak	582/582/150/159

Example Sentences

1/582	迟大夫 * 是我认识的最好的牙医。 Dr. Chi is the best dentist I know.
2/582	我叔叔的门牙是假牙。 My uncle's incisor is a false tooth.
3/582	弟弟很喜欢我给他买的新牙刷。 My younger brother really likes the new toothbrush I bought for him.
4/582	爷爷的牙很不好。他要是没了假牙，饭都吃不成。 Grandad's teeth are very bad. He can't eat without his dentures.
5/582	这把牙刷实在太旧了，牙都刷不干净，得换一把新的了。 This toothbrush is too old to brush your teeth clean. You need to get a new one.

注释 Note

* 大 (dài) 夫 means the same as 医生 (doctor).

Y 583 阳 sun yáng

Chinese	English	Character codes
太 + 阳 = 太阳	too + sun = sun	127/583
向阳	facing the sun; expose to the sun	573/583
阳刚	manly; masculine	583/411
阴阳	yin and yang	326/583
阳历	solar calendar; Western (Gregorian) calendar	583/484
阳极	anode; positive electrode; positive pole	583/436

Example Sentences

1/583	在孩子们的眼里，太阳像一个大火球，月亮像一个冰球。 In children's eye the sun is like a big fireball and the moon an ice ball.
2/583	看，那边一朵朵的向阳花就像孩子们的笑脸。 Look, the sunflowers over there are like children's smiling faces.
3/583	当太阳刚刚出来的时候，他就开车出发了。 He set off in his car just as the sun came out.
4/583	极短的头发 * 让他的脸看起来很有阳刚气。 Extremely short hair makes his face very masculine.
5/583	这个房间空气不好，终年不见太阳，没人愿意住，所以房租很便宜。 Nobody wants to live in this room because the air circulation is bad and there is no sunlight all year round, so the rent is very cheap.

注释 Note

* 发 fà=hair

爷 grandfather yé 584 Y

Chinese	English	Character codes
爷 + 爷 = 爷爷	grandfather = paternal grandfather; father's father	584/584
老爷 (ye)	(respectful) lord; master	066/584
老天爷	God; heavens	066/128/584
爷们儿	menfolk (collective term for men)	584/079/024
大爷	father's older brother; term of respect for older man; arrogant idler; self-centred show-off	014/584
少爷 (ye)	son of the boss; young master of the house; son (honorific)	109/584
老爷 (ye) 车	classic car; old car	066/584/010

Example Sentences

1/584	我爷爷和奶奶结婚七十多年了。 My grandad and grandma have been married for over 70 years.
2/584	我大爷最爱喝自家做的米酒。 My uncle loves homemade rice wine best.
3/584	爸爸的那辆老爷 (ye) 车已经有些年头了。 Dad's classic car is quite old.
4/584	我的老天爷！雨一直在下，已经下了一个多星期了！ My good heavens! It keeps raining for more than a week!
5/584	虽然爷爷已经一百岁了，可是他身体还十分健康。 Even though Grandad is 100 years old, he is still very healthy.

Y | 585 业 line of business/work/trade/industry/already yè

Chinese	English	Character codes
作 + 业 = 作业	write + school studies = homework; school consignment; work; task; operation	176/585
业务	business; professional work; service	585/306
商业	business; trade; commerce	107/585
事业	undertaking; project; career; occupation	281/585
行 * 业	industry; business	422/585
就业	look for employment; get a job; start a career	239/585
业主	owner of the business or estate	585/614
业绩	accomplishment; performance of business	585/441
安居乐业	to live in peace and work happily	352/466/246/585

注释 Note

* 行 háng=business firm; trade; line; row; MW

Example Sentences

1/585	你想去的那条商业街在市中心。 That commercial street you want to go is in the city centre.
2/585	常春蓝从小就很有商业头脑。 Chang Chunlan has had a business brain since she was little.
3/585	安居乐业是他一直向往的生活。 To live in peace and work happily is a life he always wanted.
4/585	我在午休时间完成了今天上午的作业。 I finished this morning's homework during the lunch break.
5/585	虽然我妹妹才工作了两年，然而她工作努力，业绩突出。 Although my younger sister has only been working for two years, yet she works very hard and has an outstanding performance.

姨 aunt/mother's sister yí 586 Y

Chinese	English	Character codes
阿 + 姨 = 阿姨	prefix + aunt = maternal aunt	349/586
小姨	wife's younger sister	143/586
大姨姐	wife's elder sister	014/586
姨妈	mother's sister	586/074
姨夫	husband of mother's sister	586/216
姨太太	concubine	586/127/127

Example Sentences

1/586	我们一共十个小孩，马阿姨给了我们一人一个苹果。 There are totally ten children of us, and Aunt Ma gives us each an apple.
2/586	（我）妈妈和姨妈长得一点儿都不像。 Mum and auntie don't look alike at all.
3/586	阿姨给我妹妹买了一条新裙子。 Auntie bought a new skirt for my younger sister.
4/586	今天是大姨开车把我送到飞机场的。 It was my elder auntie who drove me to the airport yesterday.
5/586	昨天姨夫来信，让姨妈假期时带上孩子一起来日本住住。 A letter came yesterday from my aunt's husband telling my aunt to take their kids to Japan on holidays.

Y | 587 议 discuss/opinion/talk over yì

Chinese	English	Character codes
会 + 议 = 会议	meeting + discuss = meeting; conference	049/587
议会	parliament; legislative assembly	587/049
议题	subject under discussion; item on the agenda	587/293
商议	to negotiate; discussion	107/587
非议	to criticise	214/587
决议	resolution	469/587
不可思议	inconceivable; unimaginable; unfathomable	007/242/286/587

Example Sentences

1/587	会议室里坐满了人，一个空位都没有了。 The meeting room is full of people. There are no spare seats.
2/587	他很“自我”，一向不理会别人的非议。 He is very self-centred, never cares about anyone's criticisms.
3/587	前两步都做完了，她们正在商议下一步应该怎么做。 The first two steps were completed. Now, they are discussing what to do next.
4/587	这个会议刚结束，他又急急忙忙地去开下一个会议了。 This meeting has just finished and he is rushing off to the next one.
5/587	总经理说在明天下午的会议上需要对这两个问题做出决议。 The general manager said that a decision would be made regarding these two problems at tomorrow afternoon's meeting.

易 easy/exchange/change yì 588 Y

Chinese	English	Character codes
容 + 易 = 容易	to hold + easy = easy; likely; liable (to)	525/588
不易	not easy to do sth; difficult; unchanging	007/588
易于	very likely; prone to	588/597
轻易	easily; lightly; rashly	519/588
简易	simple and easy; simplicity	445/588
平易近人	amiable and approachable (idiom); easy-going; modest and unassuming	513/588/236/104
《易经》	*The Book of Changes*	588/237

Example Sentences

1/588	我的女朋友是一个很容易满足的人。 My girlfriend is a very easily satisfied person.
2/588	这些题出得太容易了，大多数考生都轻易地拿到了满分。 The questions were set so easy that most of students easily got full marks.
3/588	他今天这么好的成绩来得非常不容易。 It hasn't been easy for him to achieve such good grades now.
4/588	他不单是学习好，还很平易近人，而且助人为乐，所以当选了今年的学生会会长。 He was not only a top student but was also easily approachable and generous in giving help, so he was voted as the president of the Student Union this year.
5/588	我好不容易才买到明天飞东京的票。 I just managed to buy a plane ticket to Tokyo for tomorrow.

Y | 589 音 sound/tone/news/syllable/music yīn

Chinese	English	Character codes
音 + 乐 = 音乐	sound + music = music	589/246
声音	voice; sound	533/589
音色	tone quality; timbre	589/277
音信	message	589/577
回音	echo; reply	048/589
口音	accent	475/589
发音	to pronounce; pronunciation	401/589
音响	acoustics; stereo set	589/572
音箱	speaker	589/571
音调 (diào)	tone; the pitch of the sound	589/552
知音	an understanding friend	341/589
音乐片	musical film	589/246/512

Example Sentences

1/589	他们一家都爱好音乐。 Their whole family loves music.
2/589	听口音就知道她是南方人。 By listening to her accent you can tell that she is from south China.
3/589	对大多数学习中文的法国人来说，音调是个大问题。 To most French people who are learning Chinese, tones are a big problem.
4/589	《歌舞校园》是我妹妹最爱看的音乐片，她看了很多次，把影片里的所有歌都学会唱了。 *High School Musical* is my younger sister's favourite musical; she has watched it many times and learnt to sing all the songs in it.
5/589	只要一听到音乐，我的小妹妹就跟着音乐舞动起她那胖胖的小手。 As soon as she hears the music, my little sister would start moving her chubby little hands with the tones.

银 silver yín 590 | Y

Chinese	English	Character codes
银 + 行 * = 银行 *	silver + profession = bank	590/422
银行 * 卡	bank card	590/422/470
银行 * 家	banker	590/422/053
银白	silver white	590/180
银子	general term for silver	590/172
水银	mercury	121/590

注释 Note

* 行 hána=business firm; trade; line; row; MW

Example Sentences

1/590	我们经理的女儿和一位银行 * 家结婚了。 Our manager's daughter is married to a banker.
2/590	这家银行 * 在中国有几家分行 *。 This bank has a few branches in China.
3/590	昨天晚上开始下的这场雪好大啊，今天早上起床后发现外面成了一片银白色的世界。 The snow last night was quite heavy. When I got up this morning, there was already a silvery white world outside.
4/590	你把那一笔钱放进银行 * 了吗？ Did you deposit that money in the bank?
5/590	他平时大手大脚惯了，所以经常是还没到月末，银行 * 卡就没钱了。 He's used to splurging, so he often has no money left on his bank card by the end of each month.

Y | 591 饮 drink yǐn

Chinese	English	Character codes
饮 + 料 = 饮料	drink + material = drink; beverage	591/490
饮用	drinking or drinkable (water)	591/594
饮酒	to drink wine	591/464
饮茶	to have tea and refreshments; to have dim sum lunch (Cantonese)	591/009
冷饮	cold drinks	068/591
牛饮	gulp	261/591
饮酒作乐	drinking party; to go on a binge; to paint the town red	591/464/176/246

Example Sentences

1/591	啤酒是一种最常见的饮料。 Beer is a very common drink.
2/591	绿茶是种很健康的饮料，喜欢喝的人越来越多。 Green tea is a healthy drink. More and more people like it.
3/591	今年夏天太热了，一向不喝凉东西的常老板居然也从超市买了瓶冷饮喝。 This summer was so hot that Boss Chang, who usually never takes cold drinks, bought a cold drink from the supermarket.
4/591	天太冷了，你要喝杯热饮料吗？ It's very cold. Do you want a hot drink?
5/591	你刚跑步回来，天又那么热，你可不能跟牛饮一样地喝冷水，会生病的！ You just got back from running and the weather is so hot. You shouldn't gulp down cold water, or you will get sick.

应 ought to/should/promise yīng; respond/answer/echo /meet the demand/cope with yìng 592 Y

Chinese	English	Character codes
应 + 该 = 应该	ought to + should = must	592/408
应 * 用	to use; to apply; application	592/594
相应 *	to correspond; answering (one another); to agree (among the part)	569/592
回应 *	to respond; response	048/592
应当	should; ought to	592/388
应分 (fèn)	be part of one's duty/job	592/028
照应 *	to look after; to attend to	607/592
响应 *	to respond to; answer	572/592
应 * 急	to respond to an emergency	592/437
有求必应 *	to grant whatever is asked for; to accede to every plea	158/522/363/592

Example Sentences

1/592	爱护环境是我们每一个人都应该做的。 Every one of us should care for the environment.
2/592	她的提议得到了大家的响应 *。 Everyone responded to her suggestion.
3/592	下学期他打算选一门计算机应 * 用的课。 He plans to choose a computer application lesson next term.
4/592	我真不能答应 ** 下了班和你一起去酒吧，因为我从来不喝酒。 I really can't promise to go to the pub with you after work because I never drink.
5/592	你姨妈真是个热心人，我看她整天都在帮助别人，几乎是有求必应 *。 Your aunt is a warm-hearted person; I always saw her helping others, almost never saying no to others' requests.

注释 Note

* 应 yìng=answer; echo; meet the demand; cope with (All other examples are pronounced as yīng.)

** 答应 dāying=promise

Y | 593 迎 welcome/to meet/against/towards yíng

Chinese	English	Character codes
欢 + 迎 = 欢迎	happy + to meet = to welcome; welcome	047/593
迎候	await the arrival of the guest at a place	593/045
迎接	to meet; to welcome; to greet	593/452
迎风	in the wind; facing the wind	593/405
迎新	to welcome the new guests	593/311
迎面而来	directly; head-on (collision); in one's face (wind)	593/081/399/065
送旧迎新	usher out the old, greet the new; esp. to see in the new year	287/465/593/311
笑脸相迎	to welcome sb with a smiling face	310/485/569/593

Example Sentences

1/593	马路上站满了迎候女王的人们。 The streets are full of people awaiting the arrival of the Queen.
2/593	欢迎你们来我家做客！ You are welcome to visit my house!
3/593	她不在这儿，到大门口迎接客人去了。 She is not here and has gone to the gate to greet her guests.
4/593	为了迎接新年的到来，妈妈把家打扫得干干净净。 Mum has cleaned the house inside and out for the New Year.
5/593	在迎新晚会上，大家又唱又跳，欢迎新同学的到来。 At the welcome party, everyone sang and danced to welcome the arrival of the new students.

用 to use/employ/apply/need yòng 594 Y

Chinese	English	Character codes
作 + 用 = 作用	to compose + to use = action; function; impact; effect; to play a role	176/594
用于	use in; use on; use for	594/597
不用	need not	007/594
实用	practical; functional	534/594
常用	in common usage	195/594
用来	to be used for	594/065
没用	useless	078/594
好用	useful; effective; handy; easy to use	039/594
用意	intention; purpose	594/324
别有用心	have ulterior motives	190/158/594/576

Example Sentences

1/594	这些词是常用词，请同学们一定要多练习 。 These words are commonly used, so please practise more.
2/594	你的新手机不好用，换一个吧？ Your new mobile phone is not easy to use. Would you like to swap it for another one?
3/594	她是一位作家，她所有的时间都用于写作了。 She is a writer who spends all her time writing stories.
4/594	她能说法语和西班牙语，更不用说中文了。 She can speak French and Spanish, not to mention Chinese.
5/594	这房子虽然不大但很实用，离地 * 铁又近，对单身的你来说是最理想的了。 Though the house is not big, it fits your needs and is close to the subway, so it's ideal for a single person like you.

注释 Note

* 地 dì=earth; land; ground

Y | 595 邮 post/mail yóu

Chinese	English	Character codes
邮 + 件 = 邮件	post + piece = mail; post	595/232
电子邮件	email	017/172/595/232
邮箱	mailbox; post office box	595/571
邮票	stamp	595/265
邮电	post and telecommunication	595/017
邮包	postal parcel	595/359

Example Sentences

1/595	别着急，我正在用电脑给你发邮件呢。 Don't worry, I'm using the computer to send you an email.
2/595	我经常给在国外的朋友们发电子邮件。 I often send emails to my friends who are abroad.
3/595	能留下你的电话号和邮箱吗？ Can you leave your telephone number and email address?
4/595	你马上 * 查查，我刚刚把所有文件都发到你的邮箱里了。 Please check now, I sent all the documents to your email a moment ago.
5/595	我也不清楚为什么没有收到他发来的邮件。 I'm not clear why I haven't received his email.

注释 Note

* 马上 =right away

又 again/a multi-function word yòu 596 Y

Chinese	English	Character codes
又 + 一 + 次 = 又一次	again + one + time = yet again; once again; one more	596/152/200
又来了	here we go again	596/065/067
一次又一次	repeatedly; over and over again	152/200/596/152/200
又名	also known as; alternative name; to be also called	596/083
话又说回来了	returning to our main topic...; that said...; in passing; nevertheless...; anyhow	046/596/122/ 048/065/067

Example Sentences

1/596	妈妈昨天买的苹果又大又红。 The apples Mum bought yesterday are big and red.
2/596	我家的李子树去年夏天结 (jiē) 的李子又多又甜。 The plum tree in my house bore a lot sweet plums last summer.
3/596	又来了，这些话你已经说了好几次了。 Here we go again, you've already said it many times.
4/596	第二天医生又来了，很可能他的病情又加重了。 The doctor came back the next day. Maybe his condition had worsened.
5/596	不知是哪儿来的猫，一次又一次地跑到我家院子里来。 I don't know whose cat it is, but it keeps coming to my garden.

Y | 597 于 in/on/at/suffix after an adjective or a verb… yú

Chinese	English	Character codes
关 + 于 = 关于	relate + in = pertaining to; concerning; regarding; with regards to; about; a matter of	034/597
高于	greater than; to exceed	030/597
出于	due to; to stem from	012/597
于是	thereupon; as result consequently; hence; thus	597/117
大于	greater than; bigger than; more than	014/597
相当于	equivalent to	569/388/597
终于	at last; in the end; finally; eventually	610/597
位于	to be located at; to be situated at; to lie	562/597
等于	equal to	208/597

Example Sentences

1/597	这是一本关于西班牙历史的书。 This book is about Spanish history.
2/597	早上起晚了，于是我只能饿着去上课。 I got up late so I have to go to school on an empty stomach.
3/597	他在那儿坐了三个小时，最后终于走了。 He sat there for three hours and finally left.
4/597	出于对她的照顾，老板没有让她干 * 重活。 To take care of her, the boss didn't give her any heavy duties.
5/597	他想了半天都没想出解题的思路，于是就去睡觉了。 He thought about it a long time and still couldn't figure out how to solve the problem, so he went to bed.

注释 Note

* 干 gàn=do; strike; main part

育 to raise/bring up/educate/cultivate yù 598 Y

Chinese	English	Character codes
体 + 育 = 体育	body + to raise = sports; physical education	294/598
体育运动	sports; physical culture	294/598/333/212
体育场	stadium	294/598/196
教育	to educate; to teach; education	233/598
发育	to develop; to mature; growth; development	401/598
育种	breeding	598/611
生育	to bear; to give birth; to bring up (children)	112/598
育人	educate	598/104

Example Sentences

1/598	我爸爸是一位体育老师。 My dad is a PE teacher.
2/598	我姐姐最拿手的体育运动是跳高。 My elder sister's best sport is the high jump.
3/598	每次上体育课，高大康总是找理由请假 *。 Gao Dakang always has an excuse not to go to PE lessons.
4/598	经过三年的努力尝试，大家都期望着今年育种能有满意的结果。 After three years of experiments, everyone is hoping this year's seed cultivating will have satisfactory results.
5/598	虽然学校注重文化教育，可是也要求每个学生每周必须参加三小时的体育锻炼。 Although the school pays more attention to academic education, each student is required to participate in three-hour physical exercise per week.

注释 Note

* 假 jià=vacation; holiday

Y | 599 遇 meet/encounter/run into/chance/treat yù

Chinese	English	Character codes
遇 + 到 = 遇到	to meet + to reach = to meet; to run into; to come across	599/205
遇见	to meet	599/054
机遇	opportunity; stroke of luck	051/599
境遇	circumstance	462/599
冷遇	a cold reception; to cold-shoulder sb	068/599
奇遇	happy encounter; adventure	516/599
遇难 *	to perish; to be killed	599/503
遇害	to be murdered	599/421
不期而遇	meet unexpectedly; have a chance encounter	007/096/399/599

Example Sentences

1/599	上周在北京我遇见了老朋友冷安星。 I met my old friend Leng Anxing last week in Beijing.
2/599	我们刚爬上山头，就遇到了一场大雨。 The moment we got to the top of the hill, it started to rain heavily.
3/599	在那次飞机事故中，机上所有的人员共 279 名都遇难 * 了。 All 279 passengers and crew on board died in the airline crash.
4/599	星期一上午的第一节课上，夏老师给同学们讲了他在假 ** 期里去北极旅行的奇遇。 During the first lesson on Monday moring, Teacher Xia talked about his adventures in the Arctic on holiday.
5/599	今天我在图书馆里和一位久别多年的老朋友不期而遇。 Today I ran across an old friend in the library, who I hadn't seen for years.

注释 Note

* 难 nàn=disaster; adversity; misfortune; scold

** 假 jià=vacation; holiday

元 currency unit/first/primary/unit/chief/basic/origin yuán 600 Y

Chinese	English	Character codes
元 + 月 = 元月	first + month = first month of the lunar calendar	600/162
单元	unit (forming an entity); element	387/600
元老	senior figure	600/066
公元	Common Era; Christian era	221/600
元件	element; component; unit of an instrument	600/232
元气	vitality; vigour	600/098
元音	vowel	600/589
日元	Japanese yen	275/600

Example Sentences

1/600	今天我买水果花了三十元。 I spent 30 yuan on fruit today.
2/600	对一家好的公司来说，多元化和平等化不是一个选择而是一个必须的条件。 A good company understands that diversity and equality are not optional, but are must-have criteria.
3/600	自从去年小中风后，爷爷元气一直不足，到现在还不能下地 * 行走。 Ever since Grandpa suffered a minor stroke last year, he hasn't gained his strength back and still can't walk.
4/600	汉字在公元前就出现了，已有六千多年的历史。 Chinese characters have a history of more than 6,000 years.
5/600	从这学期开始，我们每学完一个单元就有一次考试。 Starting this term, we will be tested at the end of every unit we learn.

注释 Note

* 地 dì=earth; land; ground

Y | 601 园 garden/plot/plantation/place of recreation yuán

Chinese	English	Character codes
公 + 园 = 公园	public + garden = park	221/601
校园	campus	144/601
家园	homeland	053/601
园地 *	garden area	601/390
乐园	paradise	246/601
花园	garden	426/601
果园	orchard	037/601
菜园	vegetable farm	008/601
动物园	zoo; zoological garden	212/565/601

Example Sentences

1/601	每天早上有很多人在公园里锻炼身体。 There are lots of people exercising in the park every morning.
2/601	她房子的后面有一片果园，所以她总是能吃到最新鲜的水果。 There's an orchard behind her house, so she can always have the freshest fruits.
3/601	我们的校园位于城外，又大又漂亮。 Our school campus locates at a suburb of the city. It is big and beautiful.
4/601	他是个种 ** 菜好手，自家菜园种 ** 的菜一年四季都吃不完，还拿去分给邻居们。 He is good at growing vegetables. His vegetable patch produces lots of produce, enough to feed himself and share with his neighbours all year round.
5/601	我一直不明白为什么她不愿意去动物园，后来她告诉我说她很害怕动物。 I couldn't understand why she would not go to the zoo, but later she told me that actually she was afraid of the animals.

注释 Note

* 地 dì=earth; land; ground

** 种 zhòng=plant; farm

愿 to wish/desire/be willing/vow yuàn 602 Y

Chinese	English	Character codes
愿 + 意 = 愿意	to hope + desire = to wish; to want; ready; willing (to do sth)	602/324
意愿	aspiration; wish (for); desire	324/602
不愿	unwilling; unwillingness	007/602
如愿	to have one's wishes fulfilled	526/602
自愿	voluntary	616/602
情愿	willingness; would rather (agree to X instead of Y)	270/602
但愿	if only (sth were possible)	203/602
请愿	petition (for action to be taken)	101/602
愿望	desire; aspiration; idea to achieve a certain goal in the future	602/302

Example Sentences

1/602	你和你大哥，我情愿和你一起去听音乐会。 Between you and your oldest brother, I would rather to go to the concert with you.
2/602	我真不愿意周末还去上班。 I really don't want to go to work at the weekend.
3/602	他自愿留在学校教书。 He volunteered to stay at school to teach.
4/602	她已经病了一个多星期了，但愿她能很快好起来。 She has been ill over a week now. I hope she gets better soon.
5/602	如果你不愿意坐在这儿，我可以跟你换个位子。 If you don't want to sit here, I don't mind swapping seats with you.

Y | 603 越 jump over/over step/exceed/skip a rank/surpass yuè

Chinese	English	Character codes
越 + 过 = 越过	exceed + pass = to cross over; to transcend; to overcome; to rise above	603/225
越来越……	express a deepening of degree over the passage of time	603/065/603
越……越……	the more...the more...	603/603
越来越多	more and more	603/065/603/023
越发	increasingly; ever more	603/401
越位	offside (sports)	603/562
穿越	pass through; to cross; to overcome	198/603
飞越	to fly across; to fly over; to soar	027/603

Example Sentences

1/603	雨越下越大了，看来这天气一时半会儿是不会晴的了。 The rain is getting heavier. The weather doesn't look like it will be better soon.
2/603	近年来，所有国家的天气都越来越不正常了。 In recent years, all countries' weather has become more and more abnormal.
3/603	飞机起飞后向远方飞去，变得越来越小了。 The plane took off and flew into the distance. It became smaller and smaller.
4/603	越多的人意识到要爱护环境，地 * 球的环境就会越好。 The more people are aware of caring for the environment, the better the environment for our planet will be.
5/603	经过一个时期的锻炼，他的身体越来越好了。 After a period of exercise, his health is getting better and better.

注释 Note

* 地 dì=earth; land; ground

澡 wash one's body/bath/shower zǎo 604 Z

Chinese	English	Character codes
洗 + 澡 = 洗澡	wash + bath = to bathe; to take a shower	309/604
热水澡	hot bath or shower	103/121/604
冷水澡	cold shower	068/121/604
洗澡水	bath water	309/604/121
洗澡间	bathroom	309/604/231

Example Sentences

1/604	他很喜欢一边洗澡一边唱歌。 He quite enjoys singing while taking a shower.
2/604	几十年来他一直用冷水洗澡，所以看上去身体很好。 He has been taking cold showers for decades, so he looks very well.
3/604	她很爱干净，每次洗完澡都把洗澡间清理得干干净净。 She is fussy about cleanliness and she thoroughly clean the bathroom every time after taking showers.
4/604	他几天来不是在飞机上就是在火车或者汽车上，所以一到旅馆，他马上就洗了个热水澡。 He has been on a plane, train or bus for the last few days, so as soon as he arrived at the hotel, he went straight to have a shower.
5/604	工作到很晚才回家，妈妈不但在等着我，而且把洗澡水都给我准备好了。妈妈真好！ When I came home from work late, my mum not only waited for me, but also prepared the bath water for me. Mum is so nice!

Z | 605 择 to select/choose/pick zé

Chinese	English	Character codes
选 + 择 = 选择	to pick + to select = to select; to pick; choice; option; alternative	581/605
择日	to fix a date (for an event)	605/275
择定	to select	605/392
自然选择	natural selection	616/273/581/605
不加选择	indiscriminate	007/442/581/605
不择手段	by fair means or foul; unscrupulously	007/605/284/395

Example Sentences

1/605	爸爸选择的这家宾馆已有上百年的历史。 The hotel dad chose has over a hundred years of history.
2/605	物种的进化是自然选择的结果。 The development of species was the result of natural selection.
3/605	李简和黄秋晴认识才三个月就准备择期举行婚礼，这让大家都感到很意外。 Li Jian and Huang Qiuqing have only known each other for three months, but are already choosing a date to get married, which has caught everyone by surprise.
4/605	因为方便，所以越来越多的人选择上网买东西。 More and more people choose to shop online because it is convenient.
5/605	他知道自己想要什么，而且为了这个目的而不择手段，我真的不喜欢这样的人。 He knows what he wants and is unscrupulous in reaching his goals. I really don't like such people.

张 to spread/open/a popular surname/MW zhāng 606 Z

Chinese	English	Character codes
主 + 张 = 主张	main + to spread = to advocate; to stand for; view; position	614/606
张口	to gape; to yawn; to open one's mouth; to start speaking; to talk carelessly; to talk out of place	606/475
张力	tension	606/483
舒张	to relax and expand	540/606
张开	to open up; to spread; to extend	606/061
张望	to look around; to peer at	606/302
开张	to open a business; first transaction of a business day	061/606
东张西望	to look in all direction; to glance around	019/606/135/302

Example Sentences

1/606	市中心的商场下个月开张。 The shopping centre in the city centre is opening next month.
2/606	从爱护环境出发，我们不主张用大网网鱼。 From the point of protecting the environment, we do not advocate fishing with large nets.
3/606	她站在校门口东张西望——在等她的男朋友。 She is standing at the school gate, looking around and waiting for her boyfriend.
4/606	从他发表的文字中，我们对他的主张有了进一步的了解。 From his publications, we have a bit more understanding of his views.
5/606	对于她的想法，我刚张开口想说些什么，但什么也说不出来，只好点了点头。 Concerning her suggestion, I am just about to open my mouth to say something, but I couldn't say anything, but nodded.

Z | 607 照 light up/illuminate/shine/reflect/take a picture/licence/permit zhào

Chinese	English	Character codes
照 + 顾 = 照顾	look after + attend to =to take care of; to show consideration; to attend to	607/417
护照	passport	425/607
照片	photograph; picture	607/512
照相 * 机	camera	607/596/051
照相 *	to take a photograph	607/596
对照	to contrast; to compare; to check	022/607
照明	lighting; illumination	607/082
写照	portrayal	146/607
照看	to look after; to attend to; to have in care	607/062
照旧	as before; as in the past	607/465
照常	as usual	607/195
照样	as before; (same) as usual; in the same manner; still; nevertheless	607/151

Example Sentences

1/607	A: 中文真难学！ B: 可是我认为，和法文对照起来，中文的语法简单得多。 A: Chinese is so hard to learn! B: But in my opinion, comparing to French, Chinese grammar is much simpler.
2/607	这张黑白照片已经很旧了，算是“老照片”了。 This black and white photo is very old, which can be considered as the “Old Photo”.
3/607	今晚你能帮助我照顾照顾我的孩子吗？ Can you give me a hand to look after my kids tonight?
4/607	虽然这几天一直在下雨，主办方还是决定下雨也好，不下雨也好，音乐节照常进行。 It's been raining for the last few days, but the organiser has decided that rain or shine, the musical festival will be held as scheduled.
5/607	现在大家都习惯用手机照相 *，因此很少人用照相 * 机了。 Nowadays everyone is used to using a mobile phone to take pictures; therefore, not many people use cameras anymore.

注释 Note

* 相 xiàng=appearance of a person or object; looks; posture

者 a person doing the stated work zhě 608 Z

Chinese	English	Character codes
或 + 者 = 或者	or + of this = or; possible; maybe; perhaps	434/608
作者	author; writer	176/608
记者	reporter; journalist	439/608
学者	scholar	150/608
读者	reader	021/608
前者	the former	099/608
两者	both sides	249/608
当事者	the person involved; the people holding power	388/281/608

Example Sentences

1/608	你去或者不去，都请快点儿做出决定。 Please decide quickly whether you are going or not.
2/608	我是一名中文报的记者，我得把这件事调查清楚。 I am a journalist from a Chinese newspaper. I have to investigate this issue clearly.
3/608	这本书的作者是一个才刚刚十七岁的男孩。 The author of this book is a boy who has just turned 17 years old.
4/608	她的小说发表后不久就收到了很多读者的来信。 Soon after publishing her story, she received many readers' letters
5/608	明天是周末，我们终于可以休息了，或者在家看看书，或者去看网球比赛。 It's weekend tomorrow, and finally we can rest. We shall either read a book at home, or go to watch a tennis match.

Z | 609 直 straight/vertical/straighten/upright/frank/continuedly/simply zhí

Chinese	English	Character codes
一 + 直 = 一直	one + straight = straight (in a straight line); continuously; always; all along	152/609
直到	until	609/205
正直	upright; upstanding; honest	339/609
直接	direct; immediate	609/452
直觉 (jué)	intuition	609/056
直行	to go straight; straight forward	609/422
笔直	perfectly straight; straight as a ramrod	187/609
直心眼儿	open; frank; straightforward	609/576/316/024
直到现在	even now; until now; right up to the present	609/205/141/163
一直以来	for a long time now; in the past always; until now	152/609/323/065

Example Sentences

1/609	从昨晚开始就一直下着雨。 It has been raining since last night.
2/609	我一直以来有个愿望就是去北京爬长城。 I have always wanted to go to Beijing and climb the Great Wall.
3/609	我打算去北京开完会后直接飞去东京和女朋友一起过新年。 I planned that after the meeting in Beijing, I'll fly directly to Tokyo and spend the New Year with my girlfriend.
4/609	我从一大早开始一直都在忙，直到下午三点才吃上中午饭。 I started to be busy from early morning and didn't have my lunch until three o'clock.
5/409	他很正直，但是不可爱。其实我早就想和他分手了，只是一直没找到机会而已 *。 He is an honest man, but not cute. Actually, I have wanted to break up with him for a while but just haven't found the right opportunity.

注释 Note

* 而已，that is all.

终 end/all/death/be over zhōng 610 Z

Chinese	English	Character codes
终 + 于 = 终于	end + then = at last; in the end; finally; eventually	610/597
终场	end of a performance or game	610/196
最终	final; ultimate	347/610
始终	from beginning to end; all along	280/610
年终	end of the year	090/610
终年	entire year; throughout the year; age at death	610/090
终日	all day long	610/275
终点	the end; end point; finishing line (on a race); destination; terminus	610/016
终点站	train terminal	610/016/166
终生	throughout one's life; lifetime; lifelong	610/112
终老	spend one's last years	610/066
终身	lifelong; all one's life; marriage	610/279
始终如一	consistent	280/610/526/152
有始有终	carry sth through to the end	158/280/158/610

Example Sentences

1/610	什么是天才？有人说终生努力就成了天才，你同意这个说法吗？ What makes a genius? Someone said that lifelong efforts make a genius. Do you agree?
2/610	比赛离终场还有五分钟，双方比分还是零比零，看来要加时了。 The score was nil-nil with five minutes left in the game. It's going into overtime.
3/610	他的电视机从来都不关，始终是开着的。 He never turns off his TV. It's on all the time.
4/610	我用一天的时间终于把房间打扫好了。 I took me a day to clean my room.
5/610	经过一周的调查和对比，他们最终选择了一家新的游戏公司。 After a week's surveys and comparative studies, they finally chose a new gaming company.

Z 611 种 MW/type/sort/guts zhǒng; plant/farm zhòng

Chinese	English	Character codes
一 + 种 = 一种	one + kind = one kind of; one type of	152/611
这种	this; this kind of; this sort of	167/611
那种	that; that kind of; that sort of	084/611
多种	many kinds of; multiple; diverse	023/611
种种	all kinds of	611/611
变种	mutation; variety; variant	364/611
接种	to vaccinate; to inoculate	452/611
有种	to have guts; to have courage; to be brave	158/611
种子	seed; breed	611/172
多种多样	manifold; all sorts; many and varied	023/611/023/151
种 * 西瓜	plant watermelons	611/135/223
种 * 地 **	farming	611/389

Example Sentences

1/611	那种茶是进口的，这些茶是本地 ** 种 * 的。 That type of tea is imported, these types of tea are locally produced.
2/611	妈妈很喜欢种 * 东西，今年春天她在我家后花园里开出了一块地 **，种 * 了不少种青菜。 Mum enjoys growing produce. This spring she has planted a patch of green vegetables in my back garden.
3/611	她做过多种工作，最后当了咖啡师。 She has done many jobs and finally become a barista.
4/611	在多种多样的工作中，他选择了酒店服务行 *** 业。 Among various jobs, he chose the hotel service industry.
5/611	我想了种种办法都没能最终解决这个难题，只能请教你了。 I have tried all sorts of ways, but still can't solve this problem. I can only ask you for help.

注释 Note

* 种 zhòng=plant; farm (All other examples are pronounced as zhǒng.)

** 地 dì=earth; land; ground

*** 行 háng=business firm; trade; line; row; MW

重 weight/heavy/serious zhòng; repeat/again/overlap/layer chóng 612 Z

Chinese	English	Character codes
重 + 要 = 重要	important + major = important; significant; major	612/319
重点	important point; main point; focus; key (project); to focus on; to put emphasis on	612/016
重大	great; important; major; significant	612/014
重视	to attach importance to sth; to value	612/118
着重	to put emphasis on; to stress	337/612
重用	to put in an important position	612/594
轻重	severity (of the case); degree of seriousness; whether sth is slight or serious	519/612
重 * 复	repeating	612/407
重 * 来一次	do it again	612/065/152/200
重 * 重 *	layer upon layer; a great amount	612/612
重 * 新	once more; once again; start from the very beginning	612/311

Example Sentences

1/612	这些文件非常重要，所以不能带出公司。 These documents are very important, so you can't take them out of the company.
2/612	什么是习惯？习惯就是一种长期重 * 复地、慢慢地变成不做就会难受的行为。 What is habit? A habit is a routine behaviour that is repeated for a long time and slowly becomes something hard not to do.
3/612	这么重大的决定我得要和爸爸妈妈重 * 新 ** 商量一下。 This is such a big decision I need to discuss it with my mum and dad once more.
4/612	同学们一边听课一边把重点记了下来。 The students jotted down the main points while listening to the class.
5/612	因为好用，越来越多的人开始用网上银行 *** 的业务，所以银行 *** 对安全性也越来越重视。 Because of convenience, more and more people are using online banking services, so the banks have paid more attention to banking security.

注释 **Note**

* 重 chóng=repeat; again; overlap; layer (All other examples are pronounced as zhòng.)

** 重 (chóng) 新……一下 : once more

*** 行 háng=business firm; trade; line; row; MW

Z 613 周 week/circle/round/surrounding zhōu

Chinese	English	Character codes
周 + 末 = 周末	week + end = weekend	613/499
本周	this week	006/613
每周	every week	255/613
周年	anniversary; annual	613/090
上周	last week	108/613
下周	next week	139/613
周期	cycle; period	613/096
周边	periphery	613/188
周岁	one full year of life	613/124
四周	all around	123/613
周身	all over the body	613/279
周到	thoughtful; considerate	613/205
周一	Monday	613/152
周二	Tuesday	613/025
周三	Wednesday	613/106
周四	Thursday	613/123
周五	Friday	613/133
周六	Saturday	613/072
周日	Sunday	613/275
周游	take a journey around; travel around	613/328
周而复始	go round and round; move in cycles	613/399/407/208
周长 (cháng)	girth	613/194

Example Sentences

1/613	我每周去健身房两次。 I go to the gym twice a week.
2/613	上周二我去了图书馆。 I went to the library last Tuesday.
3/613	公司大楼四周都是咖啡馆儿。 The company building is surrounded by cafes.
4/613	这个周末我飞北京，然后去西安和成都，三周后回来。 This weekend I'm flying to Beijing, then Xi'an and Chengdu, and I'll be back in three weeks.
5/613	这家酒店虽然贵了点儿，但是服务周到，有很多“回头客”。 This hotel is a bit pricey, but it provides very good services, so there are many returning customers.

主 owner/main/master zhǔ 614 Z

Chinese	English	Character codes
主 + 要 = 主要	main + major = main; principal; major; primary	614/319
主题	theme; subject	614/293
主办	organise; to host	614/357
主场	host arena; home court	614/196
主动	to take the initiative; to do sth of one's own accord; spontaneous; active	614/212
楼主	original poster (in an online forum); landlord of a building	493/614
自主	independent; to act for oneself; autonomous	616/614
主人	master; host; owner	614/104
主干 *	trunk; main; core	614/409
主教	bishop	614/233
主张	advocate	614/606/196
公主	princess	221/614
当家作主	be master in one's own affairs	388/053/176/614

Example Sentences

1/614	真没想到，这道菜的主要调料居然是可口可乐。 It really surprises me, the main flavouring ingredient for this dish is Coca-Cola.
2/614	这次活动的主办方是一家银行 **。 This event is hosted by a bank.
3/614	街头那家照相 *** 馆开了没多久就换了主人，现在是一家干洗店了。 The photo studio on that street has changed its ownership not long after it opened. It's now a dry-cleaning shop.
4/614	在中国，每年的电视春晚除了北京的主会场外，全国多地还有分会场。 For every Chinese New Year Gala, in addition to Beijing's main venue, it also has venues in other places of China.
5/614	说是去学中文，其实他这次去中国的主要目的 **** 是游山玩水。 He says he is going to learn Chinese, but in fact the main purpose of his trip to China this time is sightseeing.

注释 Note

* 干 gàn=do; strike; main part

** 行 háng=business firm; trade; line; row; MW

*** 相 xiàng=appearance of a person or object; looks; posture

**** 目的 mùdì=purpose

Z 615 注 pour/fill/concentrate/fix/stake/to inject/annotate zhù

Chinese	English	Character codes
注 + 意 = 注意	concentrate + desire = to take note of; to pay attention to	615/324
关注	to pay attention to; to follow sth closely; concern; interest; attention	034/615
注定	be doomed; be destined	615/392
注解	annotate; explain through notes	615/456
注重	to pay attention to; to emphasise; lay stress on	615/612
不注意	thoughtless; not to pay attention to	007/615/324
注意力	attention	615/324/483
下注	to pour; to lay a bet	139/615
大雨如注	the rain is pouring down	014/160/526/615

Example Sentences

1/615	住房是目前人人都最关注的问题。 Housing is the problem that everybody is most concerned about at the moment.
2/615	我们学校特别注重语言的学习。 Our school gives special emphasis to language learning.
3/615	我家的小猫很调皮，一不注意就跳到饭桌上玩儿。 My cat is very naughty. If left unattended, he'll jump onto the dining table to play.
4/615	直到昨天我才注意到这件事情，有点晚了。 I didn't notice this until yesterday. It is a bit late.
5/615	今早上班时还大雨如注，但中午已经太阳高照，这天气也变得太快了。 The rain was pouring down during rush hour this morning, but by lunchtime it was already sunny. What a changeable weather it is!

自 self/oneself/naturally zì 616 Z

Chinese	English	Character codes
自 + 己 = 自己	self + own = oneself; one's own	616/438
自行车	bicycle	616/422/010
自然	nature; natural; naturally	616/273
自身	itself; oneself; one's own	616/279
自动	automatic	616/212
来自	to come from (a place)	065/616
自我	self-; ego (psychology)	616/132
自信	to have confidence in oneself; self-confidence	616/577
自觉 (jué)	conscious; aware; on one's own initiative; conscientious	616/056
自重	to conduct oneself with dignity; to be dignified; deadweight	616/612
自力更 * 生	self-reliance	616/483/415/112
自给 ** 自足	self-sufficiency	616/220/616/346

注释 Note

* 更 gēng=change

** 给 jǐ=supply; provide

Example Sentences

1/616	这辆自行车是我刚买的。 I just bought this bicycle.
2/616	在西方国家，人们一般都认为让孩子学会自立更生是最好的教育。 In Western countries, people usually consider teaching their children to be independent is the best form of education.
3/616	新年前后他给自己在健身房办了一张年卡。 He got himself a year's gym membership around the New Year.
4/616	她对自己在这次的长跑比赛中拿第一非常自信。 She is confident that she will win the first place in this long-distance race.
5/616	他对自身的要求很高，什么事都要做到最好。 He sets himself very high standards, and everything he does must be the best.

Z | 617 总 always/assemble/sum up/general/total zǒng

Chinese	English	Character codes
总 + 是 = 总是	always + be = always	617/117
总结	sum up; to conclude; summary	617/455
总体	completely; totally; entire; overall	617/294
总机	central exchange; telephone exchange; switchboard	617/051
总得 (děi)	must; have to; be bound	617/207
总务	general matters; division of general affairs; person in overall charge	617/306
总算	at long last; finally	617/546
总的来说	all in all; as a whole; by and large; generally speaking; in a nutshell	617/015/065/122

Example Sentences

1/617	我姐姐 17 岁离开学校后就一直在电力公司的电话总机室工作。 My sister has always worked at an electricity company's switchboard since she left school at 17.
2/617	她成绩很好，总是考第一名。 She has good grades and always comes top.
3/617	雨季总算过去了，接着来的大热天对南京人来说已是司空见惯的了。 The rainy season has ended at last; the following hot weather is a common occurrence to the people in Nanjing.
4/617	放假 * 前是谢老师最忙的时候，她不但要准备开家长会的工作，还得给班里所有的同学写学期总结。 Before the school holiday starts, it's the busiest time for Teacher Xie. Not only does she have to prepare for parent-teacher meeting but she also has to write reports for all of her class.
5/617	总的来说，家里总得有些花花草草，才会有生气。 In general, a home should have some flowers and plants to enliven the place.

注释 Note

* 假 jià=vacation; holiday

嘴 mouth zuǐ 618 Z

Chinese	English	Character codes
嘴 + 脸 = 嘴脸	mouth + face = feature; face; look; appearance	618/485
满嘴	a mouthful	496/618
嘴里	mouth; in the mouth; on one's lip; speech; words	618/070
多嘴	talkative; to speak out of term; to blab; to shout one's mouth off; rumours fly	023/618
住嘴	to hold one's tongue; shut up	170/618
嘴皮子	lit. lips; fig. glib talk	618/510/172
嘴甜	sweet-talking; ingratiating	618/551

Example Sentences

1/618	大人说话时你别多嘴。 Don't speak out of turn when grown-ups are talking.
2/618	我怎样干 * 我的工作不用你来多嘴。 It is not up to you to tell me how to do my job.
3/618	你怎么会相信他呢！他总是满嘴跑火车。 How can you believe that guy! He always shoots his mouth off.
4/618	他昨晚喝了很多酒，早上起来一嘴的酒气。 He drank so much last night. He smells of alcohol this morning.
5/618	小张的哥哥很能说，别人给他起了一个外号，叫他"张铁嘴"。 Xiao Zhang's elder brother is very good at arguing that he was given a nickname of "Iron Mouth Zhang".

注释 Note

* 干 gàn=do; strike; main part

附录 Appendix

范氏序法千字文

子　汉文语言以序为本，字植于序，循“负阴而抱阳”“文以载道”之则。

“字”乃最小之单位，“序”乃串字之法则。凡字含本义与衍义者归“实字”，仅表语法之义者为“虚字”。

“序”乃“道序”、自然之序。以字为素，序“字”而生词，序“字、词”而生句，序“句”而生段，序“段”而生章。

丑　人乃物灵之首，语言之丰非他物可比。

“人”知万物本无名，无名则难分，于是上者名“天”，下者名“地”，万物亦逐一得名，物灵之首则自谓之“人”。遂“是”字始创，“是”句乃生。

人见万物之存各有其位：天在上，地在下，万物居中。于是言位之字“在”乃生，言存之字“有”始行。

人识万物各有其质，而质各有其征：天之“阔”征也，地之“实”征也，日之“耀”征也，月之“清”征也，山之“巍”、水之“滢”征也。言万物之征谓之诉性。于是“判性”之句滋生。

人困于世，饮、食、男、女皆动之所获；动则生，无动则殆。“饮”“食”“男”“女”诸动无日可离。于是“动”字句乃生。

综上所述，后世千言，皆源“是”“有”“在”“动”“判”人生五要之需、之合、之展。

寅　汉文之行止，先天后地再人。

一句伊始，先表“何时”“何地”后而“何为”。“文道”遵天道、自然之道。无天地之托依，人何存？文何有？

古占卜，天时、地利、人为；传至后世，遂成文则。概之，一言既出，天、地之需先于人，人先于动，动先于果。无天、地、人、动，则无果。盖凡言，依天地人动果之序。

卯　汉文句式。

汉文句式分三：一叙事，其序天地人动果；二言情，以情至为果，重词则后置。“去看电影院，你们**都**？”重词为“**都**”；三咏诗作赋，以辞美为果，美韵垫后。

辰　汉字库甚巨，然仅分两支，一为实，二为虚。

实者具内涵可延、外构有力之功能；**虚字**乃文法码，仅限定修饰、言简意赅之用。实、虚两支相辅相成，以天—地—人—动—果之序行文。

实字存五类：物称为**名**（包括数与量），物行为**动**，物征为**判**，评判为**度**，物串为**连**或**介**。虽五，无固，判可动，动可名，动判相构则文法出：动动；动判；判动；判判是也。

虚者文法码也：**的**，修限，码植名前。**地**，修限，码植判后、动前。**得**，修限，码植动后、判前，判后、度前。**了**，限定或言变，居位有四，于诸动、动名、名或判后。**过**，限定，码植动后，以凸名状。**在动**，以时锁动，动延。**动着**，以空锁动，动滞。“把”“被”皆具“虚实双性”：**把**，达愿，甲挚乙动求达甲愿。**被**，迫受，甲迫受乙动之果。**是……的**，以“归类”明态、释惑。**就**，主褒超常（偶贬、述）。**才**，主贬超常（偶褒、述）。**吗**，疑问。**呢**，简略疑问。**吧**，半疑问。

巳　套组。

因为……，所以……；在……上；以……为……；用……来……；……。套句需知套词之构、之用。

午　成语（习语）。

成语（习语）多四言，行文循或趋真或趋美之规，组构式达九类之多，不赘。

跋：

酝酿数年　一朝面世

自从我提出"'序法'是汉文语法"的理论，到如今能出版这套教材，前前后后经历了二十个年头。

二十年来，我一直用这段话给自己和我们的老师们鼓气："不要羁绊于西方语言学家对我们语言下的定义；作为中国人，对汉语'自性'的研究是我们义不容辞的责任。"

正源于此，我要诚心诚意地感谢外文局麾下的华语教学出版社，感谢他们的见识与勇气；也要感谢成立于 2006 年的英国子午文院（Meridian Chinese Studies）对"序法"理论的研究、开发以及长达 14 年的课堂实践，正是这些因素使得这套教材日趋成熟。

这里给"序法"冠以"范氏"做一个注脚：我是苏州范家的子孙，苏姓是家父北迁后作为艺术活动的"艺姓"。我家祖上有范蠡、范仲淹，序法这一点点小成就当属祖宗的福荫，为此称之为"范氏序法"。再，百多年前，清人马建忠首次以印欧语系解构汉文，著《马氏文通》，汉文在马氏西语"他性"的解释下流行至今。"范氏序法"力求返璞归真，重新回到汉文本身，尝试以其"自性"诠释语法规律。

整套书并非学术大著，又是针对外国学生，所以亦庄亦谐，以学习效果为主，学术依据为辅。每次碰到需用古字（甲骨文和篆体）的字符解构简化字体时，我都尽量寻找源头，但牵强乃至穿凿附会依然在所难免，还请读者和老师们谅解。

作者、主编 苏立群

2020.10 于英国伦敦

出版策划：王君校　　韩　晖
统筹协调：付　眉　　韩　颖　　彭　博
策划编辑：陆　瑜
责任编辑：陆　瑜
英文编辑：韩芙芸

图书在版编目（CIP）数据

118小时突破中级中文. 课本. 上册 : 汉英 / 苏立群主编. -- 北京 : 华语教学出版社，2021.4
ISBN 978-7-5138-2067-7

Ⅰ. ①1… Ⅱ. ①苏… Ⅲ. ①汉语—对外汉语教学—教材 Ⅳ. ①H195.4

中国版本图书馆CIP数据核字（2020）第264878号

118小时突破中级中文．课本（上册）
LIQUN SU（苏立群） 主编
*

华语教学出版社有限责任公司出版
（中国北京百万庄大街24号　邮政编码 100037）
电话：(86)10-68320585　68997826
传真：(86)10-68997826　68326333
网址：www.sinolingua.com.cn
电子信箱：hyjx@sinolingua.com.cn
北京虎彩文化传播有限公司印刷
2021年（16开）第1版
2021年第1版第1次印刷
ISBN 978-7-5138-2067-7
010000